TRANSLATION IN HONG KONG:
PAST, PRESENT AND FUTURE

W0116075

Translation in Hong Kong:
Past, Present and Future

Edited by

Chan Sin-wai

The Chinese University Press

Translation in Hong Kong: Past, Present and Future
edited by Chan Sin-wai

© **The Chinese University of Hong Kong**, 2001

ISBN 962–201–977–3

THE CHINESE UNIVERSITY PRESS
The Chinese University of Hong Kong
SHA TIN, N.T., HONG KONG
Fax: +852 2603 6692
+852 2603 7355
E-mail: cup@cuhk.edu.hk
Web-site: www.cuhk.edu.hk/cupress

Printed in Hong Kong

Contents

Introduction   vii
Chan Sin-wai

The Translations of E. J. Eitel and Others: Translators in   1
Hong Kong in the Nineteenth Century
Chan Man Sing

The Student-interpreters' Scheme and the Chinese Teacher's   9
Allowance: Translator Education in Nineteenth-century
Hong Kong
Gillian Bickley

Literary Translation in Hong Kong in the 1950s: 21
Ma Lang's Translation of *Erostratus* in *Literary*
Current Monthly Magazine
Yau Wai Ping

The Hong Kong Translation Society: A Concise History,   37
1971–1999
Liu Ching-chih

The Research Centre for Translation: A Mirror of   73
Translation Studies in Hong Kong
Eva Hung Wai Yee

Translator Training in Hong Kong: What Professional   85
Translators Can Tell Us
Li Defeng

A Higher Diploma Course of Translation and Interpretation   97
at the Crossroads — The HDTI at the City University of
Hong Kong
Mak Wai Ho

Different Formats, The Same Effect? The Experience of   119
the Open University of Hong Kong
Paul Levine

Innovative CALL Activity for Translation and Interpretation   129
Students
Carrie Chau Kam Hung and *Irene Ip Kwok Chun*

Arts Students and Technical Translation   135
David Lam Kui Kwong

Cantonese-Putonghua Sight-translation Training at the   141
City University of Hong Kong
Cheng Ting-au

From One Convention to Another — Coming out of   149
the SL Straitjacket into the TL Dancing Shoes:
On Freeing the TL Text from the SL Syntax
Evangeline S. P. Almberg

Translation Studies in Hong Kong-China and the Impact of   157
"New Translation Theories"
Leo Chan Tak-hung

Demythologizing Translation Theories   175
Alan Tse Chung

Translating: It Does Not Matter Whether You Are a Formalist   179
or a Functionalist
He Yuanjian

Translating for the Financial Market in Hong Kong   185
Kenneth Au Kim-lung

Subtitling in Hong Kong   193
Yiu Po Kwong

The Internet and Translation Studies in Hong Kong   197
Lai Swee Fo

Machine Translation in Hong Kong 205
Chan Sin-wai

Translating for the "New Age": Theoretical, Professional and 219
Pedagogic Implications
Simon S. C. Chau

Back to the Future: The Future Development of Translation 227
Studies in Hong Kong
Elsie Chan Kit-ying

Effective Bilingualism and Hong Kong Government 245
Translators — The Way Forward
Michael Chuen Kam-hung

Hong Kong's Bilingual Laws Programme 249
Tony Yen Yuen Ho

Translation and the Internationality of Hong Kong 255
Zhang Longxi

Notes on Contributors 261

Index 269

Introduction

Chan Sin-wai
Department of Translation
The Chinese University of Hong Kong

Hong Kong is a cosmopolitan city where international communication is a fact of everyday life. Translation has always played an important role in bridging the social and cultural gap between Chinese and Western civilizations. As a subject of practical, applied studies as well as an academic discipline of theoretical research, translation studies is essential to the development of the Hong Kong society as an international financial and commercial centre and a meeting place of Eastern and Western cultures.

A conference on "Translation in Hong Kong: Past, Present and Future" was held by the Department of Translation, The Chinese University of Hong Kong during March 1999 on The Chinese University campus. The present publication comes out of this two-day conference that was attended by well over 25 participants from various tertiary institutions offering translation studies. From the variety of topics, areas and periods covered in this publication, the theme that provides the linkage among the contributions is the importance of translation in the growth of Hong Kong from a small village in China to one of the best-known cosmopolitan cities in the world. This is demonstrated by the efforts of different individuals, societies and institutions that made up the world of translation in Hong Kong.

In "The Translations of E. J. Eitel and Others: Translators in Hong Kong in the Nineteenth Century," Chan Man Sing provides a tribute to the small but closely-knit community of translators who lived in nineteenth-century Hong Kong, including such luminaries as E. J. Eitel, J. Dyer Ball and Stewart Lockhart. They were all civil servants and missionaries with a common interest in Chinese middlebrow culture that many mainstream sinologues would not touch. Their translations, which reflect the colonial mindset, represent the first efforts of the West to open up the cultural world of pre-modern Hong Kong.

In a related topic, Gillian Bickley in "The Student-interpreters' Scheme and the Chinese Teacher's Allowance: Translator Education in

Nineteenth-century Hong Kong" deals with early attempts by the Hong Kong Government to create a team of Western government officers who would be useful as Chinese-English, English-Chinese interpreters and translators. Her article presents a historical overview of the introduction and implementation of these two schemes by the government in nineteenth-century Hong Kong and comments on the personalities involved and the perceived success or failure of these two schemes. This is interesting background in the light of the current policy of localisation and the lessening of the expatriate presence in the Civil Service.

Yau Wai Ping's "Literary Translation in Hong Kong in the 1950s: Ma Lang's Translation of *Erostratus* in *Literary Current Monthly Magazine*" adds both a political and literary dimension to the history of translation in Hong Kong. As editor and translator of a literary magazine based in the then British colony, Ma Lang took advantage of the freedom of expresson allowed by the colonial administration to pursue a policy that countered the prevailing literary trend in Mainland China in the 1950s. Analysing Ma Lang's rendering of the existentialist fiction of Sartre shows how translation can change the target culture through experimenting with language and extending the literary repertoire. Ma Lang was attracted to the image of the protagonist as an individual who, when confronted by a world without apparent meaning, creates an identity at odds with society. The author argues that Ma Lang's translation constitutes an alternative to the individual's subordination to society as sanctioned by the Chinese Communist Party.

The history of the Hong Kong Translation Society reflects the changing status of English and Chinese and the growing importance of translation in the territory. In "The Hong Kong Translation Society: A Concise History, 1971–1999" by Liu Ching-chih, we are told how this organization was founded in the seventies by pioneer educators and literary translators who felt a need to come together to promote research and strengthen the bonds between translators. In the eighties, the composition of the society changed to include practising translators in both the Civil Service and the commercial sector, and conferences and seminars on legal and economic translation were held. This was due to the rising status of the Chinese language after the signing of the Sino-British Joint Declaration in 1984 and the growing volume of China trade.

In "The Research Centre for Translation: A Mirror of Translation Studies in Hong Kong," its current Director, Eva Hung Wai Yee, explains that the Centre, which was not only a forerunner of all other translation groups and departments in the region, but also a reflection of the social and intellectual climate of the late 1960 and early 1970s, an era that saw strong nationalistic feelings on the status of the Chinese language. It has become internationally known through its journal of literary translation, *Renditions*, and other research activities.

The need for further training and accreditation of local translators was seen early on. The next few papers focus on the current situation of translation studies in Hong Kong. It begins with articles on translation teaching methodologies as experienced by teaching professionals from various local institutions. In "Translator Training in Hong Kong: What Professional Translators Can Tell Us," Li Defeng reported his survey on the needs of professional translators and their perceptions of translation teaching in Hong Kong. He argues their input into the translation curriculum would enhance the qualities of translators produced by these tertiary institutions. The gap between theoretical knowledge and practical needs has to be narrowed if Hong Kong is to have translators who are not only competent but who are able to change with changing market conditions. This issue is further elaborated by Mak Wai Ho in "A Higher Diploma Course of Translation and Interpretation at the Crossroads — The HDTI at the City University of Hong Kong." Here, he examines the development of the Higher Diploma Course in Translation and Interpretation at the City University of Hong Kong and highlights the challenges it now faces — changes in language environment and language needs of society that reflect the need for constant assessment and change.

The different formats that Paul Levine speaks of in his paper, "Different Formats, The Same Effect? The Experience of the Open University of Hong Kong," are the traditional style of full-time/part-time evening mode of teaching and its distance-learning, tutor-guided counterpart. He describes some of the useful experiences and comparisons gleaned from the two modes, focusing on such issues as course development and effectiveness as well as the impact on the future of translation in Hong Kong. He argues that done well, the distance mode of teaching has much to offer. And in a society where full-time study is often a luxury, he suggests that this type of format will become more and more prominent.

The application of technological invention in translation teaching has become more widespread as the new technically literate generation commence tertiary education. Carrie Chau Kam Hung and Irene Ip Kwok Chun report on "Innovative CALL Activity for Translation and Interpretation Students." The CALL (Computer-assisted Language Learning) project aims to enhance translation and interpretation students' lexical competence and knowledge in government and political affairs of Hong Kong by providing an interactive multimedia package accommodating a bilingual glossary of Chinese and English terms related to current affairs.

Lack of relevant lexical knowledge, accompanied by psychological obstacles, often prevent translation students from tackling more specialist translation courses. David Lam Kui Kwong, in "Art Students and Technical Translation," discusses effective strategies to overcome the mental blockages that non-science students have concerning technical translation. Training in interpreting between Cantonese and Putonghua is becoming more crucial with Hong Kong's increasing interaction with the Mainland. Cheng Ting-au's "Cantonese-Putonghua Sight-translation Training at the City University of Hong Kong" discusses some of the lexical, grammatical and tonal problems that occur when interpreting between the two, and demonstrates that practical, contemporary and comprehensive training is the most effective means to overcome these differences.

An article focusing on the linguistic aspects of translation teaching is a salutary warning about the dangers of complacency in translation. In "From One Convention to Another — Coming out of the SL Straitjacket into the TL Dancing Shoes: On Freeing the TL Text from the SL Syntax," Evangeline S. P. Almberg examines some common weaknesses and errors in students' attempts at Chinese-English translation. She argues that consciousness and a touch of *Zen* is required. A Chinese text is strewn with traps for a native speaker under the illusion of freedom and syntactical baggage may be carried over into the target language. The translator must understand how their own language works, especially in ways that English does not.

Leo Chan Tak-hung also takes further into the theoretical mode, discussing at length what he calls poststructuralist translation theories in his article "Translation Studies in Hong Kong-China and the Impact of 'New Translation Theories.'" From a variety of perspectives, he discusses the obstacles that beset the importation of Western poststructuralist theories into Hong Kong. Poststructuralism has been a popular subject in scholarly circles in recent decades, particularly in those societies with a longstanding cultural tradition and a history of colonisation. It is natural that this should surface in Hong Kong.

Alan Tse Chung presents an interesting discussion on translation theory and its application in "Demythologizing Translation Theories" as well as the tendency for students to believe that the translation theories taught to them will be applied in some real translation context at the end of the day. There are obviously some theories that are for discussion, while others have a more applicational nature. The "theoretical theories" aim at explicating the nature of translation, providing frameworks of principles and a background to problem-solving rather than providing the translator with hard and fast rules.

Discussion in the section is broadened from translation teaching to research in the area of translation theory. He Yuanjian, in "Translating: It Does Not Matter Whether You Are a Formalist or a Functionalist," emphasizes that the first and foremost basis for translating is that of a source language text, which is the fundamental premise for any sort of translating to happen at all. Then there is translating, a process that involves linguistic, sociolinguistic and many other principles and factors that are universal as well as specific to different languages and cultures. The goal of theories of translating, according to the author, is to uncover and investigate the system in which the universal principles and factors operate. As regards the function and usefulness of translation theory, the next series of articles shift the focus from translation theories to translation practice.

The prosperous growth of the financial market in Hong Kong creates a huge demand for translating services that are indispensable in providing all the bilingual documents necessary for the production of prospectuses, investment reports and financial newspapers. Kenneth Au Kim-lung's "Translating for the Financial Market in Hong Kong" lists some of the challenges and opportunities faced by professional financial translators in Hong Kong. Another important but neglected area is the field of subtitling. As Yiu Po Kwong says in his article, "Subtitling in Hong Kong," at least 95% of theatregoers in Hong Kong cannot understand English dialogue. Subtitling can provide them with a practical means to learn English. The nature of the work necessitates a good working knowledge of colloquial language and cultural practices. He gives us a series of examples to show just how easy misunderstandings occur through poor subtitling.

Lai Swee Fo in "The Internet and Translation Studies in Hong Kong" discusses another aspect of the application of technology in the translation process. The World Wide Web constitutes a vast network of easily accessible information and is extremely useful for translation practice and research. The proliferation of electronic texts and computer corpora will have far reaching implications for the future of translation studies. This is very much apparent in Chan Sin-wai's "Machine Translation in Hong Kong," a survey of the results achieved so far in the area of computer-assisted translation. Computer capability in the act of translation has gained increasing sophistication in recent years and the author introduces the work of the newly established Machine Translation Laboratory at the Department of Translation, The Chinese University of Hong Kong.

Simon S. C. Chau in a rather different vein takes up the issue of change in his article "Translating for the 'New Age': Theoretical, Professional and Pedagogic Implications." At this time in history when values and perceptions have shifted to a remarkable degree, he argues that some of this "new revolution" is actually a rediscovery of the past. To the author the "New Age" means a time of critical re-examination of theories and a willingness to accept a holistic approach to the act of translation.

In "Back to the Future: The Future Development of Translation Studies in Hong Kong," Elsie Chan Kit-ying traces recent local translation research which re-examines the Chinese tradition utilizing applicable Western theory and suggests ways of bringing it to a wider audience. The author proposes that a socio-political recontextualization of the Chinese tradition will provide a healthy path for translation studies in the future in this post-colonial society.

The volume concluded with three speeches that reflect Hong Kong as it is right now. In "Effective Bilingualism and Hong Kong Government Translators — The Way Forward," Principal Chinese Language Officer Michael Chuen Kam-hung explains the requirements for government Chinese Language Officers from the perspectives of language proficiency, general knowledge and cultural practices. Tony Yen Yuen Ho's "Hong Kong's Bilingual Laws Programme" also shows the rapid pace of language development in Hong Kong. Until recently, all statute laws were enacted in the English language only while judges and lawyers used English in all legal proceedings. A full understanding of the law was out of reach of most Hong Kong residents. This changed in 1989 when it was required for all new Ordinances to be drafted and enacted bilingually. This paper discusses the considerations in choosing to build a bilingual legal system and the difficulties involved.

Zhang Longxi reasserts the importance of English in Hong Kong if it is to remain a truly international city after its return to Chinese sovereignty. In "Translation and the Internationality of Hong Kong," he explores the use of Chinese and English and the crucial role that translation plays and will continue to play in the twenty-first century. The current controversy over mother tongue education shows the sensitive role that language still plays in the territory.

The twenty-four articles included in this volume can hardly tell the full story of translation in Hong Kong. We do not have an archive in which historical documents in translation are placed to substantiate some of the views expressed by contributors, and we do not have a crystal ball to look at the shape of things to come in the future. But as we all know, the future is built on the past. What is put down here will certainly serve as a guide for us to map out our future.

In the preparation of this volume, I received enormous help and support from all contributors, to whom I owe my indebtedness. My thanks are also due to other conference participants, such as Serena Jin, Wong Wang Chi, Tung Yuan-fang, Joseph Poon Hon-kwong, Fang Neng-hsun, Sin King-kui, Diana Yue, Rebecca Mok Wing Yin and John Minford, who brought interesting insights to the discussions. A note of gratitude should also be given to Miss Jennifer Eagleton, my colleague at The Chinese University, who spent many hours translating the articles and preparing the manuscript for publication.

The Translations of E. J. Eitel and Others: Translators in Hong Kong in the Nineteenth Century

Chan Man Sing
Department of Chinese
The University of Hong Kong

In the history of a colony, the position of translators should certainly be given more than superficial consideration, for translation is an indispensable link in colonial administration. It is for this reason that, in the following article, I look at the work of three translators of the colonial bureaucracy of nineteenth-century Hong Kong: E. J. Eitel (1838–1908), J. Dyer Ball (1847–1919), and J. Stewart Lockhart (1858–1937).

Eitel, a German, came to Hong Kong as a missionary in 1860. In 1879 he was appointed Inspector of Schools and Private Secretary to Governor Sir John Pope-Hennessy. Eitel was the first person to propose a government school for girls, of which proposal the Hong Kong Beliliosi Middle School was a result. He was a prolific author, producing *Chinese-English Dictionary in the Cantonese Dialect, Feng Shui*, and *Three Lectures in Buddhism* and translating the *Trimetrical Classic*《三字經》, the *Thousand-character Text*《千字文》, and a part of Ban Gu's 班固 (32–92) *Han Shu History of the Former Han Dynasty*《漢書》.[1]

J. Dyer Ball was born in Guangzhou, where his parents were missionaries. Ball came to Hong Kong in 1870. In 1878 he was appointed Assistant Interpreter to the High Court and later rose to be Chief Interpreter of the court. Toward the end of his career, he served as Registrar-General, "Protector of Chinese" (the predecessor of the office of Secretary for Chinese Affairs). Ball developed considerable expertise in Chinese dialects and published scholarly articles on the dialects of Xiangshan 香山, of Shunde 順德, of Dongquan 東筦, and of Siyi 四邑. His most well-known works were *Cantonese Made Easy* and *Things Chinese*. These two works were being reprinted right up through the 1980s. Ball also produced a little book on the art of cooking, *The English-Chinese Cookery Book* (1890). In it, two hundred Western recipes are translated into rather old-fashioned Cantonese; in the book, Ball's skill in Chinese can be seen.[2]

J. Stewart Lockhart came to Hong Kong in 1879. In 1887 he was appointed Registrar-General, "Protector of Chinese." In 1895 he also assumed the post of Colonial Secretary, a position second only to that of Governor. In 1902 he became Commissioner of Weihaiwei. Lockhart co-translated with T.W. Pearce *Enigmatic Parallelism of the Canton Dialect* and, as sole translator, produced a version of Zhao Yi's 趙翼 (1727–1814) *Cheng Yu* 《成語》*(A Manual of Chinese Quotations)*.[3]

Eitel and the other two men spent a long time in Hong Kong, so, of course, they were acquainted with one another. But Eitel's German origin naturally led to his being marginalizd in the English community of the city. Nevertheless, he became editor-in-chief of the *China Review*, a scholarly publication devoted to Chinese language, culture, and customs. The *Review* gained the respect of the sinological world. Lockhart prospered professionally in the colonial bureaucracy; he also immersed himself in Chinese culture, in 1885 forming a Chinese Reading Club which met on Wednesdays at his home to discuss literature. Dyer Ball was a member. And Lockhart, Ball, and Eitel were all regular contributors to the *China Review*.

Eitel and the others' most important purpose in their writing and translation was to teach Westerners the Chinese language and something of Chinese culture, and so to make easier their lives and work in Asia. The dictionaries and Cantonese-language textbooks which they edited need scarcely be mentioned; their translations of the *Trimetrical Classic* and the *Thousand-character Text* were also done strictly for pedagogical purposes ("exclusively tutorial")[4]. Ball's cookbook, in which he laboriously translated Western recipes to help uneducated Chinese cooks working for foreigners, is obviously another work aiming at the ease and comfort of the *kweilo* community.

In their translations (including dictionaries and Chinese-language textbooks), they did not show the kind of respect for the original text which we now have. Neither did they reveal any intention to profit from the original text to broaden experience or to extend their own horizons as translators of our time may expect from their own works. To them translation was basically to serve the dominating consciousness of colonialism and to open a road for the religious spirit, for the government, and for the economy. The result in their treatment of original texts was often an "anything goes" attitude. They simply pushed out of their minds the principle of the so-called "Occam's razor" (*Entia non sunt multiplicanda praeter necessitatem*: no more things should be presumed to exist than are absolutely necessary), which they, being missionaries and Bible scholars, should know very well and which is not unlike the Chinese "Beware of explaining classic texts by adding words to them."

At this point, we may look at some passages from Eitel's translation of the *Thousand-character Text*. According to Eitel's preface, words in parentheses were added according to the meaning of the original text, and underlined words corresponded to the words actually appearing in the text.

1. 天地玄黃，宇宙洪荒

   There is (father) *Heaven* above and (mother) *Earth* below; how *dusky* the former, how *tawny* the latter. And so there is the *universe* all around with its *aeons* all along; how *vast* the former, how *limitless* the latter.

2. 雲騰致雨，霧結為霜

   (Just see how boldly) the *clouds career up* till *down comes* (gently pattering) *rain*!
   (Just observe how quietly) the *dew congeals* till it *forms* into (beautiful, glittering) *frost*!

3. 律呂調陽

   (And likewise, in music), having discerned the *sharps* and *flats*, they have *reproduced* (in melodies) the *harmony* of nature's expanding and riveting)![5]

Inspired by the text, Eitel "adds branches and sticks in leaves" (as the saying goes), with an attitude difficult to imagine in a translator of our times. The most egregious example is his handling of "*lüe lü tiao yang*" 律呂調陽. In the Tang dynasty version of the *Thousand-character Text* by Zhi Yong 智永 (fl. sixth century), the first two characters are *lüe zhao* 律召; since the time of Huai Su 懷素 (737–?), they have been written erroneously as "*lüe lü*" 律呂. Of course, we would not be justified to require this kind of textual criticism from an amateur Sinologist like Eitel. And his rendering "sharps and flats" can even be taken as bearing a resemblance to "*lüe lü*." But when we come to the second half of the expression — to "*tiao yang*" — it is no such matter. At this point, the author of the *Thousand-character Text* is talking about an ancient method of determining the periods of the traditional twenty-four-part solar year:

pitch-pipes were stuffed with ashes of reeds at one end, and when a new period of the year arrived, the ashes of one of the pipes would fly out and the tube was cleared. So was the change from period to period in the calendar determined. With his "reproduced in melodies the harmony of nature's expanding and riveting," Eitel appears to be dragging into the text the Western concept of *musica mundana* (cosmic music). The difference is so great, it's like — well, again as the saying goes, "even when the cow is in estrus, the stallion will not mount her, nor will the bull the mare."

To understand Eitel's method of translation, violating and coercing at will the Chinese texts, we need to place it in the context of the unequal relations of power in the nineteenth century, as between East and West. Eitel and the others did not particularly respect the Chinese people, and they regarded Chinese language and literature as childish things. In his critique of H. B. Joly's English version of *Dream of the Red Chamber*, for example, Eitel takes up the matter of the great love which the Chinese have for this novel:

> How come it then, one may ask, that a book so utterly non-Confucian, so nihilistic as regards both Chinese religions and morals, is one of the most widely read novels of China? The explanation is simple. Chinese read the *Red-chamber Dream* because of its wickedness.[6]

As to their attitude toward the Chinese language, Dyer Ball's remark can be taken as representative:

> Chinese is essentially a language for infants, for children, and for simplicity of thought.[7]

Such an attitude was ubiquitous in the nineteenth century. It would probably be too much to require that our three translators deliberate carefully, mull over the essence and ponder the thought, and shilly-shally for ten days before fixing on the translation of a single word, the way Yan Fu 嚴復 (1854–1921) did. The second half of the nineteenth century was a time of widespread and vigorous translation, but the translations were done in two different cultural milieux, and the missions were so divergent, the orientations were so different, that they were virtually two different kinds of activity.

Nevertheless, the translations of Eitel, Ball, and Lockhart are not without significance in the history of translation. Ball and Eitel, for example, paid special attention to the sentence-final particles of Chinese — an attention which doubtless grew out of their needs as students of the language. Ball makes an impressive list to show various moods, various shades of feeling, which can be attached to the Cantonese word *"hai"* 係 in collocation with different particles, as follows (standard Chinese is given in parentheses after each Cantonese utterance):[8]

係咩？（是嗎）	Yes? (Oh, is it so?)
係嗎 (陰去調)（是嘛？）	Yes? (It is indeed so, is it not?)
係呀 (是呀)	Yes? (It is so indeed)
係 (是吧)	I think yes – I think it so, is it not?
係囉 (對了吧？)	It is so I think.
係唔係呢？（是不是呢？）	There, isn't it so now?
係唔係呀？（是嗎？）	Is it so?
係唔係？（是不是呀？）	There, didn't I tell you it was so?

Our feelings and intellect may be pleased and satisfied by such linguistic ingenuity, but its significance goes beyond such satisfaction and pleasure. The knowledge of Chinese which they gained through translation, from their time on, has influenced the vision which we translators have of the language. Let me offer a couple of examples.

In the first place, in his many translations of Cantonese sayings, Lockhart especially appreciated the expression *"niupi denglong* 牛皮燈籠" ("a leather lantern"). Lockhart writes:

A leather lantern — not bright.

A leather lantern as an equivalent for a dull man is emphatic. At the same time it is felt to be singularly appropriate. It calls up that kind of mental picture in which the Chinese delight.... [9]

Lockhart was not the first person to mention the imagerial tendency of the Chinese language and Chinese literature. But from the nineteenth century onward, down through energetic promotion by Ernest Fenollosa, Ezra Pound, and others, there has been in translation studies this theory that the Chinese language by its nature presents images. In psycholinguistics we have seen the theories of Hatta, Sasanuma, and others of their ilk, that it's the right hemisphere of the brain that processes Chinese characters. These are among the many theories, derived to support the notion of an imagerial tendency in the Chinese language, which have been advanced during the last hundred years and more. Since Ovid Tzeng and others offered evidence to disprove it, however, we have not heard much about the theory that the right half of the brain processes Chinese characters.[10] Still, the presentation of images by the Chinese language is a hot topic in translation studies, and there is a definite need for more precise and accurate investigation into the matter.

In the second place, we offer an example from the English and Chinese versions of the announcement that Professor Arthur Li had been appointed as Vice-Chancellor of The Chinese University of Hong Kong (1996). For the announcement, the University prepared brief biographies in Chinese and English. Neither biography, strictly speaking, is a translation of the other, but we may make a rough comparison of the two texts. The exceptional parts are the beginning and the end of each text. I give them below:

English text:

a. Beginning:

Professor Arthur K.C. Li
MA, MD, BChir (Cantab.); FRCS; FRCSEd; FRACS; FAC5; FPCS (Hon);
Hon FRCSGlas

Appointed by the Council of The Chinese University of Hong Kong as the Vice-Chancellor of the University, Professor Arthur K.C. Li assumed office on 1 August 1996.

Professor Arthur K.C. Li was born into the fourth generation of an established Hong Kong family ....

b. End:

Professor Li is 51 years old and is married with two sons.

Chinese text:

a. Beginning:

李國章教授

李國章教授生於香港，現年五十一歲，已婚，有兩子。李家原籍廣東鶴山，後定居香港，至李教授已是第四代……。

b. End:

李教授獲香港中文大學校董會聘任為大學校長，並於一九九六年八月一日到任。李教授今後將領導中大面對種種新挑戰，帶領中大邁向新紀元，為本港高等教育及社會發展作出重大貢獻。

Note. For purposes of comparison in this English version of the article, the Chinese texts are given below in English translation.

a. Beginning:

Professor K.C. Li

Professor Li was born in Hong Kong. He is fifty-one years old and married, with two children. The Li family came originally from Guangdong province and later established itself in Hong Kong. Professor K.C. Li is the fourth generation to live in Hong Kong.

b. End:

Professor Li has been appointed Vice-Chancellor of the University by the Council of The Chinese University of Hong Kong. He assumed office on 1 August 1996. Professor Li will lead The Chinese University to face all kinds of challenges, to stride toward the new century, and to make a significant contribution to tertiary education and social development in Hong Kong.

There is no adequate treatment, in textbooks of translation, of this matter — of inversion in the kinds of material ordinarily presented in introductions and in conclusions. But Ball noticed the phenomenon a hundred years ago:

They (the Chinese) are our opposite in almost every action and thought …. The end is the beginning and the beginning is the end.[11]

Ball's head was completely in the Western world when he wrote that, and apparently he disapproved of the topsy-turviness of the Chinese way. But he does point out a linguistic reality. In the 1990s, linguist Linda Yeung stated the case much more clearly:

In English, it is statement and explanation or statement and context, whereas in Chinese, there is context and at the end comes statement.[12]

which is now generally accepted to be true.

In conclusion, the translations and the research on Chinese language produced by Eitel and the others have points of value and utility even today. Not only should we read them with the attitude of respect which is due to the past; we should also think seriously about the things they have discussed.

Translated by William McNaughton

Notes

1   For Eitel's biography, see Rev. T.W. Pearce, "Ernest John Eitel, Ph.D. — An Appreciation," *The Chinese Recorder*, Vol. XL (1909), pp. 214–19; G.B. Endacott, *A Hong Kong History — Europe in China by E.J. Eitel: The Man and the Book*, Journal of Oriental Studies Monograph. Hong Kong: Hong Kong University Press, 1962.

2   For Ball's biography, see H.J. Lethbridge, introduction, *Things Chinese*, by J. Dyer Ball (Hong Kong: Oxford University Press, 1982), pp. vii–xv.

3   For Lockhart's biography, see Shiona Airlie, *Thistle and Bamboo: The Life of Sir James Stewart Lockhart* (Hong Kong: Oxford University Press, 1989).

4   See Eitel, preface, "The Trimetrical Classic." Trans. Eitel, *China Review*, Vol. 20, No. 1 (1892–93), p. 35.

5   *China Review*, Vol. 20, No. 2 (1892–93), pp. 101–8.

6   *China Review*, Vol. 20, No. 1 (1892–93), p. 66.

7   See Ball, appendix, *Cantonese Made Easy* (Taipei: Ch'eng Wen Publishing Company, 1971[Original work published 1888]), p. 4.

8   *Cantonese Made Easy*, p. 116.

9   Lockhart, "Enigmatic Parallelism of the Canton Dialect," *China Review*, Vol. 25, No.1 (1886), p. 41.

10 See Ovid Tzeng and Daisy Hung, "Psycholinguistic Issues in Reading Chinese," in Henry S.R. Kao, ed., *Psychological Studies of the Chinese Language* (Hong Kong: The Chinese Language Society of Hong Kong, 1984), pp. 230–33.

11 Ball, *Cantonese Made Easy*, p. 668. Also quoted in Linda Young, *Cross-talk and Culture in Sino-American Communication* (Cambridge: Cambridge University Press, 1994), p. 133.

12 Young, *Cross-talk and Culture in Sino-American Communication*, p. 34.

The Student-interpreters' Scheme and the Chinese Teacher's Allowance: Translator Education in Nineteenth-century Hong Kong[1]

Gillian Bickley
Department of English
Hong Kong Baptist University

While working since about 1987 on the topic of early education in Hong Kong under British administration,[2] and particularly when searching through primary sources, the present writer found and made notes also on a mass of information about interpretation and translation. Not surprisingly, the two topics of education and interpretation/translation — in Hong Kong — are inextricably intertwined.

It is particularly interesting to note that the decision of the Hong Kong Government to set up a Government Education System for the Chinese population — a decision made in 1861 — did not stand alone. It was one of two measures, which were well understood at the time to be complementary to each other. The second was the setting up of the student-interpreters' scheme, which is one of the topics of this article.

The education scheme included the establishment of the first Government school where the English language would be taught by a native speaker of English. This was the Hong Kong Government Central School for (Chinese) Boys, now Queen's College. (In 1867, however, it was opened up to all other nationalities.) The other measure involved a system of selecting a few young men from Britain, by competitive examination, to come to Hong Kong to study the Chinese Language, in the expectation that, when they had passed their Chinese Language examinations satisfactorily, they would be appointed to senior positions — when available — in the Hong Kong Government. As contemporaries said, by the one scheme, the Chinese will learn English, and by the other scheme the English will learn Chinese.

In 1841 when the British and other non-Chinese first settled in Hong Kong, there were very few people in the service of the Hong Kong Government who could act as interpreters or translators between the British administrators and the Chinese population of Hong Kong. Those that there were included missionaries, who had learnt Chinese to carry out their calling. One of these was Charles Gutzlaff, Chinese Secretary to the Hong Kong Government. Another much respected translator-interpreter was John Robert Morrison, the son of pathfinder missionary, Robert Morrison.

At least two chapters in the present book refer to the situation today and in recent past decades. C. C. Liu writes of the fact that Chinese-English, English-Chinese translation became increasingly important beginning from 1974 onwards, and again from 1984 onwards. Kenneth Au Kim-lung writes of the "huge demand for translating services" arising from the growth of the financial market in Hong Kong. In the legal area too, interpreters are constantly at work in court. Much expertise has been needed also in the recent major undertaking to translate Hong Kong laws into Chinese. In other significant domains, translation and interpretation are important requirements.

The situation in 1841 and then in 1861 was very similar. A country which had previously been comparatively inaccessible was now more accessible. There was a sudden great increase in activities involving China and other nations, in the need for communication between the Chinese and the non-Chinese. But the number of those with the language skills to facilitate these activities and communications was disproportionate to the size and variety of the tasks.

Of particular concern was the question of the legal system. English was never the *only* language used in court. The languages of defendants were always used also. And this brought the need for court interpreters and — if possible — for judges and lawyers who were bilingual in English and Chinese.

One of the arguments for the establishment of the Central School and the new focus on teaching Chinese people the English Language was that it was the duty of the Government to educate the people to understand the legal system under which they lived. On the other hand, the student-interpreters' scheme was intended to make it possible for British administrators to understand and communicate with the Chinese population.

The two linked schemes, passed by the Hong Kong Legislative Council on 23 March 1861 (almost one hundred and forty years ago), were not the first or the last initiatives that the Hong Kong Government considered in early times to improve the supply of bilinguals and hence the supply of interpreters and translators. A minute written in 1900 in the Colonial Office in London is a good indication of what the nineteenth century situation was like. It reads: "The question of how to get efficient Chinese Interpreters and Translators in Hong Kong is not a new one; in fact it is as old as the Colony itself."[3]

Before considering the introduction of the student interpreters' scheme and the Chinese teacher's scheme,[4] it should be noted that translation was a *method of teaching* at the Hong Kong Government Central School. Also, translation was taught as a *subject* at the school. The native English-speaking teachers at that school were *expected* — in fact, they were usually *required* — to learn Chinese for their work. Apart from the student-interpreters' scheme, therefore, there was another source of supply for the work of interpreters and translators in various government departments, including that of the Registrar General and the Courts. Professional interpreters came on stream as suitable graduates from the Central School became available.

Previous Work on this Topic and Method of Research

Primary English language sources have been used for this work, including Government documents and contemporary newspapers. There are however two published essays on the topic. There is a contemporary essay by E. J. Eitel, "Chinese Studies and Official Interpretation in the Colony of Hong Kong," published in *The China Review* in 1877. Although Eitel's topic relates directly to the one discussed here, his points have not been used as a basis for the present writer's own conclusions and statements; but only as one of several additional leads to the original materials. In fact, the present writer has found Reverend Dr Eitel a suspect historian of Hong Kong education. In relation to the topic of the present chapter, Eitel is an interested party. He was a member of the Board of Examiners, which examined the progress of those Hong Kong Government servants who received the Chinese Teacher's allowance. From the early 1870's, he was also Director of Studies. There is every reason, therefore, not to accept his opinions and even his assertions of fact without question. It took another century before another scholar turned his attention to this topic. In 1971, H. L. Lethbridge published an article, "Hong Kong Cadets, 1862–1941," in the *Journal of the Hong Kong Branch of the Royal Asiatic Society*. His sources are *secondary*, however. The present writer did not take his work as a starting point in any way. The original and contemporary documents indicated above were read first, to create a historical outline and interpretation. These results were then compared and contrasted with those of others, including Eitel and Lethbridge, and a final adjudication made between them.

The Two Schemes

In a Despatch dated 28 April 1855, Sir George Grey, Secretary of State for Colonial Affairs, wrote to Sir John Bowring, Governor of Hong Kong, as follows:

> I consider the knowledge of the Chinese language as essential generally for the Civil Service at Hongkong, and have to lay it down for your guidance as a rule, subject only to such very special exceptions as you may deem necessary, that no application for increase of salary in that Service is to be made for any person who has not learnt Chinese.[5]

Presumably in response to this communication, in July 1855, the Hong Kong Government published a Government Notification that "in claims for promotion a knowledge of Chinese will be considered as a recommendation to the favourable consideration of the Authorities."[6]

Six years later, in March 1861, Governor Sir Hercules Robinson referred[7] to two schemes, one already implemented and one proposed. In 1860, as Robinson reports of himself, he had "determined to defray at the public expense the cost of teachers for every public officer learning the language — about L25 per annum each." One of the conditions was a half-yearly examination. If it was found that satisfactory progress had not been made the allowance would be withdrawn.[8]

As of March 1861, three Government Clerks had made use of the scheme. However, Robinson now felt that not much good could come from it.

> To learn Chinese two things are requisite — first that the Student shall not be above a certain age — secondly that he shall give his undivided attention to the task — and in this enervating climate six hours drudgery in an office leaves neither mind nor body fitted for that close application which is necessary for acquiring so difficult a language as Chinese.[9]

Robinson now proposed a scheme for Student Interpreters, in which half-yearly examinations were also stipulated.[10] The first examination under Robinson's original scheme was conducted by James Legge, and four officers were examined.[11]

The course of studies followed by these Hong Kong Government officers — not student interpreters — while studying the Chinese language in Hong Kong from 1861 to (probably) 1874 can be garnered from reports of their examinations. Their studies included written and spoken Chinese (Cantonese). In 1863, one of them studied "the court dialect, or Mandarin." Particular areas mentioned were the radicals and colloquial phrases. In 1861 and 1862, texts studied included portions of the New Testament of the *Bible*, the first Book of the *Confucian Analects*, and the *Three-character Classic*. The report dated 6 January 1864 mentions "the colloquial" and "the written character." The report dated 15 August 1864 mentions "the character," "reading," and "the colloquial."

On 2 April 1863, Legge conducted the first examination of the student-interpreters (also known as the Civil Service Cadets). The course of studies followed by the student interpreters — while studying the Chinese language in Hong Kong from 1862 to (probably) 1874 — can also be garnered from reports of their examinations. On 2 April 1863, they were examined on reading and translating The Gospel of Saint John from the *Bible*, chapters one to seven; on the *Three-character Classic*; and on "the colloquial." Subsequently, one of them attempted to read the Confucian Classics.

In August 1863, after their examination, they were recommended to focus on spoken Chinese. They were to use their vocabulary and phrase book (each compiled by the individual student himself) and "some volumes of *Dialogues & c.*"

After their examination on 6 and 7 January 1864, they were to study the Chinese work, *The Sacred Edict*, and *Æsop's Fables* translated into Chinese.

After their examination on 15 August 1864, they were advised to read the "Works of Mencius" in Legge's *Chinese Classics* and "The History of the Three States."

On 11 March 1865, C. C. Smith's examination consisted in translating "two Notifications from an old [*Hong Kong*] *Government Gazette* in Chinese to be rendered into English" and "a few English sentences… into Chinese." He was also examined in the spoken language.

At two points during the course of the student-interpreters' studies, practical work was advised. At an early stage, it was suggested they spend time every week at the Law Courts. Towards the end of their studies, they were recommended to spend time in Canton mixing as far as possible only with Chinese people.

By September 1864 Sir Hercules Robinson was so pleased with the results of the scheme that he suggested that "arrangements might now be made for the selection at home of three additional cadets, and for their departure from England for Hong Kong in January or February next." He continued, "as it would be impossible to secure better men than those appointed on the first occasion, I would recommend that precisely similar measures should be adopted for the selection of their successors."[12] In London, one official expressed the view, "If we can but keep them in the Public Service, they will be invaluable."[13]

Examiners

Who were the examiners? Over time, three of the persons listed by Professor Chan Man Sing in his chapter — E. J. Eitel, J. Chalmers and J. Dyer Ball — were members of the Board of Examiners.

It has already been mentioned that for the first examinations conducted in Hong Kong of Government Officers who were studying Chinese — including both regular government servants and the student-interpreters — the examiner was James Legge. In August 1863, when in Hong Kong, W. J. Wade, "Secretary and Chinese Secretary to Her Majesty's Legation in this Country" gave the first batch of student interpreters their second examination. In February 1865, Legge requested "a very intelligent Chinese" to assist him in an examination. Was this perhaps Wang Tao, who lived in Hong Kong for a considerable number of years, working closely with James Legge?

As soon as the first batch of cadets passed their final examinations, Governor Sir Hercules Robinson took the view that he would no longer need to call upon the services of Legge in any further Chinese language work, and he presented him with a token of appreciation for his previous assistance, which had been given free of charge.

The next group of three new cadets was appointed in 1865. Their final examinations were taken in 1867. The examiner in this case was the Head of the Government Education Department, Frederick Stewart,[14] assisted by one other gentleman,[15] the notorious former Registrar-general, Daniel Richard Caldwell ("than whom there is, I believe no better linguist in China," as Sir Richard Macdonnell said).[16]

The next cadet was appointed in 1867. His final examination would have been due in 1869 or 1870. No record of his examinations has been found.

The Board of Examiners

A Board of Examiners was formed in 1875. No new student-interpreter was appointed until 1879. At least initially, therefore, those examined by this Board were not student-interpreters, but all other government servants studying Chinese.

As published on 27 April 1877, the Board of Examiners consisted of three former student-interpreters: passed cadet C. C. Smith as Chairman, passed cadet Alfred Lister as Secretary, and passed cadet James Russell. Also on the Board was Frederick Stewart, Head of the Government Education Department, who served as Secretary of the Board during at least March to May 1875, being replaced by Lister no later than May 1876. The fifth member was E. J. Eitel as Director of Chinese Studies.[17]

A new Board was created in 1883 by Hennessy's successor, Sir George Bowen.[18] The members were passed cadet His Honour Mr. Justice (James) Russell, passed cadet the Honourable Alfred Lister, the Honourable Frederick Stewart, LL.D., missionary the Reverend J. (John) Chalmers, LL.D. and Wong Shing, Esquire. Passed cadet James Haldane Stewart Lockhart was Honorary Secretary.[19]

Over time, the membership of the Board expanded. Of those who served in later years, mention will be made here only of J. D. Ball, who was a member of the Board of Examiners from 1898 to 1906 inclusive.[20] In 1906, he was a member of the sub-committee for the examination of candidates for posts in the Interpretation Sub-Department.[21]

The Chinese Teachers

The Chinese teachers were paid HK$10 a month per student. The rule seems to have evolved that they should teach each student for two hours a day.

There was frequently a shortage of suitable men. In 1870, Frederick Stewart wrote, "There are at present, but very few competent teachers in the Colony."[22]

In January 1886, it was agreed that the Head Master and Second Master of the Central School should share a single Chinese teacher. In Stewart's opinion, "This plan might be tried, as nothing else seems possible at present, but I am afraid it will not work. At the same time, it cannot be expected that a teacher of any standing will give his whole time to *one* man for $10 a month."[23]

The students were obviously very anxious to pass their examinations, particularly the teachers at the Central School. In 1891, Stewart's successor as Headmaster wrote as follows, presumably with *conscious* humour.

> Masters preparing for Examinations need a teacher to be at their beck and call, requiring them A.M. and P.M. sometimes at the Peak, sometimes at Kowloon; they cannot therefore be well compelled to share a master. Moreover the contre-temps that would arise through part ownership would multiply the applications for extension of time when summoned to an examination.[24]

The names of the teachers of these early government servants — whether student-interpreters or others — are not easy to find. Some of these men were Ho Alloy, Yau Lau-ting, Wong Hoi, Wong Kun-lan, Ho Fuk (brother of the later Sir Robert Ho Tung, and himself later a successful businessman), and Ho Tsung Chi.

Of Mr. Ho Tsung Chi, Frederick Stewart states, on 2 May 1882, that he had known him for twenty years "as a good scholar and successful teacher of Europeans and a man of very high character."[25] Given that this indicates that Stewart had known Mr. Ho since the time when he himself had arrived in Hong Kong (February 1862), was Ho Tsung Chi perhaps Frederick Stewart's own teacher? Certainly, we know that Mr. Ho was the teacher of J. Russell, Registrar General and later Chief Justice.

As is evident, some of these men acted as Chinese language teachers in addition to their other work, and some became extremely prominent in Hong Kong society, as their pupils did also.

The Student-interpreters

Of the student-interpreters, it has already been mentioned that one of the *second* batch — James Russell — became Chief Justice. One resigned before taking any examinations. The third man, Alfred Lister, became Postmaster General and Colonial Treasurer.[26] Of the *first* batch, Meredith Deane became Captain Superintendent of the Hong Kong Police. M. S. Tonnochy acted as Registrar General, and briefly, as Administrator of the Colony, and he was Superintendent of Victoria Gaol when he died. C. C. Smith became Registrar General of Hong Kong. Owing to a personality clash with Governor John Pope-Hennessy, however, Smith was lost to Hong Kong. Later he became Governor and Commander-in-chief of the Straits Settlements, and subsequently, Her Majesty's High Commissioner and Consul General for Borneo and Sarawak. The single student-interpreter appointed during the *third* recruitment exercise — H. E. Wodehouse — became Police Magistrate.

Chinese Teacher's Scheme

Frederick Stewart — who was not a student-interpreter — received the Chinese teacher's allowance from 1862. He became a popular hero for his work in education. Following a personality clash again with Governor John Pope-Hennessy, he became Police Magistrate, then Registrar General, and died in post as Colonial Secretary (now called Chief Secretary) of Hong Kong, the head of the permanent Hong Kong Civil Service.

To a large extent the men who have been named had been prepared for these responsible and distinguished positions by their Chinese Language studies, through the Chinese teacher's scheme. It can therefore be concluded that both the student-interpreters' scheme and the Chinese teacher's scheme were a considerable success.

Notes

[1]   The sources used for this article are mainly primary materials, found in the Public Records Office, Hong Kong. They are also available in the Hong Kong Collection at the Library of the University of Hong Kong . Many are also to be found in the libraries of other Hong Kong universities. An important and well-known source particularly used is Colonial Office Series 129, available in microfilm, containing original Despatches from the Government of Hong Kong and draft replies from the Colonial Office in the United Kingdom.

Abbreviations used in these Notes include:

CO: Colonial Office

CSO: Civil Service Order

HKGN: Hong Kong Government Notification

HKRS: Hong Kong Records Series

R: recto, v: verso: the front and back, respectively, of a manuscript sheet of paper.

[2]   This prolonged study has had numerous outputs including the monograph, *The Golden Needle: The Biography of Frederick Stewart (1836–1889)*, published by the David C. Lam Institute for East-West Studies, Hong Kong Baptist University, now available (with an optional set of CDs of the entire text) through The Chinese University Press.

[3]   Colonial Office Minute on the Report of the Committee on Official Interpretation, in Despatch No. 141, dated 3 April 1900. (CO/129/298/319–359.)

[4]   The present writer has accumulated enough material to trace government

initiatives in this area and their results *throughout* the nineteenth century, and to describe the arguments that were adduced while discussing them. The present article is necessarily brief. In due course, opportunity may arise for the presentation of a more complete description of the situation indicated by the total material that has been gathered.

5   Quoted, *Hong Kong Government Gazette*, 5 February 1881, p. 82.

6   Quoted, *Hong Kong Government Gazette*, 5 February 1881, p. 82.

7   Sir Hercules Robinson, Despatch No. 39 (Financial) to the Duke of Newcastle, dated 23 March 1861. (CO/129/80/399r.–405r., 400r.)

8   Governor Sir Hercules Robinson, Despatch No. 160 to the Duke of Newcastle, dated 26 September 1861. (CO/129/82/107r.–108v., 107v.) The stipulation described was enforced. Later, one student, whose progress was inadequate, was requested to reimburse the allowance he had received since the previous examination in August 1861, and his allowance was stopped. (See Sir Hercules Robinson, Despatch No. 65 (Miscellaneous) to the Duke of Newcastle, dated 12 April 1862. (CO/129/85/303r.–304r.))

9   Sir Hercules Robinson, Despatch No. 39 (Financial) to the Duke of Newcastle, dated 23 March 1861. (CO/129/80/399r.–405r., 401v.–402r.)

10 "Sketch of a Scheme for the Establishment of Hong Kong Cadetships" (CO/129/80/407r.–411r., 410r.), attached to Sir Hercules Robinson, Despatch No. 39 (Financial) to the Duke of Newcastle, dated 23 March 1861. (CO/129/80/339r.–405r.)

11 The four officers were T. Turner (Acting Registrar General), T. Ronald (Dispenser Civil Hospital), F. A. Sangster (Clerk and Accountant to the Superintendent of Police), F. H. Birch (Second Clerk and Accountant Colonial Treasury). (See Governor Sir Hercules Robinson, Despatch No. 160 to the Duke of Newcastle, dated 26 September 1861. (CO/129/82/107r.–108v., 108v.))

12 Governor Sir Hercules Robinson, Despatch No. 137 (Miscellaneous) to E. Cardwell, M. P., dated 20 September 1864. (CO/129/100/196r.–197v., 197v.)

13 "J. R.", Colonial Office, Minute dated 30 November [1864], on Governor Sir Hercules Robinson, Despatch No. 137 (Miscellaneous) to E. Cardwell, M. P., dated 20 September 1864. (CO/129/100/196r.–197v.)

14 Sir R. G. MacDonnell, Despatch No. 410, to the Duke of Buckingham, 13 December 1867. (CO/129/126/227r.-228v.; 227v.)

15 See Sir R. G. MacDonnell, Despatch No. 410, to the Duke of Buckingham, 13 December 1867. (CO/129/126/227r.–228v.)

16 Sir Richard MacDonnell, Despatch No. 410, dated 13 December 1867, paragraph 2. (CO/129/126/227r.–228v.) This is the D. R. Caldwell of whom E. J. Eitel writes as follows in his "Chinese Studies and Official Interpretation in the Colony of Hong Kong" (*The China Review*, 1877, pp. 1–13, p. 4, c. 2). "Even he, with his competent knowledge of the speech and customs of the Cantonese people, was but imperfectly acquainted with the written language and could therefore not do full justice to this important office [Protector of Chinese]." In the same essay, Eitel also speaks of Caldwell as being the only competent interpreter, "attached to the Police Magistracy or Supreme Court."

[17] *Daily Press*, 30 April 1877, p. 2, c. 3.

[18] Relating to the appointment of the Board of Examiners, see HKGN No. 146, dated 21 April 1883, *Hong Kong Government Gazette*, 21 April 1883, p. 364.

[19] HKGN No. 146, dated 21 April 1883, *Hong Kong Government Gazette*, 21 April 1883, p. 364.

[20] *Hong Kong Government Blue Books*, 1898 to 1906 inclusive, "Return of Members Composing the Board of Examiners."

[21] *Hong Kong Government Blue Book*, 1906, "Return of Members Composing the Board of Examiners". This sub-committee of the Board of Examiners was created on 28 March 1906. "With reference to HKGN No. 776 of the 16th December, 1902, His Excellency the Governor has been pleased to direct that the Board for the Examination of Interpreters shall from this date be incorporated with and shall form a sub-committee of the Board of Examiners." (Government Notification No. 275, dated 26 March 1906, *Hong Kong Government Gazette*, 30 March 1906, p. 368.)

[22] Frederick Stewart to J. Gardiner Austin, Colonial Secretary, 27 June 1870, HKRS 275, 1870.

[23] CSO 167, dated 19 January 1886, HKRS 275, 1885, Vol. II.

[24] George Bateson Wright, "Chinese Studies by English Masters of Victoria College," 16 November 1891. (CO/129/254/347r.–356v., 352v.) Enclosure No. 2 in Governor Sir William Robinson, Despatch No. 61 to Lord Knutsford, dated 23 February 1892. (CO/129/254/337r.–342r.)

[25] Frederick Stewart, No. 20, dated 2 May 1882, CSO No. 1477, HKRS 275, 1882, Vol. I.

[26] See HKGN No. 145, dated 21 April 1883, *Hong Kong Government Gazette*, 21 April 1883, p. 364.

Literary Translation in Hong Kong in the 1950s: Ma Lang's Translation of Erostratus in Literary Current Monthly Magazine

Yau Wai Ping
Department of English
Hong Kong Baptist University

The fictional writing of Jean-Paul Sartre first found its Chinese audience in 1956, when Ma Lang 馬朗 (the penname of Ma Boliang 馬博良, 1933–) published his translation of Sartre's short story *Erostratus* in the second issue of *Literary Current Monthly Magazine* 《文藝新潮》 — a literary magazine started in March 1956 by Ma Lang in Hong Kong. This translation in fact formed part of a project launched by this magazine to introduce French existentialist fiction to Chinese readers, which included Sartre's short story *The Wall* (translated by Ma Lang, issue 4, 1956), excerpts from Simone de Beauvoir's novel *The Mandarins* (translated by Ma Lang, issue 7, 1957), and Albert Camus's novella *The Stranger* (translated by Ma Lang and Yu Qing, issue 15, 1959).

As translator and editor, Ma Lang carefully constructed contexts for these translations in different ways — by providing commentaries on these existentialist writers, publishing Sartre's critical essay *John Dos Passos and 1919* (translated by Ma Lang, issue 11, 1957) to stress Sartre's concern with the temporal structure of narrative fiction; and publishing Ignazio Silone's interview with Camus (translated by Luo Miu, issue 14, 1958) to highlight Camus's stance on Communism. Ma Lang also planned to publish a translation of Sartre's critical essay on Camus's *The Stranger*, but this never materialised because the magazine folded shortly after the issue containing the translation of *The Stranger* came out in May 1959.

Why was Ma Lang attracted to French existentialist fiction? Focusing on his translation of *Erostratus*, this paper argues that Ma Lang was attracted to the image of the protagonist as an individual who, confronted with a world without inherent meaning, creates an identity through choices made in concrete circumstances, and who can challenge the roles and values prescribed by society. Further, this paper argues that Ma Lang sought to capture such an image through a close translation method. Finally, this paper argues that Ma Lang's translation constituted an alternative to the individual's subordination to society as sanctioned by the Chinese Communist Party (CCP).

When Ma Lang published, under the title "伊樂斯特拉士士" ("Yilesitelatushi"), his translation of a short story by Sartre in the second issue (1956) of *Literary Current Monthly Magazine*, he did not specify the source language. This was a common practice during the period when Ma Lang was translating. There is no doubt, however, that Ma Lang's translation was based on Lloyd Alexander's 1948 English translation *Erostratus* from the French original *Erostrate* (Sartre, 1939), as can be demonstrated by a detailed comparison of the Chinese and English translations. In *Erostratus*, the alienated protagonist seeks to shock a self-satisfied society and — after that fails — remains free to choose how he faces his future. The image of the protagonist as a person who creates his own values and challenges what is commonly considered self-evident is brought out in Ma Lang's translation through the close translation method. Ma Lang also calls attention to the protest launched by Sartre's alienated protagonist against a complacent society by comparing, in the translator's note, *Erostratus* to two short stories by the Chinese writer Lu Xun. This is significant because at the time when Ma Lang published his translation, Lu Xun was canonised by the CCP as a champion of Socialist Realism — the artistic credo calling for the creation of unambiguously positive characters at the service of China's socialist transformation. Placed in the context of Chinese literature in the 1950's, the image of the individual as conveyed in Ma Lang's translation constituted an alternative to the version of self constructed by the CCP.

Erostratus is a story told in the first person by the office worker Paul Hilbert, who despises society for its complacency. Hilbert lives alone in a seventh-floor apartment overlooking a busy street in Paris. He seldom leaves his home, apart from going out to eat and work. He shuns other people, whom he perceives as his enemies and persecutors. But he starts to walk the streets after he buys a revolver that makes him feel safer in the midst of the crowd. On the first Saturday every month, he pays the prostitute Lea to undress in front of him in a hotel room to satisfy his sadism and voyeurism. One night, when he fails to find Lea, he forces an unwilling prostitute to perform this sexual ritual for him by threatening to use his revolver. Pleased by his power to shock this prostitute, Hilbert plans to scandalise society by arbitrarily shooting six people in the street and then killing himself. Hilbert hopes to invent an identity for himself that will be fixed forever on the collective mind. He is encouraged by the ancient Greek legend of Erostratus, who is known for setting fire to the spectacular temple of Ephesus. But Hilbert also hopes to shock society out of its complacency. He sets out the reasons for his revolt against society in a letter addressed to 102 French writers who are praised by the public for their love of humanity. Hilbert, however, fails to carry out his plan in the cold, calm manner he has intended. In a state of panic, he shoots a pedestrian three times and fires twice on another. Pursued by a crowd, Hilbert seeks refuge in the toilet of a café. Hilbert fails to find the courage to carry out his plan to kill himself. Finally, he drops his revolver and pushes open the door of the toilet. Hilbert's loss of nerve at the crucial moment of his life shows him to be a coward, rather than the hero he imagines himself to be. But, ending with Hilbert's act of opening the door, the story also suggests that Hilbert is free to choose how he faces his future.

The protagonist of *Erostratus* is a loner who questions what is considered unquestionable and who can depart from a previously pursued path. In the Chinese translation, Ma Lang captures this image of the protagonist by retaining the plot and closely following the textual features of the English translation.

In the very first paragraph of the English translation, tension is set up between Hilbert and society as Hilbert looks at the people in the street from his seventh-floor apartment:

> You really have to see men from above. I put out the light and went to the window: they never suspected for a moment you could watch them from up there. They're careful of their fronts, sometimes of their backs, but their whole effect is calculated for spectators of about five feet eight. Who ever thought about the shape of a derby hat seen from the seventh floor? They neglect protecting their heads and shoulders with bright colors and garish clothes, they don't know how to fight this great enemy of Humanity, the downward perspective. I leaned on the windowsill and began to laugh: where was this wonderful upright stance they're so proud of: they were crushed against the sidewalk and two long legs jumped out form under their shoulders (Lloyd, 1948: 81).

Hilbert finds the pedestrians foolish: they pay particular attention to how they appear to the average person in the street but are completely unaware that they are being watched from another angle. Seeing the pedestrians as a conventional and narrow-minded bunch, Hilbert presents himself as alone and above others both physically and intellectually. The contrast between Hilbert and other people is reinforced by the repeated references to the pedestrians as *they*. The word *they* is in fact used six times in this passage. At first sight the use of this word seems quite natural given the fact that the pedestrians are strangers to the protagonist, but the passage suggests more than this, for the repetition contributes to the impression that the pedestrians are a mass of nameless, faceless people. Furthermore, Hilbert's ridicule of the stupidity of the pedestrians reveals a sadistic pleasure as he visually squeezes the pedestrians into insect-like creatures. Hilbert's criticism of and alienation from society is evident even this early in the narrative.

This is Ma Lang's translation of the opening paragraph:

> 你真應該從上面俯看人群，我熄掉燈走到窗前，他們絕不會疑心到有一刻你會由高處向下注視他們。他們只顧及前面，有時也顧及後面，但整個風貌只為五尺八寸高的觀看者計算，有誰會想到一頂圓硬氈帽從七層樓上望下去成何形狀呢?他們總是忽略了用炫目色彩和華麗衣服保護頭顱肩膀，他們不知道如何抗爭這個人性的巨敵，一幅鳥瞰的透視圖。我倚著窗臺不禁笑了：他們昂然自得的那一副端正的姿態那兒去了：他們都被擠到行人道上就從肩膀底下跳出兩條長腿。 (Ma, 1956: 22)

Back-translation (author's note: all translations from Chinese in this paper are mine):

> You really should look at the crowd from above, I put out the light and went to the window, they never suspected for a moment you would watch them from high above. They take into account only their fronts, sometimes they also take into account their backs, but the whole appearance is calculated only for a spectator of about five feet eight. Who will notice what shape a derby takes as it is seen from the seventh floor? They always neglect protecting their heads and shoulders with dazzling colours and richly ornamented clothes, they don't know how to fight this great enemy of human nature, a bird's-eye perspective drawing. I leaned on the window sill and couldn't help laughing: where was that upright stance which made them so proud and self-satisfied: they were squeezed against the sidewalk and two long legs jumped out from under their shoulders.

Ma Lang's translation is largely accurate, although the rendering of "they don't know how to fight this great enemy of Humanity, the downward perspective" as "他們不知道如何抗爭這個人性的巨敵，一幅鳥

瞰的透視圖." Back-translation: "they don't know how to fight this great enemy of human nature, a bird's-eye perspective drawing" is perhaps slightly problematic. Ma Lang renders the English word *humanity* as "人性" ("human nature"), rejecting options such as "人" and "人類" ("humankind," "people"). The expression "人性" ("human nature") can suggest the existence of an essential human quality — a notion Hilbert rejects in his letter to the French writers. The English word *downward* becomes "鳥瞰" ("bird's-eye"), a stock metaphor that suggests "from high above" and therefore preserves the primary meaning of *downward*. But the translation of the English word *perspective* as "透視圖" ("perspective drawing") is not strictly accurate, for the Chinese term refers to "a drawing showing depth and distance," rather than "a way of seeing or thinking," which makes more sense in this sentence. But, despite this mistranslation, Ma Lang's translation successfully reproduces the thrust of the English passage by closely following the textual features of the English translation. The Chinese translation generally gives the literal meanings of the English words. A departure from this procedure is the translation of the English word *men* as "人群" ("crowd") in the opening sentence. The Chinese expression evokes the picture of a large number of people and is anchored to the action of the protagonist (going to the window to look at the people in the street) in a shift in punctuation that produces a string of three sentences connected by commas. Such a shift suggests a slightly different way of opening the short story. Whereas the English translation starts with the protagonist's general comment on "men," the Chinese translation plunges the reader into the action of the protagonist and encourages the reader to extrapolate the general case from the details of the passage.

Apart from these shifts, the Chinese translation stays close to the syntax of the English sentences as far as structural differences between English and Chinese allow and largely retains the textual features of the English translation. The Chinese translation, for example, reproduces the repetition of *they*. Ma Lang uses a rather long sentence at the end of this paragraph to preserve the punctuation scheme since it stresses the sarcasm and sadism of the protagonist. The colons connecting the last three sentences provide a close link between Hilbert's laughter and his mental picture of the pedestrians being crushed into insect-like creatures. By means of the close translation method, Ma Lang is able to bring out the protagonist's criticism of and alienation from society set up in the opening paragraph of the English translation.

Hilbert constantly keeps away from other people, as he admits: "It's much harder to consider people as ants when you're on the same plane as they are: they touch you." (Lloyd, 1948: 82) This becomes "和他們在同一高低位置的時候，再把眾人視作螻蟻就很困難！他們是會接觸你的." (Ma, 1956: 22) Back-translation: "When you're on the same plane as they are, it's very difficult to look on people as moles and ants! They come into contact with you." The image of the English word *ants* as well as its sense of disdain is reproduced in the Chinese translation with the use of the stock metaphor "螻蟻," which means "moles and ants" and denotes "nonentities." The English word *touch* is more problematic because it carries an ambiguity ("to make physical contact with someone" and "to affect someone emotionally") that is supported by an event in subsequent sentences: Hilbert faints when he comes face to face with the dead body of a man in the street. What comes out clearly in the Chinese translation just quoted is, however, the central character's concern about physical contact with other people. The ambiguity of the English word *touch* is absent probably because Ma Lang was not aware of this ambiguity: Ma Lang could have reproduced the double meanings of the English word — if he had wanted—by, for example, setting out its two senses.

In the English translation, Hilbert's fear of contact with other people is in fact presented as part of his persecution complex: he stubbornly believes that there are people in the street who are constantly trying to harm him. Ma Lang again sticks to the English translation in rendering this anxiety. For example, "When they got me and knew *who* I was, they gave me the works," (Lloyd, 1948: 83) is translated as "他們一旦捉住我，知道我的底細，他們便叫我吃生活." (Ma, 1956: 23) Back-translation: "When they got me and knew who I really was, they beat the hell out of me.") Here the Chinese slang "吃生活" ("beat the hell out of") is used to capture the colloquial flavour of the English expression "gave me the works."

The English translation also shows Hilbert's sexual relationship with women to be a symptom of his general inability to relate to people. Hilbert treats women as objects of voyeurism and sadism: he cannot establish any real relationship with them. Take Hilbert's treatment of the prostitute Lea: "She undressed and I watched her without touching her. Sometimes I went off in my pants all by myself, other times I had time to get home and finish it." (Lloyd, 1948: 84) Ma Lang is able to reproduce Hilbert's anxiety to avoid contact with the woman by sticking to the English translation:

> 她寬衣解帶，而我只看住她不去碰一下，有時我自動就洩在褲裡，有時，我還及時到家加以解決。(Ma, 1956: 23)

Back-translation:

She undressed and I watched her without touching her. Sometimes, I went off in my pants all by myself, other times, I still had enough time to get home and finish it.

Hilbert is not just a pervert suffering from persecution complex, however. He challenges values most people consider to be beyond criticism. Hilbert's criticism of society is expressed most vehemently in his letter addressed to the French writers. Hilbert's letter begins: "You are a famous man and your works sell by the thousands. I am going to tell you why: because you love men. You have humanism in your blood: you are lucky." (Lloyd, 1948: 93) In Hilbert's view, these writers are popular because their works celebrate the love for people. The term *humanism* is not defined but its meaning becomes clearer when it is considered in the context of this passage: "You expand when you are with people; as soon as you see one of your fellows, even without knowing them, you feel sympathy for him." (Lloyd, 1948: 93) According to Hilbert, these writers feel comfortable when they are with other people; they feel they can understand other people since they all share a common identity as members of the human race. What Hilbert refers to as *humanism* is therefore related to a readiness to recognise an abstract human quality shared by all people, as is emphasised by the expressions "as soon as" and "even without knowing him" in the extract. These details are reproduced in Ma Lang's close translation:

當你和人群相處，你會胸襟擴大；只要你見到其中一個人，即使毫不相識，你也對他感到同情。 (Ma, 1956: 26)

Back-translation:

When you are with the crowd, your horizon broadens: as soon as you see one of them, even without knowing him, you feel sympathy for him.

In his letter to these writers, Hilbert writes of their admiration for that unique human quality that makes human beings superior to all other species: "You are delighted when your neighbor takes a cup from the table because there is a way of taking it which is strictly human and which you have often described in your works: less supple, less rapid than that of a monkey, but is it not so much more intelligent?" (Lloyd, 1948: 93) Hilbert is challenging these writers' definition of human beings in terms of an essential quality that places the human race at the centre of the world. This is the Chinese translation:

當你的鄰舍從桌上拿起一隻杯子時，你也很高興，因為手取之時也有一
種絕對的人情味，在你的作品中時有描寫；也許不及猿猴柔軟迅速，可
是不是更聰明得多嗎？(Ma, 1956: 26)

Back-translation:

When your neighbour takes a cup from the table, you are also delighted.
Because the way the hand takes an object has an absolutely human touch and
you have often described this in your works; perhaps less supple and rapid
than apes and monkeys, but is it not so much more intelligent?

Apart from the expressions "人情味" (literally, "taste of human
feelings"; here back-translated as "human touch") and "猿猴"("apes and
monkeys"), the Chinese translation closely follows the English translation
and reproduces the emphasis on human inventiveness and intelligence that
marks out humans from other animals.

Further, Hilbert suggests in his letter that this notion of an essential
human quality—celebrated in these writers' works and shared by their
readers—serves as a compensation or consolation for the frustrations facing people in everyday life: "People throw themselves greedily upon your
books, they read them in a good armchair, they think of a great love,
discreet and unhappy, which you bring them and that makes up for many
things, for being ugly, for being cowardly, for being cuckolded, for not
getting a raise on the first of January. And they say willingly of your latest
book: it's a good deed." (Lloyd, 1948: 93–4) This is the Chinese
translation:

人們貪黷地投到你的著作上去，坐在一張好好的臂椅上細讀，他們想到
一種偉大的愛情，謹慎而不快樂，那都是你帶給他們，以之彌補許多事
物的代替，使他們忘卻生成醜陋的相貌，品性懦怯，被帶上綠頭巾或正
月初一未獲加薪。於是他們情願對你的一本近著評論道：這是一大好事。
(Ma, 1956: 26)

Back-translation:

People throw themselves greedily upon your works, they read them closely in
a good armchair, they think of a great love, discreet and unhappy, which you
bring them as a substitute for many things, to make them forget being ugly,
being cowardly, being cuckolded or not getting a pay rise on the first of
January. Therefore they would rather comment on your latest work: it's really
a great deed.

The choice of the Chinese expression "愛情" (here back-translated as
love) seems strange since the term usually refers to love between a man and

a woman, whereas *love* in the English translation suggests a more general feeling of affection arising from the notion of an essential human quality shared by all people. Otherwise, the Chinese translation sticks to the English translation and clearly conveys Hilbert's criticism that these writers' works offer their readers a distraction from their day-to-day problems.

In his letter, Hilbert is also rebelling against the everyday language that has become saturated with an unquestioned notion of an essential human quality: "Even the tools I used I felt belonged to them; words, for example: I wanted *my own* words. But the ones I use have dragged through I don't know how many consciences; they arrange themselves in my head by virtue of the habits I have picked up from the others and it is not without repugnance that I use them in writing to you. But this is the last time." (Lloyd, 1948: 94) Hilbert's complaint about having to use a language saturated with opinions of other people is rendered closely in the Chinese translation:

甚至我用的器皿，我覺得也是屬於他們的；譬如說，用字上面：我就要用自己的字，結果所用者不知拖過多少人的良心了；這些字倚靠我從他處拾來的習慣，將自己安頓在我的頭裡，我現在用它來寫信給你，實際上也是十分嫌惡的，不過這是最後一次了。 (Ma, 1956: 27)

Back-translation:

Even the utensils I used, I felt they also belonged to them; take, for example, words: I wanted to use my own words. But the ones I use have dragged through I don't know how many consciences; these words have settled in my mind according to the habit I have picked up from the others. I'm now using them to write to you. Actually it's very disgusting. But this is the last time.

By arbitrarily shooting people in the street and setting out the reasons for his revolt against society in his letter to the French writers, Hilbert hopes to shake society out of its stupor.

Hilbert also hopes to invent an identity for himself that will be fixed forever on the collective mind: "I too, one day at the end of my sombre life, would explode and light the world with a flash as short and violent as magnesium." (Lloyd, 1948: 92) The protagonist strives to project a permanent self-image through an act of extreme violence. Hilbert imagines himself to explode and shine strongly for a short time before fading into nothingness. This momentary light is compared to magnesium, which is used in flash photography to freeze an instant in the flow of time. This is Ma Lang's translation:

有一天，我陰鬱的生活告終，我就會爆炸起來、短促而凶猛恰如鎂光一樣的火花會照耀世界。(Ma, 1956: 26)

Back-translation:

One day, when my dismal life ends, then I will explode, a flash as exactly short, quick, fierce and violent as magnesium will brighten up the world.

In Ma Lang's translation, Hilbert's desire for a permanent identity is rendered by a strong adjective of power and violence: "凶猛" ("fierce and violent") is frequently associated with frightening animals. Also, the connection between the protagonist and his imagined identity is effectively reproduced in the movement from "I" to "a flash" in a flow of similarly structured sentences.

Hilbert's attempt to create an immutable self-image in fact represents the culmination of his alienation from others: he desires to divorce himself completely from the concrete circumstances of human existence by transforming himself into something that will not be touched by time. In the English translation, in the paragraphs leading to the execution of Hilbert's scandalous plan, the reader is constantly reminded that this is the work of a loner. For example, the confrontation between the loner and the crowd is underlined in this English passage: "Suddenly I saw myself in the heart of this mob, horribly alone and little. How they could have hurt me if they wanted! I was afraid because of the gun in my pocket. It seemed to me they could guess it was there. They would look at me with their hard eyes and would say: 'Hey there… hey…!' with happy indignation, harpooning me with their men's paws. Lynched! They would throw me up above their heads and I would fall back in their arms like a marionette." (Lloyd, 1948: 58) This becomes

突然地我看見自己在人群中心裡了，是那麼可怕的孤單渺小；假如他們想，他們可以把我傷害得多厲害呵！因為袋中懷槍我很害怕，彷彿路人猜到我藏械似的，他們會用嚴厲的眼睛看住我，義憤填膺的說道：「喂，那邊那個……喂……」然後用他們的爪叉住我，將我擲到他們頭上一般高，像傀儡似的跌回他們懷抱裡。(Ma, 1956: 28)

Back-translation:

Suddenly I saw myself in the heart of the crowd, so horribly alone and little; how badly they could have hurt me if they wanted to! I was afraid because I was carrying a gun in my pocket. It seemed the other people in the street could guess I was armed. They would look at me with their hard eyes and would say with indignation: "Hey there … you… hey!" Then they would harpoon me with their claws. They would throw me up above their heads and let me fall into their arms like a marionette.

The adjective *happy* (qualifying "indignation") and the short but significant expression "Lynched!" are absent from the Chinese translation, although it is not clear whether it is on account of oversight or deliberate omission on the part of the translator. But, on the whole, the Chinese translation successfully conveys the confrontation between the loner and the crowd by keeping close to the English translation.

In the final scene of *Erostratus*, Hilbert locks himself in the toilet of a cafe after his bungled attempt to shock society. Failing to find the courage to shoot himself, Hilbert drops his revolver and throws open the door:

> There was silence and the same voice went on, "You know you can't get away."
>
> I didn't answer, I was still gasping for breath. To encourage myself to shoot, I told myself, "If they get me, they're going to beat me, break my teeth, maybe put an eye out." I wanted to know if the big man was dead. Maybe I only wounded him… They were getting something ready, they were dragging something heavy across the floor. I hurriedly put the barrel of the gun in my mouth, and I bit hard on it. But I couldn't shoot, I couldn't even put my finger on the trigger. Everything was dead silent.
>
> I threw away the revolver and opened the door. (Lloyd, 1948: 10)

This is Ma Lang's translation:

> 依然是寂靜無聲，同一個聲音說下去：「你知道你絕對跑不了。」
> 我沒有回答，仍在透氣。為了鼓勵自己開槍自殺，我告訴自己：「如果他們拿住我，他們要打我，敲碎我的牙，或者挖出一隻眼睛來。」我要知道那大個子是否死了，或者我只不過打傷了他……他們在預備甚麼了，在把一些沉重的東西拖過地板上來。我急忙把槍管對住我的嘴巴，用力的咬了一口。但是我總是不能開槍，我甚至無法把手指按到槍機上，一切都是死樣靜寂。
>
> 我擲下槍，打開了門。 (Ma, 1956: 29)

Back-translation:

> It was still silent, and the same voice went on, "You know for sure you can't get away."
>
> I didn't answer. I was still gasping for breath. To encourage myself to shoot, I told myself, "If they get me, they will beat me, break my teeth, or maybe gouge an eye out." I must find out if the big man was dead, maybe I just wounded him…. They were preparing for something, they were dragging

something heavy across the floor. I hurriedly pointed the barrel of the gun at my mouth and bit hard on it. But I just couldn't shoot, I couldn't even put my finger on the trigger. Everything was dead silent.

I threw away my gun and opened the door.

Ma Lang's close translation successfully captures Hilbert's thoughts, the surrounding silence, the mounting suspense and the dramatic ending. Hilbert fails to find the courage to kill himself and proves to be a coward, rather than the hero he hopes to be. But Ma Lang's translation also reproduces the sense of an opening at the end of *Erostratus*. By ending with Hilbert's act of openning the door, the short story suggests that Hilbert is free to choose how he faces his future.

Ma Lang's translation, in spite of some infelicities, is largely accurate and successful in reproducing the protagonist's revolt against society. The image of the protagonist as an individual that can reject what is commonly regarded as unquestionable is in fact a feature of *Erostratus* that Ma Lang emphasises in the translator's note. There, Ma Lang writes of *Erostratus*: "這是一部世紀末文明下新的'狂人日記',法蘭西的'阿Q正傳'." (Ma, 1956: 23) Back-translation: "This is a new *Diary of a Madman* in a fin-de-siècle civilisation, is France's *The True Story of Ah Q*."

It is necessary to provide a brief account of Lu Xun's two short stories before pursuing their parallels with *Erostratus*. Lu Xun's 1918 short story *Diary of a Madman* contains thirteen diary entries describing the deepening mental crisis of the Madman. The Madman suspects that people are trying to harm him and, after reading a number of Confucian classics, comes to the conclusion that China has always been a cannibalistic society for the past four thousand years. In the last entry, the Madman expresses his hope for a better future generation. But this hope is implied in the narrative framework: in the preface written by a friend of the Madman, it is reported that the Madman has recovered from his persecution complex and taken up an official post.

While *Diary of a Madman* concentrates on the consciousness of a lone protester, the central character in Lu Xun's 1921 short story *The True Story of Ah Q* embodies what Lu Xun sees as the weaknesses of the Chinese people. *The True Story of Ah Q* is cast in the form of biography, which is traditionally reserved for a morally elevated character. Ironically, the salient feature of the protagonist Ah Q is his lack of self-awareness. Ah Q often avoids reality by rationalising a defeat into a "spiritual victory." He claims to be a revolutionary and robs the rich during the 1911 Chinese

Revolution without knowing what the chaos is all about. Ah Q is convicted of theft and sentenced to death by public execution.

Both Hilbert and the Madman are protesters that see society as self-deceiving. Hilbert criticises people for escaping from everyday problems by subscribing to an optimistic notion of a permanent human quality. Chinese civilisation, despite its celebration of Confucian virtue and morality, is considered by the Madman as cannibalistic. While Hilbert sets out to shock a self-satisfied society by shooting people in the street, the Madman passionately appeals for an end to the widespread and unquestioned practice of eating people. Further, both Hilbert and the Madman are alienated individuals that cannot relate to other people: both fictional characters in fact suffer from the classic symptoms of persecution complex such as suspiciousness and sensitivity to rejection by others.

Whereas *Erostratus* and *Diary of a Madman* are similar in presenting the protagonist as an alienated protester against society, what is common between *Erostratus* and *The True Story of Ah Q* is not so much traits shared by the central characters, but rather the theme of society's complacency. In *Erostratus*, social criticism comes from the comments made by the central character, whereas in *The True Story of Ah Q*, the central character is the object of sarcasm and ridicule in a parody of a narrative form usually occasioned by an outstanding character. Intended by Lu Xun as a symbol for the Chinese people, Ah Q lacks self-awareness and critical judgment and continues to be complacent about the way he lives his life until, at the very end of the short story, when he realizes he has to face death alone.

By comparing *Erostratus* to Lu Xun's *Diary of a Madman* and *The True Story of Ah Q*, Ma Lang calls attention to the protest launched by the alienated protagonist of Sartre's short story against a complacent society. In the translator's note, the reader is invited to see the similarities between these stories. Ma Lang not only draws attention to what attracts him to Sartre's tale, but also brings to the foreground facets of Lu Xun's fictional writing that stand in sharp contrast to the CCP's portrait of the Chinese writer. Since Lu Xun's death in 1936, the CCP have presented him as a faithful follower of the Party and a staunch supporter of Communism. They have downplayed the tension between the individual and society in his works by depicting these features as being appropriate to a past period in history and no longer applicable to Communist China. At the time when Ma Lang published his translation of *Erostratus*, Lu Xun was in fact presented by the CCP as a champion of Socialist Realism. Feng Xuefeng 馮雪峰, a prominent Mainland critic entrusted with the task of annotating the *Lu Xun quanji*, or *The Complete Works of Lu Xun*, wrote of Lu Xun in an article first published in *Wenyi bao*《文藝報》, or *Literary Gazette*, in 1952 and later reprinted in Feng's 1981 collection of critical essays:

> 他在一九二七年之後，改變了階級立場，從一個革命民主主義者，進而成為一個共產主義者……他在後期，跟著思想的改變，在文學上成為社會主義現實主義者。(Ma, 1956: 506)

Back-translation:

> After 1927, he changed his class stand from a revolutionary democrat to a Communist.... In his later life, following the change in his thought, he became a Socialist Realist in his literary career.

Socialist Realism, adopted by the CCP from the Soviet Union in the early 1930's, was officially declared "the criterion of literary creation and criticism in China at the Second National Conference of the Representatives of Literature and Art Workers in 1953." (Yang, 1998: 17) Socialist Realism emphasized "the portrayal of new characters (heroic characters)" displaying "socialist or communist morality and ideology." (Yang, 1998: 19) Seen as servants to the state, writers were called on to create heroic characters contributing to the cause of socialist society. Such an emphasis continued to inform later slogans like "Combination of Revolutionary Realism and Revolutionary Romanticism" (革命現實主義和革命浪漫主義相結合) and reached its peak during the Cultural Revolution. (Yang, 1998: 27)

The promotion of Socialist Realism was paralleled by the emergence of a nationwide translation policy "as part of a strict educational program" adopted by CCP. (Bauer, 1964: 4) The CCP's translation policy was modelled on the Soviet Union "not only insofar as her literature was particularly translated but also as to the selection of all non-Russian translation." (Bauer, 1964: 6) In the period 1949–1960, 1,907 literary works translated from Russian were published in China, representing 56.4 per cent of the total 3,379 works of literary translations published (Bauer, 1964: 17). Literary translations from Western languages like English, French and German concentrated on nineteenth century writers; "modern or contemporary Western writers, however, were very much neglected." (Bauer, 1964: 24)

As editor and translator of a literary magazine based in the then British colony of Hong Kong, Ma Lang took advantage of the freedom of expression allowed by the colonial administration and pursued a translation policy that countered the prevailing literary trend in mainland China in the

1950's. Ma Lang's translation of *Erostratus* departed from the CCP's concentration on translations of works by contemporary Soviet writers and nineteenth century Western writers. His translation presented a protagonist who challenges values commonly considered beyond criticism, in sharp contrast to the self's subordination to society under the slogan of Socialist Realism sanctioned by the CCP. Placed in the context of Chinese literature in the 1950's, Ma Lang's translation of *Erostratus* in *Literary Current Monthly Magazine* in fact constituted an alternative to the CCP's version of self by reproducing the tension between the individual and society.

References

Bauer, Wolfgang (1964). *Western Literature and Translation Work in Communist China*. Hamburg: Institut für Asienkunde.

Feng, Xuefeng 馮雪峰 (1981).〈中國文學中從古典現實主義到社會主義現實主義的發展的一個輪廓〉(A Sketch of the Development from Classical Realism to Socialist Realism in Chinese Literature). In《馮雪峰論文集》(*Collected Critical Essays by Feng Xuefeng*). Beijing: Renmin wenxue chubanshe, pp. 478–529.

Lloyd, Alexander, tr. (1948). "Erostratus." (Original work by Sartre). *The Wall and Other Stories*. New York: New Directions, pp. 81–104.

Lu, Xun 魯迅 (1981).〈阿Q正傳〉(The True Story of Ah Q). In《魯迅小說集》(*Collected Stories of Lu Xun*). Beijing: Renmin wenxue chubanshe, pp. 69–109.

Lu, Xun 魯迅 (1981).〈狂人日記〉(The Diary of a Madman).《魯迅小說集》(*Collected Stories of Lu Xun*). Beijing: Renmin wenxue chubanshe, pp. 9–19.

Ma, Lang 馬朗 (1956).〈伊樂斯特拉士士〉(Yilesitelatushi).《文藝新潮》(*Literary Current Monthly Magazine*), Vol. 2, pp. 22–9.

Sartre, Jean-Paul (1939). *Erostrate*. In *Le Mur*. Paris: Gallimard, pp. 75–9.

Yang, Lan (1998). *Chinese Fiction of the Cultural Revolution*. Hong Kong: Hong Kong University Press.

The Hong Kong Translation Society: A Concise History, 1971–1999

Liu Ching-chih
Department of Translation
Lingnan University

The Hong Kong Translation Society (HKTS) is the only body for translators and interpreters in Hong Kong. During the past 28 years, the Society has developed from an organisation of an academic nature to a fully-fledged society for teachers and researchers as well as practitioners. The development has, to a certain extent, reflected the changes in the language scene in Hong Kong. A review of the history of the Society will help us understand more the role of the relationship between Chinese and English played in Hong Kong between 1971 and the end of the twentieth century. [1]

The Establishment of the Society

Early in 1971, a group of translators and scholars considered the possibility of establishing a translation society with an aim at promoting research and strengthening the liaison of the translation profession. After discussions, they decided to convene the first meeting on 12 March 1971 and appointed Mr. Louis Cha 查良鏞 to draft a circular letter to notify those who were interested in setting up a society for translators. The text of the letter was as follows:

> We propose to set up a Hong Kong Translation Society and sincerely hope you will join us to establish this organisation.
>
> It is envisaged that this Society will be of an academic nature. We are very much interested in translation and know very well how enjoyable and yet tedious the work is. If we are able to get together from time to time to exchange our views and experience, which will definitely help broaden our horizon and enlighten our aspirations. We will then be able to cherish the same ideals and share a common goal.

This Society could engage in work which would benefit the development of Hong Kong and promote the cultural exchanges between China and foreign countries, such as publishing books of academic value and journals, researching on issues pertaining to translation, organising conferences, *etc.*, with a view to improving the standard of translation, assisting in language training and encouraging scholars to engage in Chinese to foreign languages translation and *vice versa*. It is hoped that as a result of our work, the Society will make contributions to our community and exert a profound influence over the development of our culture.

Enclosed please find a copy of a draft of the Society's Constitution. We hope you will agree with the broad principles contained in the Constitution. It has been decided that a meeting for the founding of the Society will take place at the Top Floor of Tak Shing Building, Des Voeux Road Central on 12 March 1971. We earnestly hope you will attend this meeting. We all expect an interesting and exciting gathering. [2]

The circular letter was signed by Yu Ye-lu 余也魯, Stephen C. Soong 宋淇, Louis Cha, Alex Sun Hsu-hsien 孫述憲, Ma Meng 馬蒙, Wong Siu-kit 黃兆傑 and Lai Tim-cheong 賴恬昌.

The meeting was convened as scheduled and two resolutions were endorsed: (1) a preparatory committee be set up for the organising work; and (2) Mr. Peter Wong Chak-cheung 王澤長 be appointed Honorary Legal Advisor of the Society. Members of the Preparatory Committee consisted of Louis Cha, T. C. Lai, Ma Meng, Stephen C. Soong, Alex H. H. Sun, Phillip S. Y. Sun 孫述宇 and Wong Siu-kit. In "the Memorandum and Articles of Association" of the Hong Kong Translation Society Limited, the names of the subscribers were the seven preparatory committee members. The Society was officially incorporated on the 6th day of October 1971.

In accordance with "the Memorandum and Articles of Association," the descriptions of the seven subscribers were: Louis Cha — Newspaper Publisher, T. C. Lai — University Administrator, Ma Meng — University Professor, Stephen C. Soong — University Administrator, Alex H. H. Sun—Institute Director, Phillip S. Y. Sun — University Teacher, and Wong Siu-kit — University Teacher. Of the seven members, five were university administrators and teachers, one newspaper publisher and one business executive, a distinctive "university majority," so were members of the Society at that time.

The establishment of a translation society in Hong Kong in 1971 was indeed commendable on two grounds: In 1971, English was the only official language in Hong Kong and Chinese had no importance at all in the school curriculum as well as in the official sector; and translation was not common in Government in which English was the language of administration and law. It was not until 1974 that Chinese was made one of the two official languages in Hong Kong. Before 1974, the post of Chinese Language Officer was few in number and low in rank.

Activities 1971–1999

Membership of the first Executive Committee comprised Ma Meng as Chairman, T. C. Lai as Vice-Chairman, Stephen C. Soong as Honorary Secretary, Phillip S. Y. Sun as Honorary Editor of *Bulletin*, Lam Shan-mu 林山木 as Honorary Treasurer, Peter Wong Chak-cheung as Honorary Legal Advisor; and members included Louis Cha, Alex Sun, Wong Siu-kit and Yu Ye-lu. Of these members, T. C. Lai has always taken a keen interest in the well-being of the Society and has been sustaining his service to the Society during the past 28 years: Vice-Chairman 1971–1973; Chairman 1974–1976, 1980–1982, 1982–1984 and 1984–1986; Member of the Executive Committee 1976–1978, 1978–1980, 1986–1988 and 1988–1990; and Advisor 1990-to-date. For the full list of the Executive Committee membership, please refer to Appendix 1: Membership of the Executive Committee 1971–2000.

During the past 28 years, the Society has persistently followed the objectives of the Society as stipulated in Article 3 of the "Memorandum and Articles of Association." [3] The following is a summary of the activities of the Society during the years 1971 to 1999.

1. Publications

A. *The Bulletin*《譯訊》

Immediately after the establishment of the Society, the Executive Committee decided to publish a newsletter, the *Bulletin*, for members of the Society. Items reported in the *Bulletin* included activities such as conferences, publications, teaching and research, Government translation services, translation activities, news about members of the Society, *etc.* The first issue was published on 1 August 1972 with Phillip Sun as Editor. From then till to date, 38 issues were published. [4]

B. Conferences and Proceedings and Collected Essays

In view of the fact that it was very difficult to have sufficient items for inclusion in the *Bulletin*, the Executive Committee decided, after the combined issues 19 and 20 were published in March 1979, that the publication of the *Bulletin* be made flexible and therefore irregular and that the Society would instead organise conferences and seminars and would then publish proceedings and papers of the conferences and seminars, also on an irregular basis. The first public conference was jointly convened with the Urban Council Public Libraries and held in 1980, at which four speakers delivered four papers on literary translation, translation of economic terminology, poetry translation and legal translation. The four speakers were Mr. Stephen C. Soong, Professor D. C. Lau 劉殿爵, Dr. Y. C. Jao 饒餘慶 and Dr. Wong Kam-hung 黃金鴻. Thereafter, the Society held eight conferences during the 1980s in 1980, 1981, 1983, 1985, 1986, 1987, 1988 and 1989, except the fourth one in 1985, the other seven were jointly held with the Urban Council Public Libraries.

In addition to the conferences mentioned above, the Society also collaborated with other institutions to organise conferences, including: (2) Conference on "Translation To-day" in 1987, jointly with the University of Hong Kong, The Chinese University of Hong Kong (CUHK), the Hong Kong Polytechnic (HKP), City Polytechnic of Hong Kong (CPHK), Hong Kong Baptist College (HKBC), Lingnan College (LC) and the Centre for Promotion of Chinese Culture; (2) Conference on "Translating and Interpreting: Bridging East and West" in 1991, jointly with the College of Languages, Linguistics and Literature of the University of Hawaii and the Centre of Asian Studies of the University of Hong Kong; (3) Conference on "The Question of Reception: Martial Arts Fiction in English Translation" in 1996, jointly with Lingnan College and the Centre for Translation Studies of the Hong Kong Polytechnic University; (4) Conference on "Studies in Translating into Chinese" in 1996, jointly with the Department of Translation of The Chinese University of Hong Kong; and (5) Conference on "Translation Teaching" in 1997, jointly with the Translators Association of China (TAC) and the Department of Translation of The Chinese University of Hong Kong. [5]

As a result of these conferences, the Society was able to publish the following proceedings, papers and collected essays:

Title	Editor	Publisher	Year
The Art and Profession of Translation (258 pp.)	T. C. Lai	HKTS	1975
Essays on Translation 《翻譯論集》(387 pp.)	C. C. Liu	HK Joint Publishing	1981
Collected Essays on Translation 1983 (158 pp.) 《翻譯叢論一九八三》	Stephen C. Soong	The Chinese University Press	1983
Collected Essays on Translation 1986 (180 pp.) 《翻譯叢論一九八六》	C. C. Liu	Commercial Press HK	1986
Collected Essays on Translation 1988 (176 pp.) 《翻譯叢論一九八八》	C. C. Liu	Commercial Press HK	1988
Collected Essays on Translation 1991 (504 pp.) 《翻譯新論集》	C. C. Liu	Commercial Press HK	1991
Translation and Interpreting: Bridging East and West — Selected Conference Papers (190 pp.)	C. C. Liu and Richard K. Seymour	East-West Centre and University of Hawaii Press	1994
Translation Quarterly Nos. 5 & 6 Special Issue on Martial Arts Fiction in English Translation (236 pp.)	C. C. Liu	HKTS	1997

In addition to the publications mentioned above, the Society also published the following:

Title	Editor	Publisher	Year
A Glossary of New English 《英語新辭辭彙》	Serena Jin, *etc.*	HK Swindon	1979
A Translator's Handbook 《翻譯工作者手冊》	C. C. Liu	Commercial Press HK	1991

These publications have become important references for translators, practitioners and university students in Hong Kong as well as in Taiwan during the past two decades.

C. Translation Quarterly 《翻譯季刊》

In view of the demand for translators as a result of China's "Opening Policy" and the return of sovereignty of Hong Kong to China, six of the seven Government University Grants Committee (UGC) funded tertiary institutions provide translation courses, some with an honorary degree in translation. The Executive Committee considered that since Hong Kong had been a place where English and Chinese had been extensively used during the past one and a half centuries, Hong Kong should be regarded as an important place for English-Chinese translation and translators and scholars should therefore work hard to make Hong Kong an important place in English-Chinese translation in teaching, practice and research. The Executive Committee also considered that there was a need for a refereed journal for translators, and decided to publish the Society's journal *The Translation Quarterly* in 1994. The first issue was published in March 1995 and thereafter issue 2 in August 1995, issues 3 and 4 in December 1997, issues 5 and 6 in April 1997, issues 7 and 8 in May 1998, issues 9 and 10 in December 1998, and issues 11 and 12 in March 1999. Contributors included local and overseas scholars such as Lin Wen-yueh 林文月, Göran Malmqvist, Peter Newmark, Eugene A. Nida, Joseph S. M. Lau 劉紹銘, Eugene C. Eoyang 歐陽楨, Jin Di 金隄, Frederick Tsai 蔡濯堂, John Minford, Liu Ching-chih 劉靖之, Serena Jin 金聖華, Geremie R. Barmé, Laurence K. P. Wong 黃國彬, John Dent-Young, Leo T. H. Chan 陳德鴻, Evangeline Almberg 吳兆朋, Fan Wen-mei 范文美, Yau Pak-chun 姚柏春, *etc.*

2. Honorary Fellowship

In 1981 when the Society made plans to celebrate the tenth anniversary of its founding, the Executive Committee decided to award "Honorary Fellows" to those who have made contributions to translation. From the first award ceremony which was held on 28 November 1981 to 1999, a total of nine ceremonies were held and 24 translators and scholars were awarded the Society's Honorary Fellowship. A full list is provided below:

Ceremony/Date	Awardee
First 28 November 1981	Mr. George Kao 高克毅 Prof. D. C. Lau 劉殿爵
Second 28 May 1983	Prof. Ho Ping-yu 何丙郁 Mr. Stephen C. Soong 宋淇

Third 6 July 1985	Prof. Ma Meng 馬蒙 Madame Lin Tai-yi 林太乙
Fourth 27 September 1986	Mr. Yang Xianyi 楊憲益 Mrs. Gladys Yang 戴乃迭 Mr. T. C. Lai 賴恬昌
Fifth 26 September 1987	Prof. Lin Wen-yueh 林文月 Mr. Frederick Tsai 蔡濯堂
Sixth 8 October 1988	Madame Nancy Chang 張蘭熙 Madame Yang Jiang 楊絳
Seventh 9 September 1989	Mr. Cheng Yang-ping 鄭仰平 Prof. Guo Baoquan 戈寶權
Eighth 2 October 1991	Prof. Chang Ruogu 張若谷 Prof. Joseph S. M. Lau 劉紹銘 Prof. Liu Ching-chih 劉靖之 Mr. Xiao Qian 蕭乾 Mr. Ye Junqian 葉君健 Prof. Yu Kwang-chung 余光中
Ninth 8 October 1994	Dr. John Chen 陳佐舜 Prof. Chi Pang-yuan 齊邦媛 Prof. Serena Jin 金聖華

The eighth ceremony was held immediately after the conclusion of the Conference on "Translation and Interpreting: Bridging East and West" on 2 October 1991 at the University of Hong Kong, which was one of the activities in commemorating the twentieth anniversary of the Society's founding.

The Society believes that it is necessary to continue to award the Honorary Fellowship to those who have made outstanding contributions to the translation profession, so as to encourage more people to devote themselves to the work and help the people to understand the profession better.

3. Examinations

The development of the translation profession in Hong Kong during the past two decades, especially since the signing of the Sino-British Joint Declaration on the future of Hong Kong in 1984, has been phenomenal. We have witnessed the increasing need for translation in every sector of the Hong Kong community: the Civil Service has been expanding its use of both Chinese and English from daily communication with the public to policy papers and speeches and drafting of bills; the People's Republic of

China has become the most important trading partner of Hong Kong and therefore translation and interpreting have become an integral part of the transactions between commercial and financial firms in Hong Kong and the relevant authorities in Mainland China; there has been increasing contacts between Hong Kong and Mainland China including academic exchanges, governmental visits and regional and international conferences which require translation and interpreting; and there have been more legal and contractual documents involved in business activities. As a result, the need for translators has become a pressing issue.

In response to this development, tertiary institutions have been trying every effort to cope with the demand. Translation courses are offered by almost all the well-established academic institutions — the University of Hong Kong, The Chinese University of Hong Kong, the Hong Kong Polytechnic University, City University of Hong Kong, Hong Kong Baptist University, Lingnan University, and Shue Yan College. The Open University has also introduced translation courses. In addition, the School of Professional and Continuing Education (SPACE) at the University of Hong Kong, and the Department of Extra-mural Studies of the Chinese University of Hong Kong and Hong Kong Baptist University are providing both short and certificate courses in translation. Graduates of the translation courses at these academic institutions are awarded the B.A. degree in Translation, the M.A. degree in Translation, as well as higher diplomas, postgraduate diplomas, honours diplomas and certificates. There is yet another category which is not a product of the institutions mentioned above, *i.e.* holders of the final diploma of the Institute of Linguists (IOL) in the United Kingdom (MIL), a degree-equivalent qualification in languages. The Institute has also introduced a Diploma in Translation, which is at a level higher than the MIL. To sum up, there are therefore different levels of translation qualifications offered in Hong Kong, as follows:

1. M.A. in Translation;
2. B.A. and B.A. Honours Degree in Translation;
3. Higher Diploma in Translation;
4. Honours Diploma in Translation;
5. Certificates in Translation;
6. Elective Courses in Translation;
7. MIL (IOL); and
8. Diplomas in Translation (IOL).

The present translation profession serving Hong Kong comprises both the trained, those who have received formal training in translation; and the untrained, including both graduates and non-graduates in other disciplines.

At present, there is no coordination and uniformity in assessing the standards of translators in Hong Kong. The Civil Service has its own assessment criteria and it provides in-service training for its recruits after they joined Government. Well-established organisations such as the Hong Kong Trade Development Council, the Hong Kong Productivity Centre, and large commercial firms are able to offer competitive terms to attract trained and experienced translators. These firms may or may not require the applicants to sit for examinations, if the applicants are able to produce credentials of their academic qualifications and their working experience. However, for the bulk of the remaining private firms which are unable to afford good terms to employ well qualified translators, they have no way of telling whether the levels of their translators are up to the standard required.

During the past three decades, Hong Kong has become a highly sophisticated society, which requires specialised people to cater for the diversified needs. First of all, Hong Kong is one of the financial centres in the world, and finance and banking are daily necessities. It is also a trading centre, with trading partners in the United States, the European Union, the Middle East, Africa, China, Asia, and Russia and members of the Commonwealth of Independent States and countries in Eastern Europe. Hong Kong is also very advanced in its manufacturing industries, such as electronic components and appliances, computers, and watches. Its textile and garment industries have impressed the world markets with both their quality and quantity. Hong Kong is indeed a versatile and energetic city and its economic growth has earned it the reputation as one of the four "dragons" in Asia. It is therefore not an easy task for translators to serve such a society, as translators must also be diversified and specialised. A holder of a general degree or diploma in translation is just not adequately equipped to serve Hong Kong. The need for professional examinations, for both the academically trained and untrained translators in Hong Kong, is obvious and overdue.

The Hong Kong Translation Society has on several occasions been asked to look into the possibility of setting up a system to assess the standards of translators and interpreters in Hong Kong, including the so-called "grass-root" translators (such as untrained police interpreters). In response to these requests, the Society appointed a Working Party in 1989 to consider whether it was practicable to institute a public professional examination to assess the levels and specialisations of translators in Hong Kong, and, if it was considered necessary, how to materialise such an examination. The Working Party membership comprised teachers from the five institutions funded by the then University and Polytechnic Grants Committee (UPGC), Lingnan College, freelance translators and a Government Chief Interpreter. The Working Party envisaged that the syllabus to be designed:

1. should able to establish a certain level of professional competence;

2. should be bilingual in written papers (English and Chinese) and trilingual in oral examinations (English, Cantonese, and Putonghua), with a possibility papers of multilingual (Japanese, French, and German) in the future;

3. should demonstrate a knowledge and understanding of both contemporary language-cultures, of relevance within Hong Kong and China; and

4. should recognise language-based expertise in a particular area of professional work, such as literature, education, law, banking, accounting, economics in finance, insurance, trade and commerce, industry, medicine, telecommunications, transport, government policy and administration, international relations, publishing and the media, science and technology.

The Working Party also considered that the syllabus must be geared to Hong Kong's present needs with special reference to China, Taiwan, and Singapore.

It was hoped that when the designing work for the syllabus was eventually completed, it would achieve the following purposes:

1. it would be able to provide an assessment for the different levels of translators in Hong Kong. For example, if the syllabus was graded properly, a lower grade certificate holders could be re-cruited for jobs required a lower command of translation or inter-preting skill, such as a junior immigration officer, whereas a final diploma holder could be appointed to discharge translation work of a higher standard, translating policy papers and annual reports.

2. it would be able to assess the translators in the many specialised areas they were working. The final diploma could be designed in such a way that in addition to the all round language-cultural

elements, the candidate was also to be tested in the language-based expertise in a particular area of professional work, as mentioned above.

3. the final diploma would be able to compliment the academic qualifications offered by the various institutions in Hong Kong, the latter would provide the academic ground work and the former would enable the holder to be recognised as a specialised translator.

4. it would benefit those who do not have formal qualifications, thus providing more professionally qualified translators for Hong Kong.

The Working Party consulted the Hong Kong Examinations Authority on the physical arrangements for examinations for the Hong Kong Translation Society.

The Hong Kong Translation Society is, up to the present moment, the only organisation for translators and interpreters in Hong Kong, it realises that it should take the lead in reconciling the needs in society. There would inevitably be a recognition problem. The Hong Kong Council for Academic Accreditation was approached to advise on the design of the syllabus and the possibility of obtaining accreditations. The answer was that at that time the Council only assessed courses, but not syllabuses. The Hong Kong Translation Society was fully aware of the distinction between public examinations and accreditation of a qualification, and was not aiming at a full recognition of the professional examinations to be instituted by the Society through the Hong Kong Examinations Authority. What the Society had in mind was to require potential members to be assessed by means of professional examinations to qualify for the various categories of membership, and it hoped it would set some standards for Hong Kong translators.

After almost three years of consideration and discussions, the Executive Committee finally approved the Syllabus Working Party's proposed "Syllabus of Diploma and Advanced Diploma Examinations" which was effective from October 1991 and revised in April 1992 and again in April 1994. In the introduction of the syllabus, it specified (1) that successful candidates of the diploma examination were eligible for associate membership of the Society; (2) that the Advanced Diploma examination was set at the level of the proficiency demonstrated by a translator or interpreter in his or her specialised field; (3) that any associate members were eligible to enter the Advanced Diploma examination; and (4) that successful candidates of the Advanced Diploma examination were eligible for membership of the Society. For details, please prefer to Appendix 2: Syllabus of Diploma and Advanced Diploma Examinations (1994). The administrative arrangements were made by the Hong Kong Examinations Authority.

The first examination was held on 21 December 1991, with 127 applicants, of these two obtained exemptions, eight were absent and 117 sat for the examination.

The results were as follows: 11 candidates passed with grades A and B, 9.2% of the total member of candidates sat for the examination, quite a poor rate.

The following are relevant statistics on the three examinations:

Diploma Examination

    1991   Module 1 : 127 candidates (passed : 47)
            Module 2 : 127 candidates (passed : 12)
            Diploma awarded : 11
    1992   Module 1 : 51 (passed : 19)
            Module 1 : 64 (passed : 28)
            Diploma awarded : 22
    1993   Module 1 : 26 (passed : 5)
            Module 2 : 28 (passed : 5)
            Diploma awarded : 4

            Total diplomas awarded : 39

Advanced Diploma Examination

    1992   15 candidates registered
             9 candidates passed
             9 diplomas awarded
    1993   23 candidates registered
            14 candidates passed
             4 diplomas awarded
    1994   11 candidates registered
             6 candidates passed
             6 diplomas awarded

For further details, please refer to Appendix 3: Statistics on Diploma and Advanced Diploma Examinations 1991–1994.

In view of the declining number of applicants, the Society decided to temporarily cease to operate the two examinations and reactivate them when there were sufficient number of candidates, so as to justify the cost incurred. The Society is aware of the fact that since seven of the eight tertiary institutions offer translation courses, together with the two public examinations offered by the Institute of Linguists, London, there seems no need for the Society to re-activate the two examinations.

4. Scholarships

In 1990, the Society established the "Translation Scholarships" to award outstanding undergraduates majoring in translation at tertiary institutions in Hong Kong. The sponsors included Longman Asia Limited, the Oxford University Press (HK) Limited and Mr. William Au Weng-hei, Chairman and Managing Director of Hop Ying International Holdings Limited.

The Scholarships Scheme is a major event of the Hong Kong Translation Society with the purpose of recognising outstanding academic achievements by students of translation in tertiary institutions in Hong Kong and of promoting translation as a discipline at such institutions. Each year six scholarships are awarded to translation students, and until last year, under two categories, undergraduate and postgraduate.

Since its introduction in 1992, the Scheme has taken on different shapes. It was first launched in the form of a translation test and six scholarships were awarded. In 1993 the translation test of the postgraduate section was replaced by a research project requiring candidates to complete a 1,000-word essay on the topic "The Errors in the International News Columns of Chinese Newspapers in Hong Kong" (香港中文報章國際版中所見誤譯現象); the issue itself was perhaps too unseemly to attract any application from translators. Thus all six awards went to the undergraduate section that particular year. The whole Scheme was later renamed the "Best Translation Project Awards" where candidates were required to submit a quality translation project of about 3,500 words.

More than 40 projects were received in 1995, yet none of our honorary judges, translation teachers from various tertiary institutions, had been put off by the obviously trying grading exercises.

Starting from 1998, the Scholarships Scheme assumes a new outfit whereby nominations are invited from local universities offering a full-time undergraduate translation degree programme. All nominees are invited to attend an interview held by a judging panel appointed by the Executive Committee, and six winners are selected. The same provision will be adopted for the 1998/99 Scholarships.

The Hong Kong Translation Society acknowledged with gratitude the generosity of the following donors to the Scholarships Scheme: Sino-United Publishing (Holdings) Limited, Addison Wesley Longman China Limited, Oxford University Press, Reader's Digest Association Far East Limited, and Mr. Au Weng-hei, Chairman and Managing Director of the Hop Ying International Holdings Limited.

5. FIT, TAC and Other Professional Links

The Society has been maintaining contact with professional organisations including the International Federation of Translators (FIT), the Translators' Association of China (TAC), the Translators' Association of Taiwan (TAT), *etc.* In 1989, the Society became a full member of FIT, thus placing HKTS on the world map of Translation. In 1986, the then President and Vice-President of HKTS, Professor Liu Ching-chih and Professor Serena Jin were elected Council Member and Mr. T. C. Lai, Advisor of HKTS was elected an Honorary Council Member of TAC. The Society maintains close liaison with the Institute of Linguists, London (IOL) and the Institute of Translating and Interpreting (ITI). In view of the geographical convenience, the Society has more frequent contact with TAC and TAT. Apart from co-organising conferences, members of the Society have constant personal contact with their counter-part of TAC and TAT.

The list of conferences organised and monographs published in the foregoing paragraphs have convincingly indicated the network in Hong Kong and abroad the Society has been trying to establish during the past two decades.

6. The Fou Lei Foundation and Luncheon Meetings

In 1991, the Society celebrated its twentieth anniversary of founding and one of the many activities in commemorating this occasion was an exhibition on "Fou Lei's 傅雷 Works and Memorabilia (1908–1965)" which was jointly organised with the Commercial Press (HK) Limited from 25 to 29 October 1991. Immediately following the exhibition, a Fou Ts'ong 傅聰, the elder son of Fou Lei, Pianoforte Recital in memory of the pianist's late father was held on 29 October 1991. The recital was extremely successful and as a result the Society was able to set up a "Fou Lei Foundation" to promote translation, especially English-Chinese translation, and interpreting.

With the support of this Foundation, the Society published a publication entitled *Fou Lei and His World*; organised a number of conferences and seminars including the Seminar on Translation by Frederick Tsai, Translation Conference on Chinese-Foreign Languages Translation in 1996 and a conference in teaching of translation jointly with TAC in 1997 at The Chinese University of Hong Kong.

The long history of organising Saturday Luncheon Meetings at which translators and scholars are invited to give informal talks has persisted until today. Members of the Society welcome such luncheon meetings. We think this is a good tradition and we should continue with it. Texts of the talks delivered at some of the luncheon meetings have been included at the Society's monographs.

Concluding Remarks

It has been an eventful history of 28 years and the continued development of the Society has entirely been depending on the devotion of those members who rendered the Society their services all these years. The translation profession is not the same as other professions such as the legal, engineering, architecture, and accounting professions which are equipped well-structured examinations and proper criteria for "licensing" them to qualify in their respective professions. The translation profession is a different story. In his article "A Translation Tribunal," T. C. Lai said that "Chinese and English are supposed to be of equal status in society, politically and legally. Of course, ideally they should be in practice, the question will arise as to which version is the original and which is the translation, should any discrepancies arise." [6] Morry Schreiber in his "Some Random Thoughts about Translation" laments translators being labelled as "semi-professionals": "Most people still look upon us as, at best, semi-professionals, at worst non-professionals. Especially here in the United States, but also in other countries, the States is yet to fully include us in the ranks of white collar professionals, with all the benefits and responsibilities appertaining thereto. There are still very few schools in the United States teaching translation. And notwithstanding the great studies made by the American Translators Association (ATA), we are still without well-defined professional standards that would help us prove our competence and our professional status." [7]

In short, the professionalism of translation has, up to now, not been fully tested and therefore the qualifications have yet to be recognised. It is also because of fact that there are still people who consider those who are proficient in both English and Chinese can translate. In this context, the Society, despite its efforts in setting up well-structured examinations, is not a professional body in its strict sense, as it is not yet in a position to issue licences to qualify people to be professional translators. However, in a broader sense, the Society has always been acting as a body for translators and interpreters as evidenced by the activities it engaged in the past three decades. The only difference between the HKTS and, for example, the Hong Kong Institute of Architects, is that the former does not act as an authority to be the professional qualifications institution.

To date, there are 21 Honorary fellows, 14 fellows, 315 ordinary members, 13 associate members and one student member, totaling 364 fellows and members. It is not a large number and therefore HKTS is not a big organisation. We may need to conduct a survey to find out how many of these members are full-time translators and in which fields, and how many are taking translation as a secondary occupation. However, HKTS is a well-established, and well-structured society for translators. It has been engaging in activities along the lines of a professional translation organisation and it will eventually become a truly professional body when Hong Kong requires translators to have legal responsibilities.

Notes

1   This article is an expansion of the author's three previous articles, one written in 1981 entitled "The First Ten Years of the Hong Kong Translation Society" (*Affinity in Quintessence over Resemblance in Form: Collected Essays on Translation*, Liu Ching-chih, Taiwan: Bookman Books Ltd., 1996, pp. 49–56); one in 1991 entitled "The Twenty Years of the Hong Kong Translation Society" (*Collected Essays on Translation 1991*, ed. Liu Ching-chih, Hong Kong: Commercial Press (HK) Ltd., 1991, pp. 1–9); and one in 1990 entitled "Professional Examinations to Assess Translators." (*The Hong Kong Linguist*, No. 8, Hong Kong: Institute of Linguists Hong Kong Regional Society, Winter 1990–91, pp. 37–43). References have also been made from the following articles: (1) Liu Ching-chih's "The Language Scene in Hong Kong" (*The Translator's Handbook*, ed. Catriona Picken, published by Aslib, the Association for Information Management, 1989, pp. 149–62); (2) Liu Ching-chih's "Multi-lingual Development and Language Planning in Hong Kong" (*Languages in Education in a Bi-lingual or Multi-lingual Setting*, ed. Verner Bickley, Hong Kong: Institute of Language in Education, Education Department, Hong Kong, 1988, pp. 220–27); (3) T. C. Lai's "A Translation Tribunal?" (*Collected Essays on Translation 1991*, ed. Liu Ching-chih, Hong Kong: Commercial Press (HK)

Ltd., 1991, pp. 387–88); and (4) Ho Wai-kit's "Translation Studies Down to Earth: Western Influence and Chinese Reality" (*The Hong Kong Linguist*, No. 16, Hong Kong: Institute of Linguists Hong Kong Regional Society, 1996, pp. 40–61).

[2] The English translation is provided by the author of this article.

[3] Article 3 of the "Memorandum and Articles of Association" reads: "To raise the standard of translation by assisting in the training of Chinese and other languages and by encouraging those engaged in scholarly pursuits to translate important works in Chinese and other languages — in order to cater for the needs of a developing society and to promote cultural exchanges, and for this purpose: (1) to hold meetings of the Society; (2) to publish books or periodicals, sponsor research on various aspects of translation, organise conferences on special topics and engage in other activities compatible with the objects of the Society; and (3) to print, publish, sell, lend or distribute the proceedings or reports of the Society."

[4] The details of the 38 issues are as follows:

Year	Issue No.	Editor(s)
1972	Issues 1 and 2	Phillip Sun
1973	Issues 3, 4 and 5	Phillip Sun
		Stephen Soong
1974	Issues 6, 7 and 8	Phillip Sun, George Kao
1975	Issues 9 and 10	George Kao
1976	Issue 11	Liu Ching-chih
1977	Issues 12, 13, 14 and 15	Liu Ching-chih
1978	Issues 16, 17 and 18	Liu Ching-chih
1979	Issues 19 & 20	Liu Ching-chih
1981	Issue 21	Serena Jin
1986	Issue 22	Lo Chi-hong
		Simon Chau
1987	Issues 23 and 24	Lo Chi-hong
1988	Issues 25 and 26	Lo Chi-hong
1989	Issue 27	Ian Wong
1990	Issues 28 and 29	Ian Wong, Leung Po-chun
1991	Issues 30, 31 and 32	Ian Wong, Chan Ka-wai
1992	Issue 33	Ian Wong
1994	Issue 34	Elsie Chan
1995	Issue 35	Elsie Chan
1996	Issue 36 and 37	Elsie Chan
1998	Issue 38	Makey Au-Yeung

[5] The major conferences/seminars organised by HKTS from 1971 to 1999 are as follows:

Date	Title	Co-organiser(s)
2 February 1980	Hong Kong Translation Seminar 1980	Public Libraries, Urban Council

28 November 1981	Translation in Hong Kong	Public Libraries, Urban Council
28 May 1983	Translation and Society	Public Libraries, Urban Council
6 July 1985	Translation and Contemporary China	HKP
28 September 1985	Language Needs of Hong Kong in Future	Hong Kong Regional Society, Institute of Linguists; HKP
26 September 1986	Translation in Multilingual Society — Hong Kong	Public Libraries, Urban Council
26 September 1987	Hong Kong Translation Seminar 1987	Public Libraries, Urban Council
17–21 December 1987	Translation To-day	HKU; CUHK; HKP; CPHK; HKBC; LC; Centre for Promotion of Chinese Culture
8 October 1988	Translation in Practice	Public Libraries, Urban Council
9 September 1989	Development of Translation and Interpreting in Hong Kong	Public Libraries, Urban Council
28–30 October 1991	Translating and Interpreting: Bridging East and West University of Hawaii; Centre of Asian Studies, HKU	College of Languages, Linguistics and Literature,
22–23 March 1996	The Question of Reception: Martial Arts Fiction in English Translation	Centre for Literature, Language and translation, Lingnan College; Centre for Translation Studies, HKPU
1–3 April 1996	Translation: Studies in Translating into Chinese	Department of Translation, CUHK
2–4 December 1997	Translation Teaching	Department of Translation, CUHK; TAC

---

[6] T. C. Lai, "A Translation Tribunal?" *Collected Essays on Translation 1991*, ed. Liu Ching-chih, Hong Kong: Commercial Press (HK) Ltd., 1991, pp. 387–88.

[7] Morry Schreiber, "Some Random Thoughts about Translation," *Translation Update* (Vol. 3, No. 1), Madison: Schreiber Publishing Inc., January-February 1999, pp. 1–2. It is interesting to note that Morry Schreiber blames the lack of recognition on the following fact: "The problem, however, is not completely external. Part of it has to do with the way we perceive ourselves. The field of translation, I am sorry to say, is still dominated by people who have a primary

occupation, such as teaching, law or engineering, and who have translation as a secondary occupation. This may lie at the heart of the problem."

However, the author is of the view that, similar to the medical profession, there must be specialisations and therefore we have cardiologists, gynaecologists, orthopaedic surgeons, *etc.* In translation, we should also have legal translators, medical translators, *etc.* We may have "general translators," like the "general practitioner" in medicine, but specialists in translation are vital to a modern society, and therefore Morry Schreiber's view should be subject to further consideration.

Appendix 1

Executive Committee of
The Hong Kong Translation Society
1971 – 2000

1971–1973   1971.12

Chairman: Ma Meng 馬蒙
Vice-Chairman: Lai Tim-cheong 賴恬昌
Hon. Secretary: Chu Chi-tai 朱志泰 [Acting]
Hon. Treasurer: Yao Pak-chun 姚柏春
Members: Stephen C. Soong 宋淇
                     Alex Sun Hsu-hsien 孫述憲
                     Phillip S. Y. Sun 孫述宇
                     Yu Ye-lu 余也魯
                     Peter Wong Chak-cheung 王澤長
                     George Kao 高克毅

1973–1976   1973.7.7

Chairman: Lai Tim-cheong 賴恬昌 [1974.6.22]
Vice-Chairman: Stephen C. Soong 宋淇
Hon. Secretary: Lau Chi-ping 劉治平
Hon. Treasurer: Chu Chi-tai 朱志泰
Members: George Kao 高克毅
                     Phillip S.Y. Sun 孫述宇
                     Ma Meng 馬蒙
                     Yu Ye-lu 余也魯
                     Alex Sun Hsu-hsien 孫述憲
                     Yau Pak-chun 姚柏春
                     Cheung Ki-sun 張祺新

1976–1978   1976.5.29

Chairman: Stephen C. Soong 宋淇 [1977.3.26]
Vice-Chairman: Phillip S. Y. Sun 孫述宇
Hon. Secretary: Lau Chi-ping 劉治平
Hon. Treasurer: Lee Mein-ven 李勉民
Hon. Editor: Liu Ching-chih 劉靖之

Members:	Lai Tim-cheong 賴恬昌
	Chu Chi-tai 朱志泰
	Yu Ye-lu 余也魯
	Serena Jin 金聖華
	Pan Chiu-yin 潘朝彥

1978–1980   1978.3.18

Chairman:	Stephen C. Soong 宋淇 [1979.3.24]
Vice-Chairman:	Phillip S. Y. Sun 孫述宇
Hon. Secretary:	Lau Chi-ping 劉治平
Hon. Treasurer:	Lee Mein-ven 李勉民
Hon. Editor:	Liu Ching-chih 劉靖之
Members:	Lai Tim-cheong 賴恬昌
	Frederick Tsai 蔡濯堂
	Yu Ye-lu 余也魯
	Serena Jin 金聖華
	Leung Bo-sang 梁寶生

1980–1982

Chairman:	Lai Tim-cheong 賴恬昌
Vice-Chairman:	Liu Ching-chih 劉靖之
Hon. Secretary:	Leung Bo-sang 梁寶生
Hon. Treasurer:	Lee Mein-ven 李勉民
Hon. Editor:	Serena Jin 金聖華
Members:	Stephen C. Soong 宋淇
	Frederick Tsai 蔡濯堂
	Yu Ye-lu 余也魯
	Samuel Ding 丁紹源
	Hsu Sin-chu 許性初

1982–1984

Chairman:	Lai Tim-cheong 賴恬昌
Vice-Chairman:	Liu Ching-chih 劉靖之
Hon. Secretary:	Leung Bo-sang 梁寶生
Hon. Treasurer:	Lee Mein-ven 李勉民
Members:	Stephen C. Soong 宋淇
	Serena Jin 金聖華
	Samuel Ding 丁紹源

Hsu Sin-chu 許性初
Yau Pak-chun 姚柏春
Diana Yue 余丹

1984–1986

Chairman:	Lai Tim-cheong 賴恬昌
Vice-Chairman:	Liu Ching-chih 劉靖之
Hon. Secretary:	Leung Bo-sang 梁寶生
Hon. Treasurer:	Lee Mein-ven 李勉民
Members:	Serena Jin 金聖華
	Samuel Ding 丁紹源
	Chang Tung 張同
	Diana Yue 余丹
	Pan Chiu-yin 潘朝彥
	Simon Chau 周兆祥

1986–1988

Chairman:	Liu Ching-chih 劉靖之
Vice-Chairman:	Serena Jin 金聖華
Hon. Secretary:	Simon Chau 周兆祥 [to 1986.8.31]
	Leung Bo-sang 梁寶生 [from 1986.9.1]
Hon. Treasurer:	Ben Ho Shun-kan 何信勤
Hon. Editor:	Lo Chi-hong 羅志雄
Members:	Lai Tim-cheong 賴恬昌
	Samuel Ding 丁紹源
	Lee Mein-ven 李勉民
	Chow Oi-wah 周愛華

1988–1990   1988.3.26

Chairman:	Liu Ching-chih 劉靖之
Vice-Chairman:	Serena Jin 金聖華
Hon. Secretary:	Ho Shun-kan 何信勤
Asso. Secretary:	Raymond Lie Shing-chai 李成仔
Hon. Treasurer:	Kenneth Au Kim-lung 區劍龍
Hon. Editor:	Lo Chi-hong 羅志雄[to 1988.3.26]
	Ian Wong 黃邦傑 [from 1988.9.22]
Members:	Lai Tim-cheong 賴恬昌
	Samuel Ding 丁紹源

Lee Mein-ven 李勉民
Leung Bo-sang 梁寶生
Elizabeth Pong 龐林淑蓮

1990–1992   1990.3.24

Chairman:	Serena Jin 金聖華
Vice-Chairman:	Lee Mein-ven 李勉民
Hon. Secretary:	Ben Ho Shun-kan 何信勤
Asso. Secretary:	Kenneth Au Kim-lung 區劍龍
Hon. Treasurer:	Agnes Cheung 張燕萍
Hon. Editor:	Ian Wong 黃邦傑
Members:	Lai Tim-cheong 賴恬昌
	Liu Ching-chih 劉靖之
	Elizabeth S. L. Pong 龐林淑蓮 [to 1990.12.31]
	Alex Sun Hsu-hsien 孫述憲
	Lo Chi-hong 羅志雄
	Samuel Ding 丁紹源

1992–1994   1992.3.31

Chairman:	Alex Sun Hsu-hsien 孫述憲
Vice-Chairman:	Ian Wong 黃邦傑
Hon. Secretary:	Dominic Tang 鄧榮煜
	Jacqueline Lam 林錦薇
Asso. Secretary:	Kenneth Au Kim-lung 區劍龍
Hon. Treasurer:	Joanne Leung 梁寶珍
Hon. Editor:	Lee Mein-ven 李勉民
Members:	Serena Jin 金聖華
	Ho Shun-kan 何信勤
	Liu Ching-chih 劉靖之
Hon. Advisor:	Lai Tim-cheong 賴恬昌

1994–1996

Chairman:	Liu Ching-chih 劉靖之
Vice-Chairman:	Lo Chi-hong 羅志雄
Hon. Secretary:	Li Kam-kee 李錦祺
Hon. Treasurer:	Aman Chiu Ka-man 趙嘉文
Membership Secretary:	Elsie Chan Kit-ying 陳潔瑩
Exec. Editor:	Poon Hon-kwong 潘漢光

Investment Secretary:	Dominic Tang 鄧榮煜
Members:	Kenneth Au Kim-lung 區劍龍
	Serena Jin 金聖華
	Jane C. C. Lai 黎翠珍
	Diana Yue 余丹
Hon. Adviser:	Lai Tim-cheong 賴恬昌
Hon. Auditor:	Kenneth Chau 蔡天助
Hon. Legal Adviser:	Henry Woo 胡家為

1996–1998   1996.6.8

Chairman:	Lo Chi-hong 羅志雄
Vice-Chairman:	Jane C. C. Lai 黎翠珍
Hon. Secretary:	Li Kam-kee 李錦祺
Hon. Treasurer:	Aman Chiu Ka-man 趙嘉文
Membership Secretary:	Elsie Chan Kit-ying 陳潔瑩
Execu. Editor:	Poon Hon-kwong 潘漢光
Members:	Liu Ching-chih 劉靖之
	Serena Jin 金聖華
	Diana Yue 余丹
	Evangeline Almberg 吳兆朋
	Jacqueline Lam 林錦薇
	Chen Longgen 陳龍根
Hon. Adviser:	Lai Tim-cheong 賴恬昌

1998–2000   1998.6.27

Chairman:	Liu Ching-chih 劉靖之
Vice-Chairman:	Lo Chi-hong 羅志雄
Hon. Secretary:	Bosco Wong 黃承義
Hon. Treasurer:	Candy Wong 黃紹顏
Execu. Editor:	Liu Ching-chih 劉靖之
Bulletin Editor:	Makey Au-Yeung 歐陽漢玉
Members:	Evangeline Almberg 吳兆朋
	Elsie Chan Kit-ying 陳潔瑩
	Jane C. C. Lai 黎翠珍
	Serena Jin 金聖華
	Jacqueline Lam 林錦薇
	Li Kam-kee 李錦祺
	Sarah Tsou 盧毓文

Hon. Adviser: Lai Tim-cheong 賴恬昌
Hon. Auditor: Kenneth T. C. Chua & Co.
                            蔡天助會計師事務所
Hon. Legal Advisor: Eddie Yiu 姚棟華

Appendix 2

Syllabus of Diploma and Advanced Diploma Examinations

Effective from October 1991
Revised April 1994

Preface

The Hong Kong Translation Society believes that the introduction of its Diploma and Advanced Diploma takes place at a very significant time as the Society celebrates its twentieth anniversary. As Hong Kong prepares to become a Special Administrative Region of the People's Republic of China, the time is appropriate for the Society to make another contribution to the future development of Hong Kong. There is no doubt that Hong Kong will continue to play a major role in the international world of business and communication, as well as occupying a key position in South-East Asia. High-level translators and interpreters will continue to be in great demand if Hong Kong is to remain an effective bridge between China and the rest of the world.

The new Diploma and Advanced Diploma examinations are the result of two years' research and development by a working party composed of leading academics and translators. The examinations have been deliberately designed to be exacting, practical tests of translation and interpreting at a high level for two main reasons: firstly, the Society believes it has a duty to establish high professional standards for translators and interpreters; secondly, successful candidates will be able to adduce the diploma as objective evidence of their translating and interpreting skills. These examinations also offer the opportunity to translators and interpreters lacking formal qualifications to obtain diplomas aimed at undergraduate and graduate levels. Furthermore, successful candidates of the Diploma examination will be eligible to apply for associate membership of the Hong Kong Translation Society, and successful candidates of the Advanced Diploma examination will be eligible to apply for full membership.

The Executive Committee
The Hong Kong Translation Society
August 1991

1. Introduction

1.1   The Hong Kong Translation Society was established in 1971 with the aim of raising the standard of translation in Hong Kong. It is a prestigious organization, with several hundred members representing the major academic institutions and government departments, as well as the business sector. In 1989, the Society Appointed a working party to investigate the need for a public examination and to advise the executive committee accordingly. The Working Party under the chairmanship of Dr. C. C. Liu, came to the conclusion that there was a need for public examinations specifically designed to meet needs of translators and interpreters in Hong Kong. It also felt that the Hong Kong Translation Society contained the expertise essential for the ongoing maintenance of the high standards of design, preparation, examining and oversight of this nature. These syllabuses represent the product of two years' research and planning by the Working Party who believe the examinations offer Hong Kong's translators and interpreters the opportunity to gain diplomas and membership of a highly-regarded, academic organization.

1.2   The Diploma examination of the Society is set at a level of translation skills commensurate with the level attained by an undergraduate at the end of the first year of a translation degree/diploma course. Successful candidates are eligible for associate membership of the Society. Graduates of translation departments of tertiary institutes and members of the Institute of Linguists may be exempt from this examination as a qualification for associate membership.

1.3   The Advanced Diploma examination is set at the level of the proficiency demonstrated by a translator or interpreter in his or her specialized field. Only associate members are eligible to enter the Advanced Diploma examination. Successful candidates are eligible for membership of the Society.

1.4   Associate members and members are entitled to enjoy all the benefits of membership of an active society concerned with the needs of translators and interpreters in the academic, commercial, literary, government and cultural circles of Hong Kong. Activities include regular meetings, the opportunity to meet and hear distinguished people in the translation field, cultural exchanges, seminars and conferences.

2. Aims and Objectives

2.1 The Diploma examination is a bilingual test of translation skills offering candidates the opportunity to demonstrate their competence in moving easily between English and Chinese. Its objectives are as follows:-
  (1) To test written fluency in English and Chinese within a contemporary context.
  (2) To test accurate translation of the written language from and into each language.
  (3) To demonstrate an awareness and knowledge of areas of cultural and topical relevance within Hong Kong, China and the broad spectrum of international affairs.

2.2 The Advanced Diploma examination is a high specialized test of a specific translation skill. Candidates are free to choose their area of specialization and to resit the examination in order to demonstrate their competence in other areas. The objective is as follows:-
  To test performance at an advanced level in an area of specialist knowledge of skill involving translating or interpreting from Chinese to English or English to Chinese.

3. Examination Design

3.1 The Diploma examination is bilingual, testing English and Chinese in an identical way in the two modules. Candidates should be familiar with both traditional and simplified characters: they are permitted to write both forms of characters. Dictionaries are permitted. A high standard of performance is demanded.

3.2 The Advanced Diploma examination offers a choice of eight modules enabling candidates to choose one as their own area of specialization. Candidates should be familiar with both traditional and simplified characters. Dictionaries are permitted. An advanced level of performance is demanded.

4. Diploma Examination

4.1 Module 1 — Translation from Chinese to English (3 hours)
  In this module candidates are required to translate two texts into English. One text will reflect an area of current interest in Hong

Kong. The other text will reflect an area of current interest in China. Traditional or simplified characters may be encountered. Each passage will contain about 500 characters.

Candidates will be required to demonstrate that they have fully understood the source texts. Other assessment criteria will include the choice of vocabulary, sentence construction and punctuation in the target language, as well as the ability to reflect the style of the original passage.

4.2   Module 2 — Translation from English to Chinese (3 hours)
This module has an identical structure to Module 1. The source texts will be in English: each passage will reflect an area of current international interest. Each passage will contain not more than 500 words. Candidates may use both traditional and simplified characters.

5. Advanced Diploma Examination

Candidates will be required to choose one module and state their choice on the entry form.

5.1   Module 3 — Translation from Chinese to English [Arts] (3 hours)
This module is a test of translation skills at an advanced level. Candidates will be expected to demonstrate their familiarity with the arts and to produce translations which accurately reflect the content and style of the original passages. Traditional or simplified characters may be encountered. The passages will contain about 1,000 characters.

5.2   Module 4 — Translation from Chinese to English [Social Sciences] (3 hours)
This module is a test of translation skills at an advanced level. Candidates will be expected to demonstrate their familiarity with social sciences and to produce translations which accurately reflect the content and style of the original passages. Traditional or simplified characters may be encountered. The passages will contain about 1,000 characters.

5.3   Module 5 — Translation from Chinese to English [Science and Technology] (3 hours)
This module is a test of translation skills at an advanced level. Candidates will be expected to demonstrate their familiarity with

science and technology and to produce translations which accurately reflect the content and style of the original passages. Traditional or simplified characters may be encountered. The passages will contain about 1,000 characters.

5.4   Module 6 — Translation from English to Chinese [Business and Management] (3 hours)

This module is a test of translation skills at an advanced level. Candidates will be expected to demonstrate their familiarity with business and management and to produce translations which accurately reflect the content and style of the original passages. Traditional or simplified characters may be used. The passages will contain not more than 1,000 words.

5.5   Module 7 — Translation from English to Chinese [Arts] (3 hours)

This module is a test of translation skills at an advanced level. Candidates will be expected to demonstrate their familiarity with the arts and to produce translations which accurately reflect the content and style of the original passages. Traditional or simplified characters may be used. The passages will contain not more than 1,000 words.

5.6   Module 8 — Translation from English to Chinese [Social Science] (3 hours)

This module is a test of translation skills at an advanced level. Candidates will be expected to demonstrate their familiarity with social sciences and to produce translations which accurately reflect the content and style of the original passages. Traditional or simplified characters may be used. The passages will contain not more than 1,000 words.

5.7   Module 9 — Translation from English to Chinese [Science and Technology] (3 hours)

This module is a test of translation skills at an advanced level. Candidates will be expected to demonstrate their familiarity with science and technology and to produce translations which accurately reflect the content and style of the original passages. Traditional or simplified characters may be used. The passages will contain not more than 1,000 words.

5.8   Module 10 — Translation from English to Chinese [Business and Management] (3 hours)

This module is a test of translation skills at an advanced level. Candidates will be expected to demonstrate their familiarity with business and management and to produce translations which accurately reflect the content and style of the original passages. Traditional or simplified characters may be used. The passages will contain not more than 1,000 words.

6. Diplomas and Membership

6.1   On successful completion of the Diploma examination, candidates will be eligible to apply for Associate Membership of the Society. Candidates who pass one module only will be required to resit the other module in order to gain the diploma.

6.2   On successful completion of the Advanced Diploma examination, candidates will be eligible to apply for Membership of the Society.

6.3   Successful candidates will be placed in one of two categories: Distinction or Pass — in each module of the Diploma and Advanced Diploma examinations. The Advanced Diploma will record the candidate's area of specialization.

7. Administrative Arrangements

The Diploma examination is held each year in December and the Advanced Diploma each year in July. Closing dates for entries is approximately six weeks before the examinations. Entry forms and further details about entry procedures are available from:

> Hong Kong Examinations Authority
> San Po Kong Sub-Office
> 17 Tseuk Luk Street
> San Po Kong
> Kowloon

8. Fees

The entry fee for each examination is stated on the entry form. Candidates will be entered for examinations only after payment of the appropriate entry fee.

9. Examination Results

Notification to candidates of their results will take place as soon as possible, normally within about three months of the examination.

10. Further Information

Further information about the Hong Kong Translation Society can be obtained from:

The Honorary Secretary
Hong Kong Translation Society
P. O. Box 70335
Kowloon Central Post Office
Kowloon

Appendix 3

Diploma and Advanced Diploma Examinations

The Diploma and Advanced Diploma Examinations has been conducted for three years commencing in the year 1991. In the past years, the Diploma Examinations were held in December and the Advanced Diploma Examinations were held in July. A summarised profile of the candidates in those three years is shown as follows:

1. Diploma Examinations

Year	No. of Candidates Registered	No. of Candidates Passed	Diplomas Awarded	No. of Membership Approved
1991	Module 1: 127 Module 2: 127	Module 1: 47 Module 2: 12 Full Pass: 11	11	Life: 4 Ordinary: 14 Associate: 15
1992	Module 1: 51 Module 2: 64	Module 1: 19 Module 2: 28 Full Pass in 1st Attempt: 11 Full Pass in 2nd Attempt: 11	22	Life: 2 Ordinary: 9 Associate: 11
1993	Module 1: 26 Module 2: 28	Module 1: 5 Module 2: 5 Full Pass in 1st Attempt: 3 Full Pass in 2nd Attempt: 1	4	Associate: 3

2. Advanced Diploma Examinations

Year	No. of Candidates Registered	No. of Candidates Passed	Diplomas Awarded	No. of Membership Approved
1992	15	9	9	Life: 1 Ordinary: 3
1993	23	14	14	Ordinary: 1
1994	11	6	6	Associate: 1

Names of Candidates Awarded Diploma

There were altogether 37 candidates are awarded Diplomas from 1991 to 1993, details are as follows:

1991

1　Ho Chiu Louis
2　Cheung Wai Hing
3　Wong Kwan Cheung
4　Wun Siu Lun
5　Lee Yuen Nar Susanna
6　Leung Po Sing
7　Chung Bing She
8　Fung Siu Tin
9　Wong Pak Kwan Patrick
10　Cheng Tsan Wah
11　Li Kin Keung

1992

		1991	1992
1	Kwok Chun Man		Full Pass
2	Hung Yik Sing		Ditto
3	Lee Kan Yung Robert		Ditto
4	Kho Sin Tek Henry		Ditto
5	Ling Ka Wai		Ditto
6	Tam Lai King Peggy		Ditto
7	Hung Tak Ming		Ditto
8	Lam Kwok Cheung		Ditto
9	Ha Kit Yi Iris		Ditto
10	Tien Kai Hong		Ditto
11	Kong Yuk On		Ditto
12	Lo Shu Wing Peter	Module 1	Module 2
13	Lee Hou Yuen Cecil		Ditto
14	Wong Kui Chin		Ditto
15	Lam Kam Shan		Ditto
16	Choy Mou Ching		Ditto
17	Chan Wing Evelyn		Ditto
18	Tan Sai Kwong Peter Stephen		Ditto
19	Lam Siu Ming		Ditto

20	Lai Man Kit		Ditto
21	Yuen Sea Ching Mary Margaret		Ditto
22	Wong To Kang	Module 2	Module 1

1993

		1991	**1993**
1	Fung Sui Lin		Full Pass
2	Tsang Hon San		Ditto
3	Li Kan Nung		Ditto
4	Liu Wai Lok	Module 1	Module 2

Lists of Candidates Awarded Advanced Diploma

There were altogether 29 candidates awarded the Advanced Diploma from 1992 to 1994. Details are as follows:

1992

1	Fung Yeung Pik Yan Yolanda	Module 3: Chinese-English, Arts
2	Li Kin Keung	Ditto
3	Lee Yuen Nar Susanna	Ditto
4	Li Kam Cheong	Module 4: Chinese-English, S. S.
5	Cheng Tsan Wah	Ditto
6	Fung Siu Tin	Ditto
7	Wong Kwan Cheung	Ditto
8	Fan Chi Wai	Module 7: English-Chinese, S. S.
9	Chan Tak Wai	Ditto

1993

1	Cheung Wai Hing	Module 3: Chinese-English, Arts
2	Lam Siu Ming	Ditto
3	Lee Kan Yung Robert	Module 4: Chinese-English, S. S.
4	Tam Lai King Peggy	Ditto
5	Wong Kwan Cheung	Module 5: Chinese-English, S & T
6	Kong Yuk On	Ditto
7	Chau Hing Kwan	Ditto
8	Chan Wing Evelyn	Module 6: English-Chinese, Arts
9	Yuen Sea Ching Mary Margaret	Ditto

10	Ho Chiu Louis	Module 7: English-Chinese, S. S.
11	Choy Mou Ching	Ditto
12	Wong To Kang	Ditto
13	Lai Man Kit	Module 8: English-Chinese, S & T
14	Hung Yik Sing	Ditto

1994

1	Chu Jacob Shing-Tsu	Module 5: Chinese-English, S & T
2	Wong Kwan Cheung	Module 6: Chinese-English, B & M
3	Tsang Hon San	Module 8: English-Chinese, S. S.
4	Wong Hon Keung	Ditto
5	Cheung Yun Yu	Ditto
6	Wong Kui Chin	Module 10: English-Chinese, B & M

The Research Centre for Translation: A Mirror of Translation Studies in Hong Kong

Eva Hung Wai Yee
Research Centre for Translation
The Chinese University of Hong Kong

The Historical Context

The Research Centre for Translation (hereafter RCT) at The Chinese University of Hong Kong was set up in 1971. With a 30-year history, it is not only the oldest centre of its kind in the region,[1] but also predates the establishment of all local T & I full degree courses.[2]

RCT was founded before Chinese became an official language in Hong Kong. Its establishment, to a large degree, was a reflection of the social and intellectual climate of the late 1960s and early 1970s. It was an era that saw strong nationalistic feelings focussed on the issue of the status of the Chinese language, which was finally given official status comparable to English in 1973. The Chinese University of Hong Kong, founded in 1965 with enhancing the study and dissemination of Chinese culture as a clear mission, saw it as the university's duty to explore ways in which to serve the community in this crucial phase of its development. The founding of RCT can be seen as a response to the questions arising from the social milieu of the early 1970s: how to strengthen the position of Chinese language and culture, and how best to address the practical issues involved. RCT, which has become best known internationally for its work in literary translation, was in fact founded with practical issues in mind.

The Centre's initial conception also benefited indirectly from the cultural role translation work had played locally during the 1950s and 1960s. Since the turn of the twentieth century literary translation had been a conspicuous tool in China's efforts at cultural and social modernization, a tradition that had considerable influence on the intellectual orientation of

Hong Kong at mid-century. Amongst the various literary and translation activities then current were several series of translated literature launched by the US-sponsored World Today Press. Members of the Centre in its early years such as Stephen Soong and George Kao had played an important role in the World Today books and journal. They brought with them their editorial experience in terms of culturally oriented translation work which had substantial influence on the nature of the projects undertaken in RCT's early years. Their ability to attract funding from private foundations also meant that the Centre's projects were supported by outside funding from the start. This reliance on grants, sponsorships and donations for all centre projects is now an RCT tradition.

Three Phases of Development

In terms of self-conception as well as research orientation, the development of RCT can be divided roughly into three phases. This is to a certain extent reflected in the change of the Centre's name:

> Centre for Translation Projects 1971–1977.
> Centre for Comparative Literature and Translation 1978–1983.
> Research Centre for Translation 1983–present.

However, it must be emphasized that there has been no abrupt break between individual phases, no sudden decisions that effected a severance of ties with the past or a quantum leap into the future. While new developments always had their seeds planted in a previous phase, the characteristics of one phase also carried on into the next. This is because any lasting impact can only be achieved through continuous and sustained endeavours that respond sensitively to shifting internal academic strengths and the changes in the larger intellectual climate. Thus one may even argue that the seeds of RCT's various activities were all planted within the first decade of its establishment, and that while some germinated and grew almost immediately, others awaited their time, not emerging into prominence until both the external environment and internal strengths became favourable.

The following account highlights the main characteristic of RCT in each of the three phases that form its history up to mid-2000.

Phase 1: Short-term Projects and Short-term Courses

RCT was founded when the academic and funding structures at the

Chinese University were still developing.[3] The name "Centre for Translation Projects" reflects such realities: there was little long-term funding for continuous work; individual projects, including those related directly to teaching, were supported by external grants, mostly from U.S. foundations. Applications were made and approved on an annual basis. Even *Renditions*, RCT's flagship journal conceived by George Kao, had a far from smooth early childhood because of the uncertainties of funding.[4]

1. Book Projects

The projects, which formed the core of RCT's activities in its early years, were of a varied nature, covering such areas as bilingual glossaries, bibliographies and case studies. The English-Chinese glossary series includes titles in anthropology, psychology, legal terminology and sociology. This fits in with the Centre's mission of facilitating Hong Kong's new, officially bilingual needs. Translations of English books into Chinese such as Bernard Gallin's *Hsin Hsing: Taiwan, A Chinese Village in Change* were undertaken; there was also bibliographical work in translation such as the *Bibliography of Sino-Japanese and Japanese-Chinese Translation*, to date still a significant reference work for early twentieth-century translation activities. In some cases RCT's role was that of research initiator, in others the Centre acted more as funding applicant and provided administrative, editing and publication support. However, the fact that there was a Centre devoted specifically to translation-related work certainly eased the way for the application of foundation support in all cases.

2. Teaching

Teaching was one of the primary concerns of RCT in its early days. As mentioned above, the founding of the Centre had a strong practical side, and providing much needed training to a rapidly expanding field was one of the immediate needs. Though as a research unit the Centre was never expected to provide regular undergraduate teaching, it took on an important function as organizer of short-term practical courses. For six consecutive years, diploma courses in "advanced translation" offered by The Chinese University's extramural arm were actually run and managed by RCT, which was responsible for securing foundation funding and recruiting teachers. The number of courses offered per year varied from one to four, and with an enrolment of 30 per course, RCT's indirect role in teaching was substantial. The students came from a varied background, including government language officers, teachers, journalists, university administrators, and one university lecturer. These short courses, aimed at filling an immediate need by providing instruction in translation approaches and techniques, were not meant to replace the development of regular degree courses which would improve both the standard and status of translation work. As the two universities and the Hong Kong Polytechnic all took measures to address the need for translation teaching at the undergraduate level, by 1977 RCT considered its role in translation instruction fulfilled. It was then able to direct its attention and energy to more long-term developments.

Phase 2: Literary Translation

Since the late 1970s most people have identified RCT with its flagship journal *Renditions.* While successive directors of the Centre have indeed dedicated a significant amount of their time and energy to building up the journal, in fact at no point in RCT's history did it represent the bulk of the Centre's work. In the Centre's early years non-literary work accounted for a substantial amount of its activities and output. There was, however, a period when it did seem that RCT would concentrate on literature-related activities. This coincided roughly with RCT's changing its name — and therefore identity — into that of the Centre for Comparative Literature and Translation (1978–1983).

   In the international translation studies scene, the late 1970s and early 1980s saw the emergence of scholars originally in comparative literature become one of the leading forces in the search for a new direction for the fledgling field of translation studies. While one cannot claim that those in charge of RCT at that time were familiar with the work of this group of young scholars[5], the major restructuring of RCT to incorporate comparative literature as a primary growth direction did take place in exactly the same period. Rather than a coincidence, this reflects the influence of a general trend in the Humanities then current. On the one hand, it was a time when the comparatists had begun to find a strong voice in academia; on the other hand, the development of translation studies locally had taken on a decidedly literary direction. The prominence of literary studies in the local degree programmes of the late 1970s and early 1980s —— and to a certain extant, even today — is a reflection of this. Unlike in the west, linguistics never at any time dominated translation studies in Hong Kong. One of the reasons for this was of course the background of university teachers who either volunteered or were conscripted to join the staff of the translation programmes in the 1970s: the majority of them had received their training in the literary field. However, if one looks at the larger picture of Chinese culture in general and the positioning of translation activities in that culture in the last century[6], one would realize that the literary bias reflects the tendency of Chinese culture itself, not just that of local academic culture.

Given the factors listed above, it was no surprise that a "marriage" was made at The Chinese University of Hong Kong between comparative literature and translation research. Since the Centre had become well known for its work in literary translation, it was perhaps logical to think that a viable direction for future development would be an interdisciplinary one, with comparative studies built on a solid basis of translated Chinese literature. However, even with this new possibility being given administrative and structural support, the Centre's non-literary work continued in the form of glossaries and dictionary projects. While there is definitely com mon ground between translation studies and comparative literature, that is not necessarily a guarantee that a common developmental direction can be forged. When two vibrant new disciplines, each coming from its own background with its specific concerns, attempt to discover a new, common path, success can be elusive. In the case of RCT, it became obvious that translation studies had its non-literary side that was important for the development of the discipline, and comparative literature did not have to concern itself necessarily with applied literary translation. The strain showed when the Centre's flagship journal lagged further and further behind its publication schedule. As the divergence between the goals and the needs of the two branches of the Centre became obvious, it was decided that they each deserved a separate identity.

Phase 3: Basic Research and the China Connection

The third phase of RCT's development shows a stronger research orientation than the previous phases, thus reflecting that the new name effected in 1983 indicated a real change in the Centre's orientation. This, however, represented an expansion of activities rather than a change of direction, for RCT did not cut back in areas of proven strength. On the contrary, literary translation received a boost from the mid-1980s onwards with the launch of a paperback series which is commercially distributed worldwide.[7] Hong Kong literature, in particularly, became one of the main focuses of the

Centre's literary publishing work. The shift in the Centre's developmental direction since 1985 can be best summed up as follows: the emphasis between 1985 and 1991 was in applied translation, while the year 1992 marked a definite turn to basic historical research.

1. Conferences, Lectures and Workshops

One aspect of RCT's multi-faceted concern since its inception has been the development of translation as an academic discipline. Starting from the mid-1980s, RCT began to devote more energy to the field's intellectual and disciplinary aspects. The Centre was one of the first local academic units to organize conferences and seminars on translation, and also the first to bring international scholars of translation studies to address the local academic community. The latter step was especially significant as it transcended the usual boundaries of the Chinese-English language pair that had so far dominated the translation discourse in Hong Kong.

The conference "Interdisciplinary Approaches to Translation and Translation Teaching" and a series of workshops organized in 1985 brought together scholars who were primarily in literary translation. This marked the beginning of the Centre's decade-long efforts at developing the intellectual aspects of Chinese translation studies. The years since 1996 have seen RCT's role as conference organizer expanding to truly international proportions: most conferences organized by RCT were arranged to take place in other Chinese communities rather than locally. This development, built on RCT's excellent working relationship with sister institutions in Mainland China and Taiwan, also reflects the Centre's new research orientation in terms of China's translation tradition.

Lectures and workshops given by visiting scholars were an important part of RCT activities in the late 1980s and early 1990s; among these, the lecture series organized in 1993–94 is perhaps worth a special mention. In bringing to Hong Kong four international scholars from three generations[8], all with different approaches to the subject, RCT offered to the local translation academic community substantial exposure to the expanding potentials of this fast-developing field. One of the most important issues we were faced with was the need to bridge the gap between actual translation work and translation studies as an intellectual discipline; another was to transcend language-specific concerns. While continuing to build on its reputation in literary translation, through its lectures and conferences, the Centre also took a firm direction in defining its mission in the non-literary areas of the field.

2. Collaboration with China

In 1985 RCT signed an agreement with Nankai University in China for collaborative work in the translation field. With RCT's assistance, Nankai University set up a new Research Centre for Translation. Though this collaboration did not rank as a great success[9], it gave RCT early exposure to the pitfalls of such collaboration, and therefore the experience on which future success would be built. The Nankai connection also brought RCT into direct contact with the "translation and social sciences fever" that swept across China in the mid-1980s.[10] One of main projects of the Nankai Centre was a series entitled "Modern Classics in the Social Sciences" and another was an English language journal translating the latest research in social sciences for the international academic community. With substantial help from RCT, both projects bore fruit, but as they never received enough support — whether financial or logistic — from Nankai University itself, both were discontinued when external funding ran out.

The lesson RCT learned from this was that at that stage, individual collaboration was probably more fruitful and easier to manage than institutional ones, not the least because the Centre, as a small unit, could not afford the manpower and energy which institutional collaboration with China always demanded. Thus, when RCT rapidly expanded its contacts with the mainland in the 1990s, collaborative work has been done on a project rather than long term basis,[11] with extremely encouraging results.

3. Historical and Cultural Research

RCT's new research orientation since 1992 focuses on the Chinese translation tradition from the second century onwards, particularly on its relations to mainstream Chinese culture. While this reflects the 'cultural turn' of translation studies in the 1990s internationally, this research direction also coincides with the ideals that led to the founding of the Centre and the cultural mission of the University. The bridging of cultures has to start with a thorough understanding of a particular culture's self-perception in relation to cross-cultural activities. China, which has been given to pendulous swings between cultural arrogance and a sense of crisis, provides an extremely fertile field of investigation. In addition to research initiated at the Centre, RCT also contributes to the expansion of the field with the launching of the Translation Studies Research Series[12] and annual Translation Studies Awards for the best research papers in the cultural and historical aspects of translation in China.

The Cultural Mission

The concern for reinforcing the role of Chinese language and culture locally, which informed the founding principles of RCT, also constantly underlined the direction of its development. Hong Kong's unique history offers academics here several advantages unavailable to their colleagues in other Chinese communities. In terms of language and cultural environment, despite its elitist and flawed education system, Hong Kong did provide the opportunities for the nurturing of bilingual and bicultural individuals, albeit in no great numbers. If we consider this against the background of the Chinese mainland since 1949, where the culture was monolingual, education opportunities conditioned by the government's ideological policies,[13] and the educational system wrecked by the havoc of the Cultural Revolution, the bicultural heritage of Hong Kong is truly exceptional. In terms of academic freedom, Hong Kong has a strong edge in the investigation of all topics that are taboo in China. In terms of information access, Hong Kong is ideally situated to acquire knowledge of the latest developments in the West as well as in China. For several decades, Hong Kong has also enjoyed similar advantages over other major Chinese communities. Taiwan, which until the mid-1980s had its own yoke of ideologically based taboos, is, like China, a society that functions primarily on Chinese languages and norms. Singapore, despite its many official languages, is in effect dominated by English as *lingua franca* culturally and socially.

Given such a background, it is not surprising that Hong Kong academics should see themselves as uniquely positioned to play the role of cultural intermediary. RCT's literary translation work benefits from Hong Kong's linguistic and cultural advantages as well as from free access to material banned in the mainland or Taiwan.[14] What is particularly noteworthy is that literary translation at RCT started during the Cultural Revolution, when China's cultural heritage seemed in great peril. In interpreting China's literary tradition for an English readership, RCT in effect undertook to preserve and recreate that tradition.

The Centre's early cultural mission was not limited to Chinese literature; it also included the dissemination of Western knowledge through Chinese translations. This was very much part of the reformist/ modernization legacy which dates back to the turn-of-the-century. However worthy this second cause, it clashed with the realities of a fast changing world. For the Centre, a major test came in the late 1970s, when it was faced with a dwindling market demand for Chinese translations of English material. The Centre's director made the following remarks:

> The Chinese University and the Centre are obligated to produce books in Chinese even though there seems to be no market for Chinese books in Hong Kong, Taiwan and South East Asia.[15]

This obligation was not externally imposed, but was part of the sense of mission that informed the Centre's role in relation to Chinese culture. The heart of the matter, as it were, was revealed in the early 1980s, when the Centre was faced with a succession crisis. Stephen Soong, generally considered to be the founder of RCT, and who was then suffering from serious health problems, had a firm opinion about the kind of candidate who should be given responsibility of the Centre. He argued strongly for a Chinese person, knowing full well that by then RCT was internationally known for literary translation from Chinese into *English*. Soong was not oblivious to the fact that very few Chinese persons in academia had the necessary language and cultural command of English to shoulder the burden of *Renditions*. He therefore made the following suggestion: a native English-speaker could serve as Editor of *Renditions*, provided that he/she would work under a Chinese director.[16] This preference was cultural rather than racial. In Soong's opinion, however successful *Renditions* was it only represented a part of RCT's mission. Since it was a mission rooted in Chinese culture, someone grounded in that culture should therefore carry the torch. Students of translation studies will probably find this an illuminating example of the cultural forces that shape and position translation and related activities.

Towards a Conclusion

Both in terms of the range and the quality of its work, RCT can be considered an academic success story. While the most important ingredient for success is always the hard work of a long-serving and dedicated staff, RCT's experience also shows that there are other factors crucial to the long-term viability of a research unit. In terms of conception, to have been founded in the right place and at the right time may be a case of serendipity, but it also reveals the founders' perspicacity. In terms of funding, the Centre was able to make a virtue of necessity and establish a tradition of diversification of resources. In terms of academic activities, new developmental directions had always been undertaken in recognition of variations in internal strengths, and unsuccessful experiments (of which there have been quite a number) were truncated. Lastly, the pursuit of excellence (which ensures a high international reputation) does not limit RCT's activities to one particular sphere: the Centre straddles the two fields of Chinese literature and translation studies, and manages to have a considerable international presence in both. This academic diversity will allow the Centre considerable flexibility in its future development.

Notes

[1]   To the best of our knowledge there is no academic centre of a comparable nature or history in East and Southeast Asia.

[2]   The University of Hong Kong started the first local B.A. degree course in translation in 1974. Though the Chinese Department at Hong Kong University had an established lectureship/assistant lectureship in translation as early as 1927, translation had only been offered as a minor course until 1974.

[3]   This was also reflected in the initial affiliation of the Centre, which was founded as part of the Institute of Social Sciences and Humanities, and was transferred to the Institute of Chinese Studies in 1976.

[4]   It was not until 1976 that it received an endowment from the local Wing Lung Bank, thus becoming the first Centre project to see a more secure future.

[5]   Among them numbered André Lefevere, Susan Bassnett and Theo Hermans.

[6]   Prior to the twentieth century, China's major translation activities were all non-literary. The fact that literature was hailed as a means to save and strengthen the nation at the end of the nineteenth century saw new norms emerged in terms of the visibility of literary work (particularly fiction) in translation. The dominant role of literature received a boost, perhaps ironically, from the utilitarian approach of reformers and revolutionaries alike. As a propaganda tool it remained at centre stage in the first decades of the PRC. For more details see Eva Hung, "Several Issues Relating to Translation Studies in China." (中國翻譯研究的幾個問題), in *Translation, Culture and Literature* (《翻譯‧文化‧文學》), Beijing: Peking University Press 北京大學出版社, 1999.

[7]   The Renditions Paperpacks series was launched in December 1986.

[8]   They were Eugene Nida, Gideon Toury, Eugene Eoyang and Tejaswini Niranjana.

[9]   The mid-1980s saw a mass exodus of Chinese academics to the West. The majority of the Nakai Centre personnel left China and did not return.

[10]   See, for example, Chen Fong-ching and Jin Guantao, *From Youthful Manuscripts to River Elegy*, Hong Kong: The Chinese University Press, 1997.

[11]   Including three international conferences, one working academic conference, an academic book series and the annual Stephen C. Soong Translation Studies Awards.

[12]   Initiated at RCT; published and distributed by Peking University Press.

[13]   One notable example of how ideology and politics influenced foreign language

education was the transfer of students and teachers of Russian to English departments after the PRC's relationship with the Soviet Union turned sour. Until the early 1980s, foreign language learning in mainland China was a highly sensitive and strictly controlled area.

[14] The mutual hostilities between the Taiwan and mainland Chinese governments was reflected in a substantial amount of literary censorship on both sides of the Taiwain Straits until the mid-1980s.

[15] RCT Annual Report 1976–77. The Centre finally decided to discontinue its work in this area not just because of financial considerations, but also because of extremely limited human resources.

[16] RCT Annual Report 1982–83. This arrangement would have entailed considerably more resources than RCT ever commanded, so the actual setup at the Centre has always demanded that one person do both jobs.

Translator Training in Hong Kong: What Professional Translators Can Tell Us

Li Defeng
Department of Translation
The Chinese University of Hong Kong

Studies on translation teaching have been gaining momentum in recent years. While plenty has been written on translator's competence and proficiency (Shreve, 1997), approaches to teaching translation (Gile, 1995a), the role of theory in translation teaching (Gentile, 1991) and empirical study of translation process and its pedagogical implications (Lorscher, 1991), several other important aspects of translation teaching have been un- or under-explored. For example, there has been little study on the design and planning of translation curricula and yet curriculum design and planning most directly affects the quality of translators turned out by translation programmes. Therefore, how to conduct curriculum design and inject innovation in translation programmes, I believe, merits our attention.

There is general, though not universal, agreement among educators that curriculum design and innovation should be based on learner needs (Pratt, 1994:35). Therefore, in an effort to study the design of translation curriculum, an assessment of learner needs would be a good point to start, hence this study of professional translators' needs and perceptions of translation teaching in Hong Kong, particularly on the areas where changes and improvement are necessary.

The Study

Design

The present study of professional translators in Hong Kong consisted of two parts: a questionnaire survey and a follow-up interview with selected informants.

The first part of the study was a questionnaire survey. In the survey, 65 questionnaires were sent out and 42 questionnaires were completed and returned, with a return rate of 64.6 percent. Following the questionnaire survey, in-depth interviews were carried out with 12 of the respondents to further explore their background and their understanding of being translators/interpreters and also their perceptions of translator training in Hong Kong.

Participants

Participants of the study were 42 professional translators in Hong Kong, among whom were 24 Chinese Language Officers, 16 translators and interpreters in private companies and two police translators. Most of them were in their 20s and 30s and had B.A. and M.A. degrees from local tertiary institutions. Many had worked as translators for around 8 years when this study was conducted.

Data Analysis

In data analysis, following the strategy of analytic induction (Bogdan and Biklen, 1992), I repeatedly read through the completed questionnaires and the interview transcripts during and after the study. In this process, recurrent themes and salient comments were identified and noted for the final report.

Findings of the Study

As the result of my going through the data several times, the following emerged as the major themes of this study.

Most Helpful Courses

What were the most helpful courses? The respondents were requested to choose three courses that they took in translation and language training programmes that proved most useful. These were specialized translation/interpretation courses, English language and literature courses and Chinese language and literature courses. Among the 42 translators surveyed, 38 (90.5%) reported that English language and literature courses were the most helpful. 36 respondents (85.7%) reported that Chinese language and literature courses were most helpful. 30 respondents (71.4%) mentioned specialized, practical translation courses as most helpful, which included such courses as commercial translation, news translation, translation of government materials, scientific and legal translation.

Best and Least Prepared Areas

What were their best-prepared areas before joining the translation/interpreting profession? 24 people (57%) considered proficiency in both English and Chinese as one of the areas they felt competent. 16 people (38%) mentioned their being equipped with good translation skills as another such area.

Regarding least prepared areas, 24 out of 42 respondents (57.1%) cited subject matter knowledge as the area where they felt least prepared when they first became translators and interpreters. Such lack of subject matter knowledge ranged from knowledge of the structures of the government, knowledge of science and technology, knowledge of current affairs, to knowledge of the stock market and financial world. To use the words of one of the respondents, "It is knowledge other than that related to language, literature and translation that we are lacking."

The other least prepared area referred to by the respondents was oral interpreting. It was mentioned 8 times (19%).

Challenges at Work

According to the respondents, one of the biggest challenges they had at work was to choose the right style for translating a particular text. The right style, for them, included proper format, register, and terminology for a particular type of text. 31 respondents (73.8%) referred to it as their biggest challenge. Choosing the right style of translating remained their biggest challenge throughout their years in the profession.

The second biggest challenge for them was interpretation in general. 26 people cited interpreting as challenging no matter how long they had worked in the profession. Topics that they were unfamiliar with gave them particular difficulty. Stage fright and short notice of assignments were two other reasons why they found interpreting difficult.

The third biggest challenge was the time constraint with both translation and interpretation assignments. 24 respondents referred to it as the biggest challenge. Generally they had too much work but too little time.

This was especially true for Chinese Language Officers. They were often asked to finish translation "within an almost unreasonable time."

24 respondents cited language competence as a challenge. In general, they constantly felt that they run out of "the right phrases and words" for the right text. Besides they seemed to have difficulty in understanding the original English text as well when they were engaged in English-Chinese translation. As one respondent said, "the English sentences are so complicated in structure in some technical texts that it is really very difficult to figure out the meaning."

Another challenge reported by the informants was that they did not know where to find the references to help with their translation. 19 people referred to it as a challenge for them. This was especially true for those who were relatively new to the profession. Finding references here includes both seeking references for the subject matter and also the terminology in the target language. According to the respondents, they were very seldom taught how to find related references in completing a translation assignment. It seems that finding references to help with translation is assumed to be fairly easy by many teachers. But, it is not the case in actuality. As one informant commented, "when we get to the job, it is really not easy to find good references at all. We don't even know where and how to start."

Changes in the Translation World

Another theme that has come out of this study is that great changes have taken place in the translation market over the years and that such changes have considerably affected the job of professional translators. The respondents identified three major changes: more Chinese-to-English translation, more selective translation, and rapid appearance of new terms in almost all subject areas. 34 out of the 42 informants reported that they were obviously doing more translation from Chinese into English, which was quite different from years ago when they mostly translated from English to Chinese. According to the respondents, this change has affected them in two ways. First, as mentioned earlier, they need to have better Chinese and English writing skills because there are now more translation assignments from Chinese into English, thus making it necessary for them to change English from the passive language into the active language. Secondly, because of the higher status and wider use of Chinese since the handover to Chinese sovereignty in 1997, they are now sometimes required to draft documents in Chinese. This also makes it essential for them to have better Chinese writing skills.

The second major change the respondents have seen in translation is that in addition to complete translation, they are receiving more assignments of selective translation, such as vetting, abstract translation, summary translation and abridged translation. In such cases, they are not required to translate the entire text, but to translate the main ideas of the text or only parts of the text. For some, they are asked to do oral translation of a written text or what they have noted down at board meetings. This is an area that the respondents felt that they did not have much preparation at university and therefore needed more training.

The third change seen by the informants is that they are translating more China-related documents than ever before. Even before 1997, they were often required to translate more Mainland documents. They generally found such translation assignments challenging because "we really don't know much about the Mainland, especially its political-social systems." Also, "we are not familiar with the terms that are used in the Mainland and therefore it is difficult to put them into proper English." Others also felt that because of the closer relationship between Hong Kong and the Mainland, there had been an increasing number of translation assignments that deal with China-related business. They felt "it's time for us to take a course in China studies."

Disparities between Translator Training and the Real World of Translation Practice

The respondents were also asked how well their training as translators and linguists reflected the reality of the translation profession. Most of them thought that their training somehow reflected the real needs of professional translators. 16 out of 42 believed that their training adequately reflected the reality, 20 believed that their training somewhat reflected the reality, and six believed that their training did not reflect the reality very well.

When asked for their comments on how well the present training programmes reflected the actual needs of the profession, 20 out of 42 respondents thought that the programmes did not reflect the reality very well, 12 thought it somehow reflected the reality and the rest chose not to answer this question since they graduated quite a long time ago and felt unfamiliar about translation programmes today.

The examples that the respondents cited as disparities between translation teaching and the real world of translation practice included context versus teamwork, time constraints versus translation procedures, and complete translation versus selective translation. At university, teachers like to stress the importance and the use of context in translation. However, in reality, according to the informants of the study, when there is a large amount of translation work, the original text is often chopped up and divided among a team of translators. At other times, in order to meet tight deadlines, the work has to be shared among a group of translators. Sometimes, one translator may only get a couple of sentences to translate and therefore the translation is then totally decontextualized. As one respondent said, "then there is no context to help with the comprehension. The best we can do at such times is to make wise and educated guesses."

Teachers and researchers often talk about the proper procedures of translation. For instance, Jin (1991) suggested a three-step procedure, which begins with a thorough and careful reading of the entire SL text plus reading about the author and other background information related to the SL text. However, due to time constraint, professional translators in the real world seldom have time to read the whole text before translating. Instead, they start translating right away in order to get it finished in time. Also, Jin suggested that when the draft is completed, it should be set aside for about two weeks before the translator tries to revise it. Unfortunately, very seldom can professional translators afford such luxury in reality. Almost always they have to submit the translation to the client as soon as it is finished. In fact, during my interviews with the informants, several of them mentioned that one of their first challenges as translators was that they had to learn to "be satisfied with an acceptable but not perfect translation."

In all translation departments and programmes, students are taught how to do complete translation. They hardly get a chance to learn how to do summary or abridged translation, let alone vetting. However, professional translators nowadays are often required to do selective translation. This is especially true in the commercial field. According to some of the respondents, they were sometimes requested to do translation that might be different from the traditional definition of translation. For instance, they might be asked to attend a Board of Directors meeting conducted entirely in Cantonese and produce its minutes in English or vice versa. They might be requested to summary-translate a document of hundreds of pages. Since such skills are seldom taught in traditional translation programmes, these changes have posed new challenges for traditionally trained translators and interpreters.

Further Training

When asked what they would like to learn more if they have a chance to enrol in an in-service training programme, 28 out of 42 respondents believed that they would like to study more English language and literature in order to improve their English. 26 respondents cited Chinese language and literature as an area that they would like to study more. Many of them specifically stressed that they would like to work more on Chinese grammar, since they had to translate more from Chinese into English and even draft manuscripts in Chinese.

Another subject that the respondents would like to learn more is Putonghua. 19 out of 42 placed this as their subject of choice. Many of them found that they were now often assigned to interpret for visitors from the Mainland.

Implications of the Study

The implications of this study are fairly straightforward. Basically, we should teach and strengthen what learners need for the job, and make necessary changes in teaching methods with the express aim to help students smooth the transition from study to work.

Practical Training

It was found in this study that there are considerable discrepancies between translation training and the real world of translation practice. The examples given by respondents include contextualized translation versus team translation, time constraint versus proper translation procedures and complete translation versus selective translation. These were also the biggest challenges that the respondents had when they first joined the translation/ interpretation profession. How do we smooth the transition and reduce the "real world shock" for our graduates? I believe one of the solutions is to provide them with more practical training.

Practical training includes at least two parts: authentic training materials and improved training methods. The first is very obvious. We should use materials from the real translation world rather than contrived materials for translation practice. Also, we should use up-to-date rather than out-dated materials for practice.

Another aspect of *authentic* translation relates to the methods of training. Instead of using the model of freelance literary translation as the training model, we should give students more practice in simulated real-world situations, such as translating within limited time and collaborative group translation.

Authentic training should also include training on selective translation such as summary and abridged translation. This study shows that the translation world has changed dramatically over the last few years. Rather than the traditional complete text-text translation, translators today are often assigned to do oral-written or written-oral translation. Rather than doing complete translation, they may be asked to do selective translation. However, at present, such skills are rarely taught in translation programmes. At most they are only briefly touched upon. It seems that it is time that the skills of abridged translation, summary translation and abstract translation be taught in translation programmes.

Enhanced Language Training

The respondents found that although their language training was most useful for them at work they still found it insufficient for their professional needs. We can also see from the present study that the respondents seemed to have prized language skills and therefore training in language skills over translation skills training. Therefore, a strong message from this study is that bilingual competence is the most important to the translator and that language training for translation students needs to be strengthened.

More Training in Cantonese and Putonghua

This may seem repetitious to the previous section of Enhanced Language Training. However, I would like to single it out because it has particular significance in this context. First, even in programmes that do provide intensive language training before translation training, stress is put mostly on training of the foreign language while training of one's mother tongue is always kept minimal. However, as we are all aware, training in students' mother tongue is just as important, if not more, than the foreign language. This is especially important for translation programmes in Hong Kong. The respondents believed that it is essential for them to have good Chinese writing skills to be a competent translator in Hong Kong today. They also found that the need to learn Putonghua, because they receive more interpretation assignments between Cantonese and Putonghua, or they simply need to carry out assignments in Putonghua, as the result of more exchanges between Mainland China and Hong Kong.

Recent socio-political changes in Hong Kong have also brought about another implication for translation teaching: the need for a course of China Studies for translation students. As a result of more interactions between the Mainland and Hong Kong, translators need to do more China-related translation in all sectors of the translation and interpretation market. Therefore a course to help them know more about Mainland China seems to be in order.

Enhanced Interpretation Training

Interpreting seems to be a skill that needs enhanced training in all translation programmes. The respondents in general found interpreting challenging and the training they received inadequate. From my own experience teaching at The Chinese University of Hong Kong, students are usually afraid of taking advanced interpretation courses. So how to encourage students to take more advanced interpretation courses and reduce their anxiety by creating a more supportive learning environment is then crucial. Compared with countries in other parts of the world, there has been little research on interpreting and interpreter training in Hong Kong and Mainland China. I believe more study on this topic should be done as we advance into the next millennium.

Teaching of Subject Matter Knowledge

How do we respond to students' needs for more subject matter knowledge? Obviously, there is no easy answer. However, efforts can probably be made in at least two areas. First, in teaching specialized translation courses, we should also teach as much related background knowledge as it is possible. Many of us are already doing this but I think it is worth reiterating here. Secondly, we as teachers need to encourage students to read more and read everything. Plenty has been said on the importance of subject matter knowledge to translators (Lü, 1984; Gile, 1995b) and therefore it needs no stress here. However, one of the respondents' comments seemed to have said it all: "common sense is the name of the game." Aside from the above two measures, we can probably only let students accumulate such meta-translational knowledge gradually in practice.

Reference-finding in Translation Teaching

Teaching students how to seek references seems to be overlooked in translation teaching. Therefore, it is time that we teachers, particularly those teaching specialized translation courses, take up the responsibility to inform students of useful references in translating texts of different subjects. In addition to traditional references such as glossaries and dictionaries, students should also be taught how to make use of modern technology to seek useful information for translation. For instance, how to locate the website of a commercial company and find necessary information to help with an assignment of commercial translation, or how to make use of the websites set up by the Hong Kong SAR Government to help with translation of government documents. It will also be very helpful to students if we can inform them of the websites of some international, regional and national translation and interpretation organizations, various translation links and on-line discussion groups. All this information would be invaluable to our students.

Conclusion

First, this study has yielded interesting findings about the real world of professional translators and provided important implications for translator training. Therefore studies of this sort should be done regularly to gather feedback from our graduates so as to inform future training. We as translation teachers, must reach out to the real world of translation practitioners, so that when "...constructing a bridge between theory and practice is attempted from both sides, it will be completed before long." (Bühler, 1987: 110)

References

Bogdan, Robert and Sari Knopp Biklen (1992). *Qualitative Research for Education: An Introduction to Theory and Methods.* London: Allyn and Bacon.
Bühler, Hildegund (1987). "Language and Translation: Translating and Interpreting as a Profession." In R.B. Kaplan *et al.* eds., *Language and Professions: Annual Review of Applied Linguistics,* Vol. 7. Cambridge: Cambridge University Press.

Gentile, A. (1991). "The Application of Theoretical Constructs from a Number of Disciplines for the Development of a Methodology of Teaching in Interpreting and Translating." *Meta*, Vol. 36, Nos. 2–3, pp. 344–51.

Gile, D. (1995a). *Basic Concepts and Models for Interpreter and Translator Training*. Amsterdam: John Benjamins Publishing Company.

Gile, D. (1995b). "Mirror Mirror on the Wall: An Introduction." *Target*, Vol. 7, No.1, pp. 1–5.

Jin, Di (1991). "Contra-Bly States of Translation." *Translation Review*, Vols. 36–37, pp. 22–4.

Lörscher, W. (1991). *Translation Performance, Translation Process, and Translation Strategies: A Psycholinguistic Investigation*. Tubingen: Narr.

Lü, S. (1984). "Translation and Miscellaneous Knowledge." In Luo Xinzhang, ed., *On Translation*. Beijing: The Commercial Press.

Pratt, D. (1994). *Curriculum Planning: A Handbook for Professionals*. FL, Orlando: Harcourt Brace Javanovich, Inc.

Shreve, G. M. (1997). "Cognition and the Evolution of Translation Competence." In J. H. Danks, G. M. Shreve, S. B. Fountain and M. K. McBeath, eds., *Cognitive Processes in Translation and Interpreting*. London: Sage Publications.

A Higher Diploma Course of Translation and Interpretation at the Crossroads — The HDTI at the City University of Hong Kong

Mak Wai Ho
Division of Language Studies
City University of Hong Kong

Introduction

In the last decade, Hong Kong has undergone far-reaching political and social changes. As a result of the much-anticipated realignment of language uses in different domains, translation courses have been booming in all tertiary institutes. The development of the Higher Diploma of Translation and Interpretation (HDTI) at the City University of Hong Kong is a good example of the social and institutional intricacies that a higher diploma course of Translation and Interpretation in Hong Kong has faced. This paper will first outline some major steps in the development of the HDTI and then highlight some of the formative forces behind these changes. Keeping to the theme of this conference, the emphasis of this paper is on the future. I will discuss the challenges that the HDTI is currently facing and explore possibilities for its future development. I will concentrate on the following three areas: (1) Course objectives and aims, (2) Course design, and (3) Career paths of graduates.

Part I: From Past to Present

A Brief History of HDTI at City University

The Higher Diploma of Translation and Interpretation (HDTI) at the City University of Hong Kong, now under the Division of Language Studies of the College of Higher Vocational Studies, was first offered by the then Department of Languages in 1985–86. It continued to be offered by the Department of Applied Linguistics (renamed the Department of Chinese, Translation and Linguistics in January 1992), which came into being as the result of the splitting of the Department of Languages into two separate departments; the other being the Department of English. In summer 1991, the responsibility for the course was passed to the Division of Humanities and Social Sciences of the newly created College of Higher Vocational Studies, which would run, with few exceptions, all sub-degree courses of the then City Polytechnic (renamed City University in 1994). The course is now offered by the Division of Language Studies, which resulted from a splitting of the Division of Humanities and Social Sciences into this Division and the Division of Social Studies in 1994.

Mission and Role of HDTI

The objectives of the pre-college HDTI were:

> To provide balanced training in translation and interpretation designed to reflect advances in language studies, translation theory and practice and to provide knowledge of Putonghua/Mandarin or Japanese as a third language/ dialect other than English and Cantonese.

and

> To prepare students for full time translation/interpretation work. (City Polytechnic, 1987)

The founding of the College of Higher Vocational Studies provided a good opportunity for the HDTI to reconsider its identity, mission and course design; and these were largely reflected in its first course revalidation exercise at 1991. The College's main mission is for form five leavers and for "graduates to take up employment in the public and private sectors as senior vocational staff usually with middle management responsibilities." (Chan and Imrie, 1995: 119–29) The Mission Statement of the College emphasizes: "excellence in teaching," "student competency with communication and learning skills," "fitness for purpose of vocational programmes to ensure graduate capability," and "operation and interaction with the practicing profession and employers." (Imrie, 1995: 7)

To be in line with this statement, it was deemed that HDTI should be "vocational" and "practical" or "applied" in nature. The aims and objectives of the new HDTI syllabus have become:

> To provide students with the language skills, cultural awareness, analytical capability, and confidence acquired through constant practice, to enable them to enter the employment market on graduation with a broad-based foundation upon which, after two or three years of work experience and/or further study, they can rapidly build a solid competence as fully-fledged translators and interpreters, or as practitioners of other translation-centered activities. (City Polytechnic, 1992)

A quick comparison of the two syllabuses will reveal that while both stress the relevance to employment, the objectives of the new syllabus are more "focused" and "less ambitious," stressing the need for a "broad-based foundation" for "further development" instead of a "ready made full-fledged product." In addition, the target professions have been broadened from translation and interpretation jobs to "practitioners of other translation centered activities." Furthermore, the "balanced training of translation and interpretation" has been downgraded. In the revalidation exercise, a lot of factors were required to be taken into consideration including employment surveys, the target students, feedback from past students and so on. We can see that the new syllabus is more "down-to-earth" in the way that the capability (thus a stress on foundation and preparation, and confidence) as well as career path (e.g. more diversified job nature, further studies) of prospective students have been taken into consideration. The implications to syllabus design will be discussed in the following section.

Course Design

In order to realize the new objectives and aims of the HDTI, the programme was restructured in a way so as to steer clear of the linguistic dominance of its precursor and to give more weight to "cultural awareness" and "practicality." A comparison of the "old" (Appendix 1) and the "new" (Appendix 2) syllabus will show the following (for more detailed comparison, please refer to Appendix 4):

1. To realize the "foundation" objective, there were more "introduction" and "preparation'' components to suit the level of prospective candidates, who were supposed to be form five leavers.
2. Linguistics and "theoretical'' subjects (e.g. Semantics, Sociolinguistics, Introduction to Language Studies) and supporting modules (e.g. Introduction to Law, Elements of Office Administration) were drastically reduced: the former from 32.5% to 10.96% and the latter from 7.21% to 1.99%.

3. The reduced hours were mainly used for more translation courses (note particularly the hours devoted to the third year project, from 40 hours to 150 hours), English Communication /Writing modules (from 5% to 12%) and cultural modules (from 3.6% to 8. 64%).

4. A Chinese word-processing module was also included as a formal module.

As a result of this restructuring, the identity and image of a "professional" translation course were much more enhanced. The proportion of translation and interpretation components increased from 25.88% to 42.52% in the new syllabus. However, the hours in Putonghua were reduced from 240 to 150 hours, which seems undesirable if the objective of "mastering three languages Chinese, English and Putonghua" is to be realized. This issue has come up recurrently in subsequent staff-consultative meetings as students expressed the need for more Putonghua hours.

Career Development

Before B.A. degrees in translation were offered (BATI at the City University of Hong Kong was offered in 1992), the HDTI was often considered as a "degree equivalent" qualification in the territory and overseas. Indeed it is not uncommon that graduates have been directly admitted to M.A. Degrees by local and overseas Universities. Traditional jobs for our students are in translating (e.g. Police Interpreters, Chinese Language Officers, and Court Interpreters) and in the mass media. As 1997 approached, translating and translation-related jobs abounded. This was reflected in the employment figures (see Appendix 5). As a matter of fact, in 1995, HDTI students had the highest rate of entering government posts (44.2%) among all City University students (BATI only 29.8%).

The employment rate of our students is more than satisfactory. The unemployment rate has been low and their average income is usually higher than the Higher Diploma mean (nearly 26% higher in 95 due to higher government salaries).

Part II: From Present to Future

In part I, I have shown how the HDTI has responded to social demands for bilingual professionals through its course objectives and design. Now it has been two years since the change of sovereignty and economically, Hong Kong has been severely enervated by the "financial storm." The controversies over declining language standards and whether English or Chinese should be the medium of instruction can be taken as the backdrop to the discussion of the challenges that the HDTI is facing.

Course Objectives and Aims

We have noted, in admission interviews for example, that more and more students have said that they take our programme not because they want to be professional translators but because they want to improve their Chinese and English language skills. Added to this, the trend that more and more students will further their studies (34.3% in 1998) instead of becoming "vocational" will surely challenge the mission and identity of the College. Are the present objectives of HDTI flexible enough to cater for the very divergent needs and aspirations of our students? The following directions are worth exploring:

1. Should we still emphasize vocational training? If not, what are the subjects that should be offered? It seems that we need to broaden our ideas about employment beyond the traditional "translation" jobs such as police interpreters, Chinese language officers etc. (no graduates entered these jobs in 1997). We may need more comprehensive surveys on the language needs of our graduates.

2. Should we emphasize professional (specialized) translation? Or just bilingual skills and gear our programme towards a course of "bilingual communication" like the Polytechnic University? As far as language skills are concerned, we may as well ask what are translation skills and what are bilingual skills? It is stunning to note that in a recent survey (see Appendix 5), 45.5% of graduates said the course was irrelevant to their job. But it is also interesting to see that 80% of the same batch of students maintained that what they have learned is very useful in their daily work. (City University, 1998). It seems that the way that Chinese and English languages are used needs to be examined more carefully. A recent survey on the language used at work of our graduates may give us some clues:

	English skills			Chinese Skills				Translating skills	
	Speaking	Writing	Reading	Putonghua	Cantonese	Writing	Reading	Translating	Interpreting
Frequently or often used	50% (18)	55% (20)	69% (25)	36% (13)	90% (32)	61% (21)	61% (22)	31% (11)	0% (0)
Not often or seldom used	50% (18)	45% (16)	30% (11)	64% (23)	9% (3)	40% (14)	39% (14)	69% (25)	100 % (35)
	100% (36)	100% (36)	99% (35)	100% (35)	99% (35)	101% (36)	100% (36)	100% (36)	100% (35)

Source: 1997 Employment Survey by HDTI, internal document.

In the 1999 University Calendar (City University, 1998: 265), the objectives of the HDTI were rewritten as:

> The programme provides the language skills, background knowledge, capacity for analysis and practice in translation and interpretation to prepare students for the employment market and for their further professional and academic development. Graduates will find employment in the public and private sectors in jobs which require information transfer skills, such as translation and interpretation, between English and Chinese (Cantonese and Putonghua) and/or good communication skills in both languages generally. Apart from working specifically as translators or interpreters, graduates will also find employment in journalism, publishing, marketing, advertising, education, office management, the judiciary and mass communications.

To a certain extent, I think the programme coordinator has already taken into consideration the issues I have raised above and these shifts in emphasis will aptly pave the way for future course revalidation.

3.   There was proposal of for a Higher Diploma of Language Studies, but because the HDTI has a well-established reputation among employers and professionals in the field we are unsure that it would bring much benefit. A Diploma in Translation and Interpretation gives our students a better professional image and edge over other language streams. However, a Higher Diploma in Language Studies may sound more academic and broader in scope, and may give our students wider choice in BA or MA courses.

Or should we consider the issue from a broader perspective, i.e. the role and status of the Higher Diploma in the whole education system of Hong Kong? We have seen how the mission of College has helped define the objectives of the HDTI. What will be the role and status of the College and Higher Diplomas in the future? The issue indeed has been high on the agenda. For example, in a paper on the future of sub-degree Education, it was suggested that:

> Higher Diploma does not reflect fairly the quality of the programmes offered by CHVS. The breadth and depth of coverage of the programmes have effectively exceeded those offered by Technical Colleges and granting the same award would be de-motivating for students and staff alike. (Working Party, 1998:7)

And

> To this end, the Working Party is firmly of the view that a new title of "Associate Degree" will best suit the present academic quality and standard achieved at the Higher Diploma programmes offered at CHVS. (Working Party, 1998:15)

Course Design

Undoubtedly a significant factor in shaping course design is the Credit Unit System, which was implemented across all Universities in 1997. "Flexibility" and "choices'" seem to be the two biggest advantages of the system. For example, it may allow multiple entry possibilities and offer different modes and different paces of study. Its easily transferable credits can also facilitate academic recognition and transfer of qualifications, and may allow the offer of awards at different stages (e.g. 1 year for a certificate, 2 years for a diploma). By opting for different electives, students then can place more emphasis on intellectual training or vocational knowledge to suit their own aspirations.

While the potential is yet to be explored, the impact of the Credit Unit System on the present syllabus should not be taken lightly. Institutional requirements already takes up nearly 22 credits (Chinese Civilization 6, Out of Discipline 6, University language requirement 6, College language requirement 4, refer to Appendix 3 for more details) out of the minimum 93 credits, amounting to 23.7% of the whole syllabus. As our students are usually exempted from the 6 University language credits, they tend to take up more out of discipline modules, Japanese and French being the most popular. The taking of more out of discipline courses will further reduce the proportion of core courses (see Appendix 4). Overall translation and interpretation elements are still high (about 46 %). However, translation courses have been cut to the bone. "Linguistic" and "theoretical" courses have either been cut or absorbed in other courses. For example, Discourse Analysis is cut. Many of the cultural modules have become electives and the yearlong Structure of English is regrouped into a one-semester course.

The following possibilities can be further explored:

1. Considering that more and more students will further their studies, should we re-introduce some more "linguistic" or "theoretical" modules to give them a broader foundation so as to facilitate their future intellectual pursuits? I think at least an "Introduction to Language Studies" module covering basic linguistic concepts should be reintroduced.

2. Since our students are usually exempted from English requirements, why can't we offer them "Advanced Putonghua" or "Putonghua for Specific Purposes"?

3. What about specialization? We now offer three areas: Commercial Translation, Literary Translation and Technical Translation. How can we help students specialize? In what areas? Again, surveys on the language needs of target jobs are important. I am very happy to hear Prof. Li Defeng's stress on authentic materials in the training of translators at this conference.

4. As translation modules have been cut, it seems that the only room for manipulation is the Project, which amounts to 210 hours and takes up nearly 45.1% (210/465) of all translation component hours. Should we add research, desktop publishing, editing, and glossary compiling components? Or can we consider other formats apart from the traditional extended essay? Say a portfolio approach?

5. In order to counteract the diluting effect of the Credit Unit System, can we rename some courses to highlight its translation identity? For example "Structure of English" and "Text Production" can be renamed "Translation and Advanced Grammar" and "Advanced English Writing Skills for Translators."

Career Development

Despite the severe economic situation, employment prospects of our graduates appear to be satisfactory. Unemployment rate is low, only at 1. 5% of the 98 survey (the average rate for all graduates is 11.2%). This shows that people with good bilingual skills are still in great demand, though they need not necessarily be called a "translator" or "interpreter." The average income is still HK$500 higher than the HD average. About 62. 9% said they were satisfied with their present job in last year's survey.

Browsing through the employment figures (see Appendix 5), the following trends are evident:

1. More and more graduates work in the private sector.
2. Graduates work in more divergent, less well-defined fields. This may explain why 45% of graduates said their work was not relevant to their course.
3. More and more graduates have opted to further their studies locally or abroad (34.3% at 98). Is this due to the harsh employment situation?

To look ahead, how can we help our graduates establish more vocational links and open up further studies opportunities? I suggest the following possibilities:

1. As our past graduates have been our valuable information sources, it is important to get them organized. One option would be to form a network of HDTI alumni, which would surely strengthen the identity of HDTI graduates and students. We can invite past graduates to share their experiences with present undergraduates.
2. Employment surveys should be conducted to obtain the most updated employment information. It may be useful to conduct longitudinal studies to research into the typical career path of our graduates apart from the annual employment survey, which only focuses on the fresh graduates.
3. One suggestion from past graduates is that students should get some work experience before they graduate. How can we help students get more "relevant" and "meaningful" work experience, which may include part-time, voluntary or placement positions?
4. Since the advantage of the credit unit system is its flexibility and easy transferability of credits, we should take a more proactive role in establishing formal links and recognition with professional bodies (e.g. MIL, NAATI) and other universities (e.g. The Open University, Leeds). The part-time top-up degree, the B.A. in Professional Communication, jointly offered by SCOPE (School of

Continuing and Professional Education of the City University of Hong Kong) and the University of New England, serves as a bridging course tailored made for graduates of the Division of Language Studies. This is a move in the right direction.

Conclusion

In this paper, I have shown that the development of a Higher Diploma course in translation and interpretation is subject to many constraints. The experiences of HDTI at City University of Hong Kong demonstrates well how a HD course juggles the ever-changing needs of society and students with institutional constraints (e.g. the Mission Statement of the College, the Credit Unit System) and still maintain its integrity as a "professional translation course." A review of the role and status of Higher Diploma courses in the tertiary education system is high on the agenda, and the potential of the Credit Unit System is yet to be fully evaluated. A four-year university degree and a two-year higher diploma course are also topics for discussion. No doubt, the HDTI stands at the crossroads, but one thing is sure—we need to meet the future with confidence and innovation.

Appendix 1: Course Structure 1987 (pre-College era)

*One term equals 10 weeks

Year 1

Term 1	Hrs	Term 2	Hrs	Term 3	Hrs
EN0131 English Communication Skills for Translation and Interpretation I	30	EN0132 English Communication Skills for Translation and Interpretation II	30	EN0133 English Communication Skills for Translation and Interpretation III	30
AL0231 Chinese Communication Skills for Translation and Interpretation I	30	AL0232 Chinese Communication Skills for Translation and Interpretation II	30	AL0233 Chinese Communication Skills for Translation and Interpretation III	30
AL0301 Introduction to the Study of Language	30	AL0302 Language, Culture and Thought	30	En0451 Contemporary English Literature	30
AL0801 Beginning Putonghua/Mandarin/ Mandarin I*	30	AL0802 Beginning Putonghua/Mandarin/ Mandarin II	30	AL0803 Beginning Putonghua/ Mandarin/ Mandarin III	30
ACO521 Elements of Office Administration I	30	AL0002 Beginning Putonghua/Mandarin Laboratory (continued to term 3)	15	AL0002 Beginning Putonghua/Mandarin Laboratory (continued from term 2)	30
BM 0407 Business Functi ons	30	AL0701 Introduction to Translation I	30	AL0702 Introduction to Translation II	30
		LW0613 Introduction to Hong Kong Law	30	AL0551 Contemporary Chinese Literature	30
	180		195		195

*Those exempted from Putonghua can take a comparable Japanese course.

Year 2

Term 1	Hrs	Term 2	Hrs	Term 3	Hrs
AL0304 Foundations of Language Study	30	AL0401 Structure of English I	30	AL0402 Structure of English II	30
AL0305 Language and Society in Hong Kong	30	AL0501 Structure of Chinese I	30	AL0502 Structrue of Chinese II	30

Year 2 (Cont'd)

Term 1	Hrs	Term 2	Hrs	Term 3	Hrs
AL0704 Principles of Translation and Interpretation	30	AL0071 Methods in Translation and Interpretation Laboratory (to be continued interm 3)	15	AL 0071 Methods in Translation and interpretation Laboratory (to be continued from term 2)	15
AL0804 Putonghua/ Mandarin I	30	AL0805 Putonghua/ Mandarin II	30	AL0806 Putonghua/ Mandarin III	30
SS0102 Hong Kong Society	30	AL005 Putonghua Laboratory (to be continued in term 3)	15	AL005 Putonghua Laboratory (to be continued from term 2)	15
		AL0717 Cultural Background to Translation I	30	AL0718 Cultural Background to Translation II	30
	180		180		180

Year 3

Term 1	Hrs	Term 2	Hrs	Term 3	Hrs
AL0306 Socioloinguists	30	AL0403 English Semantics	30	AL0503 Lexical Studies	30
AL0311 Discourse Analysis and Stylistics	30	AL0710 Comparative Studies in Translation	30	AL0613 Comparative Studies: Chinese and English Language Strutures	30
AL0314 Project	40	AL0711 Specialized Translation and Interpretation 1 (Commerce and Law)	15	AL0712 Specialized Translation and interpretation 2 (Commerce and Law)	30
EN0452 English Liberary Tradition	30	AL0713 Specialized Translation and Interpretation 1 (Science and Technology) Or AL0715 Splecialized Translation and Interpretation 1 (Media and Literature)	30	AL0714 Specialized Translation and Interpretation 2 (Science and Technology) Or AL0716 Specialized Translation and Interpretation 2 (Media and Literature)	30

Year 3 (Cont'd)

Term 1	Hrs	Term 2	Hrs	Term 3	Hrs
AL0503 Chinese Syntactic and Semantic Structure	30	AL0719 Approaches to Interpretation Or AL0091 Interpretation Laboratory	15	AL0720 Consecutive Interpretation Or AL0093 Simultaneous Interpretation Laboratory	30
				AL0092 Consecutive Interpretation Laboratory Or AL0721 Simultaneous Interpretation	30
	180		150		180

Source: *Higher Diploma in Translation and Interpretation, Higher Certificate in Translation and Interpretation Definitive Course Document,* Vols. 1 and 2 (1987). Hong Kong: City Polytechnic of Hong Kong.

Appendix 2: Course Structure 1992

*There were 15 weeks in each semester.

Year 1

Sem A	Sem Hrs	Sem B	Sem Hrs
HS 4000 Introduction to Translation	45	HS4000 Introduction to Translation	45
HS 4100 Preparation for Interpretation	30	HS4100 Preparation for Interpretation	30
HS 0131 English Languag Skills	45	HS0131 English Language Skills	45
HS2231 Chinese Language Skills	45	HS2231 Chinese Language Skills	45
HS2801 Beginning Putonghua	45	HS2801Beginning Putonghua	45
HS2551 Contemporary Chinese Literature	45	HS4400 Literary and Cultural Background: Europe	30
		HS2920 Chinese Language Computer Editing	30
	255		270

Year 2

Sem A	Sem Hrs	Sem B	Sem Hrs
HS4001 General Translation	30	HS4001 General Translation	30
HS4101 Introduction to Interpretation	30	HS4101 Preparation for Interpretation	30
HS2803 Putonghua	30	HS4003 Commercial and Government Translation	45
HS4403 Contemporary Chinese World	30	HS8212 Hong Kong Society	30
HS4200 Introduction to English Text Productions	45	HS2803 Putonghua	30
HS4401 Literary and Cultural Background : N. America	30	HS2501 Structure of Chinese	45
HS4502 Structure of English	45	HS4502 Structure of English	45
	270		255

Year 3

Sem A	Sem Hrs	Sem B	Sem Hrs
HS4005 Semi-technical Translation	45	HS4004 Translation of Literature	45
HS4102 Interpretation Workshop	30	HS4201 English Text Production	45
HS4002 Translation Theory and Criticism	45	HS4102 Interpretation Workshop	45
HS4504 Discourse Analysis	30	HS4404 Contemporary Western World	40
HS4007 Project	75	HS4007 Project	75
	225		240

Source: *Higher Diploma in Translation and Interpretation Course Document*, Vols. 1 and 2 (1992). Hong Kong: City Polytechnic of Hong Kong.

Appendix 3: Course Structure under the Credit Unit System (as at 1998)

In order to graduate, a student needs at least 93 credits from these four categories:

1. University language requirement   (6 credits)
2. College language requirement   (4 credits)
3. University Chinese Civilization   (6 credits)
4. Out of Discipline Requirement   (at least 6 credits)
5. Programme Core   (61 credits)

A typical schedule as suggested by the Programme Coordinator is used here:

Year One

Sem A	Crds	Hrs	Sem B	Crds	Hrs
Introduction to Translation	2	30	Introduction to Translation	2	30
Preparation for Interpretation	2	30	Preparation for Interpretation	2	30
Beginning Putonghua/ I	3	45	Beginning Putonghua II	3	45
English Language Activation	3	45	Eff. Eng. Lang. Learning Strategies	3	45
Essentials of Chinese Language	3	45	Elements of Chinese Writing	3	45
Fundamentals of Communication	2	30	Language and Society in HK	2	30
Practical Psychology for Everyday Life	2	30			
Core	13	195		15	225
Out of Discipline	4	60			

Year Two

Sem A	Crds	Hrs	Sem B	Crds	Hrs
General Translation	2	30	General Translation	2	30
Introduction to Interpretation	2	30	Introduction to Interpretation	2	30
Advanced Putonghua/Mandarin	2	30	Advanced Putonghua/Mandarin	2	30
English Text Production I	3	45	English Text Production II	3	45
Structure of English	3	45	Structure of Chinese	3	45
			Commercial Translation	3	45
Core	12	180		15	225
Out of Discipline	4	60			

Year Three

Sem A	Crds	Hrs	Sem B	Crds	Hrs
Project	7	105	Project	7	105
Technical Translation	3	45	Literary Translation Theory and Practice	3	45
Interpretation Workshop	2	30	Consecutive Interpretation or Simultaneous Interpretation	2	30
Core	12	180		12	180

Credit Units from core subjects: 28 (year 1)+27 (year 2)+24 (year 3)	=	79
Compulsory 6 Credits in Chinese Civilization	=	6
2+2 required Out of Discipline credits from year 1	=	4
4 more Credits from other Out of Discipline courses	=	4
Total	=	93

Note:

1. Maximun credits is 108 (or 18 per semester).
2. Students also have 6 Credits to satisfy the University Language requirement but all HDTI students are exempted.
3. Possible Electives make up 93 credits:

LS1243 Readings in Contemporary Chinese Literature	3 credits
LS 1271 Computer Skills in Chinese	3 credits
LS 1801 Structure of Japanese Language	6 credits
LS 1802 Japanese Communication Skills	6 credits
LS 1803 Outline of Japanese History	4 credits
LS 3440 European Background	2 credits
LS 3441 American Background	2 credits
LS 3631 Building a Professional Image	6 credits
LS 3634 Advanced textual Studies	4 credits
CM 1341 Elements of Business	3 credits
CM 1343 Introduction to Marketing	3 credits
DSS1104 Practical Psychology for Management	2 credits
DSS1602 Analytical Techniques for Decision-Making	3 credits
DSS2601 Sociology of Popular Culture	3 credits
DSS2601 Contemporary China and Hong Kong: Issues and Context	3 credits

Sources: (1). *Higher Diploma in Translation and Interpretation, Course Handbook 1998–99.* (1998). Hong Kong: City University of Hong Kong. (2). *Calendar.* (1998). Hong Kong: City University of Hong Kong. (3). Unpublished Internal Circular from Programme Coordinator.

Appendix 4: A Comparison of the Three Syllabuses

Components	87 syllabus		92 syllabus		99 syllabus	
	%	hours	%	hours	%	hours
Putonghua modules	14.45	240	9.97	150	10.75	150
English Communication Skills (excluding literature and linguistic modules)	5.42	90	11.96	180	12.90	180
Chinese communication Skills (excluding literature and linguistic modules)	5.42	90	5.98	90	6.45	90
English Literature and Background	3.61	0	0	0	0	0
Chinese Literature and Background	1.81	30	2.99	45	0	0
Linguistic modules (including structure of English and linguistic modules)	32.50	540	10.96	165	8.60	120
Translation modules (including project + specialized translation)	28.67	310	32.56	490	33.33	465
Interpretation modules	7.21	120	12.96	195	12.95	180
Cultural Background Modules	3.61	60	8.64	130	6.45*	90
Supporting modules# (e.g offered by other departments)	7.21	120	1.99	30	8.60	120
Computing Modules	0	0	1.99	30	0	0
		1660		1505		1395

+The hours of project was 40 in 87 but increased to 210 in 92 and 98 syllabuses

*Chinese Civilization

For list of electives see Appendix 3

Appendix 5: Employment Figures

(a) Number of Graduates:

	89	95	98	Remarks
No of graduates	41	57	72	A rise of 75% in 9 years, about 8.3% per year

(b) Employment by Sector

	89	95	98
Employed	95.1%	76.8%	58.2%
Self-employed	–	–	–
Unemployed	–	3.6%	1.5%
Underemployed	–	–	6%
Further studies	4.9%	17.9%	34.3%
Not seeking employment	–	1.8%	–
	100%	100.1%	100%

(c) Job Nature by Employment Sector

	89	95		98	
Government	26.8%	44.2%#		7.7%*	
Education	2.4%	–		15.4%	
Non-profit organ.	9.8%	–		10.3%	
Private	53.7%	55.8%		66%	
Commerce			46.5		46.2
Industry			7		2.6
Public utilities			2.3		17.9

#HDTI has got the highest rate among all City U graduates
* (0% for the year of 97.)

(d) Employment by Job Nature

	89	95	98
Translation and interpretation	46.2	65.1	7.7
Mass communication	20.5	2.3	7.7
Marketing and sales	12.8	4.7	17.9
General Administration	10.2	2.3	10.3
Customer Services	–	4.7	15.4
Secretary/ General Clerical	2.6	7.0	5.1

(d) Employment by Job Nature (Cont'd)

	89	95	98
Trading and purchasing	–	7.0	7.7
Property Development	–	2.3	–
Teaching/Training	–	–	7.7
Research	5.1	4.6	–
Taxation	–	–	2.6
Medical health	–	–	2.6
Legal services	–	–	2.6
Religious work	–	–	2.6
Finance	–	–	5.1
Public relation	–	–	5.1
Disciplined forces	2.6	–	–
	100	100	100.1

(e) Relevance of Course

	89	95	98
Relevant	71.1	(46.5) 90.7	(6.1) 54.6
Quite relevant		(44.2)	(48.5)
Quite irrelevant	28.9	(9.3) 9.3	(18.2) 45.5
Irrelevant		–	(27.3)

(f) Income

	89	95	98
Min	4300	8000	7350
Max	12360	17270	24320
Average	6640	11376	10333
HD average	5612	9029	9586

(g) Job Satisfaction

	89	95	98
v. satisfied	Na	56.1	2.9
Satisfied	Na		60.0
Dissatisfied	Na	43.9	37.1
Very dissatisfied	Na		0

Na=not available

(h) Further Studies

	89		95		98#	
Local	0%		20%	(2)	8.6%	(2)
City U	0%		0%		4.3%	
HKU			20%*		4.3%	
Overseas	100%	(2)	80%	(8)	90.3%	(21)
UK			80%		82.6%	
Australia			–		8.7%	
		2		10		23

* One of the students was admitted direct to M.A. (literary and cultural studies) of HKU

Among the 23 students, 19 (82.6%) studied for a B.A. degree and 4 (17.4%) for a M.A.

Source: Graduate Employment Surveys conducted by Student Affairs Office, City University of Hong Kong.

References

Chan, D. and B. W. Imrie (1995). "Marketing Higher Diploma Courses in the Hong Kong Context." In B.W. Imrie *et al.*, eds., *Commitment to Higher Vocational Education to Hong Kong*. Hong Kong: City University of Hong Kong, pp. 119–29.

City Polytechnic of Hong Kong (1987, 1992). *Higher Diploma in Translation and Interpretation Course Document*. Hong Kong: City Polytechnic.

City University of Hong Kong (1999). *Calendar*. Hong Kong: City University of Hong Kong.

City University of Hong Kong (1998). *Employment Survey, 1998*. HDTI internal document.

Imrie, B. W. (1995). "College of Higher Prevocational Studies Commitment." In B. W. Imrie *et al.*, eds., *Commitment to Higher Vocational Education to Hong Kong*. Hong Kong: City University of Hong Kong.

Working Party on the Future of Sub-degree Education, The (1998). *The Future of Sub-degree Education Offered by the CHVS of the City University of Hong Kong*. Hong Kong: City University of Hong Kong.

Different Formats, The Same Effect? The Experience of the Open University of Hong Kong

Paul Levine
School of Arts and Social Sciences
The Open University of Hong Kong

Introduction: Formats

Since the 1970s the translation and interpretation (hereafter T & I) profession has experienced rapid growth in Hong Kong both in interest and numbers of practitioners. With a population of over seven million, Hong Kong, for its size, produces more translation students than many countries.[1] This popularity has led to a profusion of courses, offered in both the public tertiary and private sectors. The range of programme choices may be great, but in general, it is the public tertiary institutions that are the breeding ground for a large number of T & I practitioners. These institutions deliver their offerings in formats that include both the full-time traditional daytime classroom lecture/tutorial leading to the B.A. degree as well as the part-time, evening degree/diploma, lecture/tutorial course. Supplementing these core courses are the higher degree M.A. level courses that are taught by seminar/lecture as well as supervisor/ post-graduate student formats.

Of course, B.A. final-year translation projects are also delivered on a one-to-one basis of supervisor to undergraduate student. The above choices represent the traditional formats that have become established academic practice both in Hong Kong and the world.

The purpose of this paper is to compare the delivery of translation courses (and the above-mentioned, traditional academic formats in which I have taught for more than a decade at the City University of Hong Kong) to a distance-learning non-traditional format, as delivered at the Open

University of Hong Kong, where I currently work. The areas that will be discussed include: programme goals, class format and goals, student backgrounds, quality-control, assignments and assignment-monitoring and examinations.

Since all of these topics really require separate in-depth treatments, I shall only touch on a few interesting features in this brief treatment.

What I hope to delineate are some of the similarities and differences between traditional programmes and their "open" counterpart. By so doing, it is hoped that light can be shed on how programme delivery can be designed so future student learning requirements can be further addressed.[2]

Programme Goals

During my time at City University, the Translation and Interpretation programmes were upgraded several times, as a response to the demand for better and higher qualifications as the market for T & I graduates widened from the 1980's into the early 1990's. The certificate/diploma offered during the 1980's was upgraded to the B.A. level, while at the same time, an M.A. programme was being drafted. The goal of the B.A. was to produce translation professionals who would pursue careers either in the public or private sectors. The express aim of the Open University B.A. Programme in Languages and Translation is to upgrade language skills and provide training for students in translation skills.[3] Although both programme goals seem quite similar, those of the Open University are much more modest, as befits its relatively fewer course selections and more recent introduction. In reality the two differ greatly in operation. The delivery system of a programme can affect the way that programme's goals are achieved. So even though the goals can be found in course prospectuses, what do they actually mean when compared with their delivery systems?

Class Format

No doubt, most readers are familiar with the traditional lecture/tutorial/seminar format, so I shall only mention a few salient areas that are useful for comparison. At City University, the traditional format for undergraduate lecture/tutorial classes in T & I (with the exception of one-on-one or language laboratory interpretation classes) consists of 12 and 40 students plus teacher.[4] Either a combination of class notes, photocopied material/off-prints and/or textbooks provide the greater part of class content. The teacher stimulates the class by posing problems/questions/tasks for the class to consider. Then, notes are taken or students are asked to perform particular tasks such as text translation, and to report on them. This means that there is minimal face-to-face interaction in the classroom.

By contrast at the Open University, there is one optional monthly tutorial that is supposed to cover the key skills or areas covered in the course material and one-to-one over-the-telephone question-and-answer sessions as a usual practice. The keys to making this system work are the motivation and self-discipline of adult learners. Should they not possess these key ingredients, it would be difficult for them to pass even foundation-level courses. What motivates them? As working adults, more often than not, distance-learning students have a definite "agenda" and "issues" that they want to resolve, not to just get a paper qualification.[5]

Course material then becomes the centre of the learning process for adult students. This makes the writing of course materials the most important part of the course-preparation process. Since the course (the author) must adopt the stance of a tutor, rather than a lecturer, the voice and tone of the course materials are informal and less dense than traditional academic presentation. The aim is to elicit students' interest in the material, by getting the student to question the material as they go along, and not just to mechanically read it. This precludes simple linear processing and makes the student work back and forth within the material. In a translation course material, for example, a translation theory is described, but at the same time, various questions are raised concerning the text to test the student's understanding and ability to summarize and apply what has been learned at each step in the reading process. Activities and self-tests are included to make the student reinforce what has been learned. The purpose is to integrate material as it is presented.

This approach to the presenting course material has the advantage of being immediately evident to the students. Other than self-learning, optional once-a-month tutorials, held at times and locations as convenient to students as possible, are one of the other two main means where distance learners interact with educators. These two-to-three-hour tutorials are set up so that they cover the main points in the course material and also cover translation and language practice. One aspect of the distance tutorial that echoes its traditional counterpart is that the tutor goes over course assignments with the students. However, since these tutorials are optional, students are not obliged to attend them and are not penalized for doing so. There are many reasons for this.[6]

The coordination of class assignments and their marking is actually the major responsibility of a tutor at Open University because the students depend on detailed marking of their assignments to correct errors and prepare themselves for future assignments.

Lastly, there is time set aside by tutors every week to answer the telephone at home when the students call up with problems. This format allows busy students to call in the evening, when they are working through course materials on their own as they encounter problems.

Student Backgrounds and Student Needs

The reasons that adults give for enrolling in the BALT programme range from upgrading their language skills to career-related ones. Interestingly, students often express pure interest in language and translation as subjects in themselves, rather than for simply practical job-related ends. The Language and Translation programme is designed to deal with distance-learning students by having them take more language-centred courses at the lower levels and concentrate on translation only in the middle and upper-level courses. The students seem to be more confident with language skills by the time they have to face translation and linguistics courses. Lastly, the class sizes vary, but the average is about 32–35 registered, with 15–20 per tutorial.

By comparison, undergraduate students at the City University represent the traditional intake from middle school who come straight out of an academic format and are quite used to studying. They are further used to ingesting material, but find the freedom of the tertiary system a bit daunting because they are used to having choices made for them by their secondary-school teachers. The problems of discipline and study habits are less pronounced at this level. Students tend to retain material more quickly, but their motivation and expressiveness may not be as great as adult learners, particularly during tutorials.

Quality Control

The concept of quality control as applied to course offerings within a programme deals with the standard of the course design as well as course content, teacher competence and student quality. The T & I courses in the

City University programme, as at most universities, must be validated both internally and externally by matching them against other tertiary T & I courses in Hong Kong. The prevailing standards of what is considered the "right" design and course content are then assessed by committees of professionals both in and out of the field. In addition, annual course reports, course updates and other monitoring exercises are run, chiefly to ensure that standards are being maintained. But, no matter how well designed course offerings are, they can often only be as good as the students who are their "target audience."

Each year while at City University, I attended numerous course-related meetings to consider the course results and content. In addition, course reports were submitted by course leaders to the T & I section within the Chinese Translation and Linguistics Department, in order to record the progress of the course. These reports were then integrated into an overall report that was submitted by each programme leader to the faculty. Current course syllabi were usually kept on file in the department so that they can be checked and modified. All of the above steps are taken in attempt to keep standards up.

At the Open University, quality control is also built into course content. When a new course is proposed, the vetting process first enlists the services of an external course assessor, who must be a recognized professional in the field. This person plays a key role in the development of course content, being a final arbiter as to what is or is not included in the syllabus. Usually, the contents of Open University syllabi are pitched at a fairly high academic level due to the requirements of the external course accessor who is another expert in the field. In fact, external requirements for course quality control can only be useful when they are balanced against the views of the other key internal development monitors, who are more familiar with student needs and capabilities.[7]

A further element is missing, and that are the tasks that the student has to complete to obtain a classwork grade.

Assignments and Assignment Monitoring

At City University, courses are weighted by their relationship to the programme as a whole whether they are introductory or not. The assignments are set by each course examiner and usually, because class sizes are relatively small, are marked by the same person (or collection of persons). Assignments range along a spectrum of complexity from simple translation tasks all the way up to short papers and dissertation-length long transla-tions at the B.A. level. In-class assignments and laboratory practice are also included in the programme as well. After assignments are returned to students, there is often a question-answering session. Marks are awarded according to the course syllabus set by the course examiner, who deter-mines the weighting of assignments vis-a-vis the final examination.

The one exception is the student final-year project, which has to be vetted by two assessors, who agree on the grade to be awarded. Usually, at the end of the semester, programme-level meetings are held to look at the grade distribution in each course.

The Open University system is much more complex and driven by two exigencies: first, the need to keep the course standards in line with those of other Hong Kong tertiary institutions; and second, the need to keep tutor remarks on tutor-marked assignments handed in by the students up to a useful level for the students. Because the amount of face-to-face contact is minimal, it is necessary for tutors in distance-learning courses to supply the maximum amount of information on student tutor-marked assessments. This kind of feedback, usually written in laborious detail, helps the inde-pendent student to understand the nature of their errors, so as to improve performance. Unfortunately, this kind of detail is quite demanding in terms of the time needed by the tutor to process student papers, so anywhere from 1-3 hours on one paper is the norm.

In order to ensure that course standards are upheld as far as possible, the role of the course coordinator, the counterpart of the course examiner in the traditional City University course, is crucial. The course coordinator is responsible for personally monitoring tutor-marked assignments, which are processed through the mail to the Open University before they are returned to the student. In addition, random samples of student tutor-marked assignments and tutor comments and marks are sent to external course examiners, who further comment on the grades assigned to students. Of course, the question of whether any grade can be considered "fair" is always open to interpretation, but usually major deviations in marking are picked up by the course coordinator and dealt with after the course exami-nation has been held.

Examination and Examination Monitoring

Without going into great detail, the most that can be said about the tradi-tional university examination-system is that it is given varying weights according to the type of course and the marking method of the course examiner. Since translation and interpretation skills are cumulatively acquired over time, many traditional courses assign more weighting to the exam than to course work. However, for courses in which there is continual assessment, marks are assigned as student assignments are processed by the course examiner, and only at the end of the course is a final grade assigned, together with a final examination grade.

In other courses, the examination is counted separately and weighted against the in-class grade. At the end of the semester, course grades are determined by the course examiner.

The Open University uses the above formats as well, and the process is scrutinized quite carefully due to the importance attached by students to course results. End-of-course final grade award meetings go to great lengths to process marks and look at their distribution. In both systems, course results are also assessed at higher levels (usually the faculty). As is done with the course assignments, sample examination scripts are sent to the external examiner for comment as to the marks given and the quality of the exam as a whole.

Conclusion

The title of this paper, "Different Formats, The Same Effect? The Experience of the Open University of Hong Kong," implies that the delivery of translation skills through a distance format is open to question. Throughout my description of the various selected facets of the traditional and distance-learning format course, I have tried to stay within a factual mode of presentation as much as possible. But the in some sense the crucial question is: "Can the distance-learning of translation skills be effective?" I think that the above evidence suggests that not only can it be done, but given the right students and teacher, it can be done well. In addition, the adult learner for whom these courses are designed is one who is highly motivated, not just by the desire to learn, but by a definite agenda with particular issues in mind.

This then changes the focus of learning from just "qualification-based" student needs to "issue-and-agenda"-based student desires. This conclusion may seem simplistic, but it has implications for the future delivery and design of courses in non-traditional formats, including those delivered at great distance over the World Wide Web. Traditionalists often say that nothing can take the place of face-to-face interaction, and in some cases this may be true (for instance, in the teaching of intermediate and advanced

interpretation skills), but for basic translation skills (and even some interpretation ones), it seems that the course structure and quality control as
well as assessment can be comparable to the traditional format. The key
component seems to me to be the ability of students to handle the material
they are given.

Notes

[1]   According to the *Routledge Encylopedia of Translation Studies*, the United
      States, with a population of about 350 million, has a total of 17 programmes that
      produce translators and interpreters. There are about 5,500 practitioners who
      are registered with the American Translators Association and about 1,000
      translators who belong to the American Literary Translators Association. So, by
      a rough estimate, if there are about 10,000 or more practicing translators in the
      US, there is a ratio of 1:35,000, while in Hong Kong the ratio is probably about
      1:2,000.

[2]   In his recent article, "Translation Syllabuses at the Tertiary Level in Hong
      Kong," Prof. Liu Ching-chih compares the seven tertiary institutions, including
      the Open University (Liu, 1998: 37–46), but makes the comment that much is
      not known about the Open University syllabus. In this paper I shall not deal
      with the syllabus, because I wish to concentrate on several micro-processes as
      they relate to Open University students, versus those of City University, in
      order to keep the perspective on course delivery as opposed to planning. The
      Open University programme is still under development, while that of the City
      University has been established for almost fifteen years. Thus, there are many
      facets of the Open University programme that are still unclear because it is
      "under construction." Since the advent of the World Wide Web, many univer-
      sity-level courses, including translation courses, are becoming available to a
      new generation of "distance learners." Thus, the Open University format has
      relevance for the growing audience of web-based learners.

[3]   See the unpublished internal BATI Course Validation Document, City Univer-
      sity of Hong Kong, Department of Applied Linguistics (1989) and *Prospectus*,
      The Open University of Hong Kong, *Prospectus*, 1998–9 and Liu, 1998: 40.

[4]   This ratio of 1:12 or 1:40 has undergone a transformation due to the new credit-
      unit system, so class size at City University, may actually be greater than 1:45
      because two or three classes may be simultaneously taking one course.

[5]   Adult distance learners, unlike traditional undergraduate format learners, have
      usually worked or are working full-time, and are motivated whether by job
      needs, directed personal interest or a perceived lack of language and translation
      skills to address specific concerns. Their agenda is usually work-related. Even
      those students who study in the distance mode out of "interest" usually perceive
      themselves as lacking certain language/translation skills. Thus, the motivation
      to succeed relates to specific agendas rather than just the piece of paper. It was
      my experience, when asking undergraduate students in the City University

about why they chose the T & I programme, the answer was often that it was a "soft" arts option and led to a paper qualification, rather than any specific agenda.

6   Typical reasons for student nonattendance: work demands that clash with tutorial time/venues, child-minding and family-related tasks, and travel outside Hong Kong.

7   The discrepancy between the comprehensive coverage of course-content and the actual levels and abilities of distance learners is one ongoing problem for Open University students, but is not true in all cases, but rather more often found in broad survey courses that relate to one or two subject areas.

References

Baker, Mona (1998). *The Routledge Encyclopedia of Translation Studies*. London: Routledge.

Department of Applied Linguistics (1989). *Internal BATI Course Validation Document*. Hong Kong: City University of Hong Kong.

Liu, Ching-chih (1998). "Translation Syllabuses at the Tertiary Level in Hong Kong." *Translation Quarterly*, Vols. 9–10, pp. 29–83.

Open University of Hong Kong, The (1998–99). *Prospectus*. Hong Kong: The Open University of Hong Kong.

Open University of Hong Kong, The (1998–99). *Factbook*. Hong Kong: The Open University of Hong Kong.

Innovative CALL Activity for Translation and Interpretation Students

Carrie Chau Kam Hung and Irene Ip Kwok Chun
Division of Language Studies
City University of Hong Kong

Introduction: Background and Rationale

Based on the teaching experience of the investigators, students often have problems in learning difficult glossary and special terms, especially in the field of translation and interpretation. Their usual method is through rote-memory (like memorising word lists) which is both inefficient and temporary. Drills and practices alone can be quite tedious and boring.

In order to motivate students to learn special terms which are an integral part of the training of translation and interpretation and to enable them to learn more effectively, there is a need to design learning activities with the use of computers which are popular among students. Computer-assisted Learning (CAL) was first introduced in the early 1960s. The development of the microcomputer provides a new vehicle for the purpose of computer-assisted language learning (CALL). As pointed out by Cameron, CALL vocabulary materials provide "multiple exposures in various contexts, so as to give the learner the opportunity to use his normal vocabulary learning faculties… as well as the knowledge of the world." (Cameron, 1989:9) Challenge and curiosity are two of the motivating elements identified by Malone in computer educational software. (Cameron, 1989)

Aim

The aim of the study is to make use of this new vehicle of CALL to provide students of translation and interpretation with an innovative computer package that they can use for self-study. The focus of this package is on a bilingual glossary in the area of government and political affairs, which is of much significance to Hong Kong students, especially with the handover of Hong Kong back to China.

Among the students, those from the translation and interpretation field may be most affected by the change of these terms. This is because their prospective career is highly related to the social context. As suggested by Pan, the translator "moulds his mind with the social, political and cultural needs of his time and environment." (Pan, 1975: 40) Acquiring lexical competence of new government and political terms is thus very important for the students who are potential professional translators/interpreters.

Methodology

The content of the package is based on journals, newspapers and magazines. There are one hundred terms in the package with twenty terms in one test. The terms fall into 5 categories and they are *China-related affairs*; *electoral, legal and judicial affairs*; *general terms*; *government structure;* and *public figures and organisations*. One English or Chinese term is shown on the computer screen at one time and the user is given 50 seconds to provide either an English or a Chinese translation. Such arrangement is based on two criteria of good translation — accuracy and adequacy — as proposed by Pan (1975). The whole process will be timed automatically by the computer and the scores indicated immediately so that the user will have a better idea of his/her performance.

In order to evaluate the effectiveness of the package and to enhance students' knowledge in government and political affairs, 30 students of Higher Diploma in Translation and Interpretation Programme, City University of Hong Kong, were recruited on a voluntary basis as subjects. Fifteen of them were Year 2 students and the rest were Year 3 students. The main hypotheses include the following:

(1) Year 3 students will perform better than Year 2 students,
(2) all the participating students will improve in their test scores, and
(3) computer-assisted language learning is effective and favourable.

General Design

The general design is a within-group matched-subject one (pre-test and post-test) and also involves between-year comparison. Basically there are two parts of the project, a test session (to check the existing knowledge of the subjects about the 5 categories of terms) and a game workshop (to enable the subjects to learn these terms). These two parts may have different arrangements. The procedures of the present study are reported in the following.

During their first visit, students were given a test (Test 1) on 20 terms randomly drawn from the 5 categories mentioned above. Afterwards they attended a 30-minute game session, which is a workshop of interactive learning, drills and practice. The participants were asked to attend another similar session about two weeks after the first visit, so as to check if the knowledge could be recalled within a short period of time. During the second visit, they were asked to attend the same game session first and then take the test (Test 2). After that, they were asked to fill in a questionnaire (Questionnaire 1) in order to get their feedback. Each participating student was provided with a printed list of the 100 terms for their reference.

As the success of any translation programme is highly related to the "initiative and incentive behind it," (Pan, 1975) the test provides challenges and the game session arouses incentive and curiosity. The speed of learning mainly depends on the individual student. In an attempt to verify whether learning had really taken place and that the newly-gained knowledge of the glossary could be retained over a longer period of time, we invited students, 5 from Year 2 and 5 from Year 3, to come again around six months after Test 2. This time there was no game session and only the test (Test 3) was given to the participating students, together with a follow-up questionnaire (Questionnaire 2). Results were compiled, compared and analysed.

Findings — Test and Questionnaire Results

In general, the hypotheses were supported.

The following table shows the results of the tests more clearly:

Table 1. Mean percentage of accuracy in tests

Students	Test 1	Test 2	Test 3
	Mean %	*Mean %*	*Mean %*
Year 2	26.7	45.7	54
Year 3	30.7	52.7	40

Test 1 and Test 2

1. It can be seen from these results that the Translation & Interpretation Year 3 students, who have received one more year of training than the Translation & Interpretation Year 2 students, performed better. In Test 1, their mean accuracy percentage is 30.7, which is 4% higher than that of the Year 2 students.

2. As for Test 2, the results are similar: Translation and Interpretation Year 3 students again performed better. Their mean accuracy percentage is 52.7, which is 7% higher than that of Year 2 students. They showed greater improvement than Year 2 students. Their improvement rate is 22%. Translation and Interpretation Year 2 students had an increase of 19%, and their correct percentage is 45.7 % this time. This corresponds with one of our hypotheses, i.e. students in general will improve in their test scores.

Test 3

From the results of Test 3, it is verified that learning has really taken place, and the following findings are noted:

1. Translation and Interpretation Year 2 students got a higher percentage of accuracy (14%) over Year 3.

2. Translation and Interpretation Year 2 students are generally more positive towards CALL, learning through the list of 100 terms, and getting more other exposure. This is possibly due to the fact that they still are translation students. As for the former Year 3 students who are now working, they have to handle language-related tasks, but they are not exactly translators/interpreters. The relatively poorer performance of Year 3 students is possibly due to less exposure and practice with translation tasks. Moreover, now that they have already got a job that is not directly related to translation, they may not find the glossary so relevant to them (as compared to Year 2 students who need to prepare themselves for their potential job later). As a result, Year 3 students tend to attach less importance to the CALL activity. In a way, it fits in with the suggested significance of exposure and motivation mentioned earlier.

    In terms of exposure within the six months after Test 2, 80% of the 10 participants (5 Year 3 and 5 Year 2 students) of Test 3 had exposure by reading newspapers. The most common English paper was *South China Morning Post* and the most popular Chinese paper was *Ming Pao*. Some had exposure from television, one got exposure from interpretation lessons and one from textbooks.

4. Half of the subjects had compiled a glossary but those who had not done so thought that they would do so in the future.

Conclusions and Recommendations

In conclusion, we find that our hypotheses have been generally supported by our findings. The students have gained knowledge of the glossary, and learning has really taken place. As for the recommendations, the content of the package can be revised with new items added to the existing list. In the future, the database of the CALL package can be further extended to other aspects like mass media and business that are in line with students' preferences. It is also recommended that the CALL activity should be integrated as part of the teaching programme as it would help to motivate students and enhance their learning effectiveness. In the long run, the content of the CALL activity may extend from learning glossary to other areas of language learning as well. As the sample size of the present study is quite small, it is possible to recruit more students to join the CALL activity in order to further evaluate its effectiveness.

References

Cameron, K. (1989). *Computer Assisted Language Learning*. Norwood: ABLEX Publishing Corporation.

Pan, F. K. (1975). "Towards a Formal Training Program." In T.C. Lai, ed. *The Art and Profession of Translation: Proceedings of the Asia Foundation Conference on Chinese-English Translation*. Hong Kong: The Hong Kong Translation Society.

Arts Students and Technical Translation

David Lam Kui Kwong
Department of Translation
The Chinese University of Hong Kong

Psychological obstacles are the main barriers that prevent arts students from undertaking science and technical (S & T) translation. This paper suggests some effective measures to arouse students' interest in working with S & T materials. The author has in fact applied those measures successfully in his university teaching.

The New Millenium Beckons Us to Develop Technology

Political leaders in Beijing and Hong Kong have repeatedly stressed the importance of science and technology in their respective societies. In 1986 the father of Chinese reform, Deng Xiaoping, claimed that the twenty-first century would be a hi-tech era and that China must occupy a place on the frontline if it was to be considered one of the world's superpowers. The Hong Kong Government launched the Cyberport project in 1999. This project was to be a specially designated site devoted to fostering research and development of hi-tech communication systems. This project received an enthusiastic response from local entrepreneurs in prominent local businesses such as Pacific Century CyberWorks, Cable and Wireless HKT, Star TV, and Legend.

Hong Kong's culture is now firmly rooted in the Information Age. We are bombarded with Western science and technical publications on a daily basis. Books, magazines, catalogues, manuals, home pages, technical contracts and sales agreements all need accurate translation before reaching their target audience — the general public and those in industry who are eager to obtain timely information. At present these publications, for the most part are translated by engineers, scientists and sales personnel because local translators prefer doing literary/political translation to technical translation. A limited number of science fiction books, like those written by Asimov, Sagan and Hancock, which sell well in Hong Kong today, have been translated by Taiwanese, not Hong Kong scholars.

The author is aware that science and technical translation is becoming a major subject in translation studies. Its importance will grow as science and technology achieves an even higher profile in everyday life. Therefore this area is a fertile ground for further research.

Psychological Barriers

The author has been assigned the duty of attracting young translators to science and technical translation. Third year students at The Chinese University of Hong Kong in general have a reasonable command of English and Chinese as well as a fair knowledge of translation techniques. Yet in attempting hi-tech translation, they encounter new problems. As a result they feel uncomfortable, frustrated and discouraged. This leaves them with little incentive to pursue translation projects in this area. The following are some typical comments from students:

> "I am no good at mathematics. I don't have a logical mind, so how can I do technical translation?"

> "I am in the arts stream in college. I shouldn't have to worry about science if I don't want to."

> "My skill level in translating science and technical articles will never be comparable to those of engineers and scientists. I would rather let them do the translation."

> "Applied translation is too time-consuming, too commercial and there is too much effort required. It does not contribute as much as theoretical work or translating fiction."

These barriers are more psychological than real.

1. *Students overestimate the difficulties involved in technical translation.* It is natural to expect that arts students will have problems in comprehension in this area. This is mainly due to their unfamiliarity with the specialized vocabulary necessary to express scientific and technical concepts in a precise and succinct manner. These students do not realize that these concepts are easily accessible in technical books and dictionaries and that they should utilize them in their work. Students should not be afraid to seek help from instructors and friends, since consultation is an absolute necessary

step in translation even for hi-tech professionals. Persistent effort will ultimately pay off.

2. *Students underestimate their own ability.* They have already entered the university, so they are considered to have the ability to think in a logical and systematic way. They are also trained bilinguals who are capable of carrying out literary translation. Nothing should prevent them from doing competent hi-tech translation. Bill Gates is a good example. He did not graduate from university, yet he has managed to set up a hi-tech firm and become one of the richest men on the planet. This demonstrates that a B.Sc. degree is not always necessary to successfully work in the hi-tech field.

Suggestions for Teaching Science and Technical Translation to Arts Students

These are some suggestions and examples that have proved successful in the author's many years of university teaching.

1. The instructor should make it clear to the students that in this information age, nobody is immune from using hi-tech or digital equipment. Arts students should be prepared to write articles describing the modern world, in which the Internet and interactive digital television have become commonplace, and where space travel will one day be a reality. Arts students edit their drafts using a word processor, search for information on the World Wide Web, and store files on computer discs. Their whole world is hi-tech.

2. Statements that are related to science and technology are subject to the same grammatical rules and sentence structure as literary expressions. The only difference is that S & T statements are objective, straightforward, and use non-emotive language to get their message across. For example, if the instructor draws a geometrical shape like figure 1 on the blackboard he asks the students "What have I drawn?" The students may answer "You have drawn a pyramid" or "You have drawn a tetrahedron." Both answers are correct except that both have involved personal judgements, hence they are less scientific. The straightforward scientific statement is "You have just drawn five connected straight lines." There is nothing complicated about the words used in this sentence.

Fig 1   Fig 2

3. The instructor should use translation terminology. For example when the term *El Nino* is used, it should be explained that the term is a derivation from Spanish meaning a child born at Christmas time. Translation students are familiar with derived terms. This term is therefore understood, because the warm spell, or *El Nino*, hits Central America regularly every four years, especially at Christmas time, like the child. Another example is to introduce a string of numbers called the *Fabionacci Series* — 2, 3, 5, 8,13, 21.... Usually arts students tune out when confronted with such mathematical concepts. The instructor then explains that these numbers have formed a Golden Section Rule of Beauty used in building design since the time of the ancient Greece. This rule is also used to judge how skillfully a woman's makeup has been applied. This information piques the students' interest, since this topic is now related to their daily life.

4. Technical terms are difficult to remember unless they are bundled up in a tree-structure, and relations between terms are clearly mapped out. For example *bitumen* is not an easy word for arts students to remember. The term *non-renewable natural resources* should be introduced first and that this concept includes *coal* and *petroleum*. Petroleum is extracted from underground as *crude oil*, which is then refined to yield *gasoline, diesel* and *bitumen*. The terms *hydropower, wind power, tidal energy* and *solar power* can also be introduced as *renewable natural resources*. With proper explanation and illustration, a whole set of new words can be linked together in the long-term memory. It should also be noted that some computer databases are constructed on a relational network, containing many tree-structures formed according to the semantic relationship between words.

5. Transparency and illustrations should be used extensively, since the more senses are used in the learning process, the more likely the retention of the concept.

6. The students should be urged to exercise logical thinking. An example is the sentence "雞三足" which can be literally translated as "a chicken with three legs." This remark was used by scholars around 500 B.C. when Chinese philosophy had not yet reached its golden age. Philosophers liked to show their erudition by the use of bizarre argument. The sentence above indicated a physical rule that any object, say a table, must have more than two legs to support itself in the upright position. Now "a chicken can hold its upright position by itself, shall we still say that a chicken has two legs, or else more legs?"

7. Interactive teaching should be used to assist lectures in science and technical translation. When this instructor found students' attention wandering in the course of a lecture, he decided to enliven his approach. After asking "Do you love travelling?" "How about travelling to Egypt?" "Would you like to hear how I went inside the pyramid?" A lively atmosphere then returned to the classroom. Figure 2 was then projected onto the screen to show a map of the three Giza pyramids. He then posed some further questions; "Can you guess why the pyramids were not built in a straight line?" "Why are two of them larger than the third one?" The students tried out a number of hypotheses: "Perhaps the younger pharaoh was willing to build pyramids smaller than his forefathers to show humility;" "the large granite blocks were exhausted after building the two pyramids, so the younger Pharaoh had to build a smaller one;" and "the Egyptians did not have accurate surveying tools at that time."

The instructor replied:

> All your guesses are wrong. We know that people can provide different explanations for a particular event. The right explanation should be the most logical and most suitable for the historical background and geographical conditions at that time. As in translation, a word usually has multiple meanings listed in the dictionary, but we have to choose the one that is most suitable for the sentence and for the article.

As the instructor was giving the above remarks, the students pressed him impatiently for an answer. "Please tell us why the pyramids are unequal in size." The instructor's reply was this:

"Now I see that you are genuinely interested in science and technology. I would like to give you time to think about it a bit more...so I'll give you the answer in the next lecture!"[1]

Note

[1] The three pyramids were planned to reflect the position and brightness of the three stars on the hunter's belt in the constellation of Orion.

Cantonese-Putonghua Sight-translation Training at the City University of Hong Kong

Cheng Ting-au
Department of Chinese, Translation and Linguistics
City University of Hong Kong

This article is an introduction to the Cantonese and Putonghua sight-translation training that has been given to students by the Department of Chinese, Translation and Linguistics, City University of Hong Kong for a number of years. The targeted students are those who have had at least ninety hours of training in basic Putonghua. The context of teaching Putonghua is to link it up with its ultimate goal: translation. The initial goal, however, is to enhance the listening and speaking of the language.[1]

Background

There are two things that should be mentioned here. Firstly, the return of Hong Kong to Chinese sovereignty has brought the China factor into the economic environment, and systematic training in interpretation between Cantonese and Putonghua has become a matter of utmost importance. The *Apple Daily* is used here as an example. On 2 March 1996, before the Handover, we read that "because of the enormous work of the China-Britain Liaison group and the Infrastructure Coordination Committee, there is an urgent need for Putonghua interpretation, and it is estimated that more than 1,700 meetings will need simultaneous Putonghua interpretation this year." On 3 September 1999, after the Handover, Chen Lingqin, Director and General Manager of Standard and Poor's, pointed out in an interview that new employees "must speak Putonghua," adding that "a local who can speak fluent Putonghua has more chance of getting into our company than a foreigner who has many years of work experience." We have to face this more utilitarian trend and continually revise our training so that it conforms with these recent developments. Secondly, the understanding of the specific characteristics of Cantonese as well as the special points of interpretation between Cantonese and Putonghua has been deepened. The blanket statement that "the greatest differences are in sound, followed by the lexicon, and their grammatical differences are the least" is being replaced by scientific, empirical and quantitative studies.

People have now realized that there are lexical and grammatical differences between the two dialects which cannot be overcome by Chinese characters nor by the cultural commonness of the Han race today. Lui Shu Ching (1984), when discussing language mistakes in the compositions of Hong Kong secondary school students, points out: "one key mistake that emerged from the statistics is the misleading transfer of Cantonese words (50.9 %)."

Ouyang Ruying (1996) put it even more clearly: "The most serious problem is how to prevent Hong Kong students from using words in Cantonese dialect with the sounds of Putonghua."[2] We have to address this speech habit in order to change it, which naturally leads to a number of pedagogical considerations. Firstly, we have to bear in mind that in second language learning, translation is one of the effective ways of internalizing language rules. Secondly, there is not necessarily a natural connection between listening and speaking ability and translation competence. Thirdly, translation between Cantonese and Putonghua is primarily oral interpretation; in view of this, a more practical teaching model should be designed in order to train better qualified interpreters.

Further Discussion

Three things will be discussed here, namely, the nature, position and quantity of interpreter training. Since the nature of training is interpreting, or pedagogical interpreting, and in the context of the present situation, we will now focus on the early stage of interpreting training, sight-interpretation. The problem of positioning is more complicated. For a more micro-perspective, as we have just mentioned, the Chinese language cannot surpass the lexical and grammatical differences between dialects. For a macro-perspective, a survey is needed. We carried out a statistical investigation into the distribution of Cantonese words in different sections of the *Apple Daily* and came up with the following results.[3]

Number	Section	Title Percentage of Cantonese Words (%)
1.	Trends of daily life	95.5
2.	Entertainment	90.1
3.	Property	81.8
4.	Special columns	70.8
5.	Hong Kong news	52.6
6.	Children	42.1
7.	Society	40.9
8.	Finance	26.1
9.	Sport	26.0
10.	Cross-strait news	12.7
11.	International news	8.5

The findings of this survey have many implications for applied linguistics. The first is that interpretation content should not be separated from the language that the community actually uses and so we should stress the effectiveness of authentic materials in interpreter training. Secondly, interpreter training must focus on vocabulary and by using these words in real sentences and situations the grammar of the target lexical group will be obvious. After all, language is a grammaticalized lexical entity. Thirdly, there has to be a large proportion of dialectal components in interpretation materials; if we do not carry out such surveys and limit our vision to items 6 to 11, then interpreter training mostly seems superfluous. All these implications set the foundation for working out the teaching model and the selection of course materials. We emphasize the contemporariness of the material so students could relate to it visually and physically. We emphasize the temporality of the material so that students could work on things fresh in their memory. And we emphasize the relevancy to their life so that students could share the feelings of the common people in Hong Kong. Naturally, the subject matter should not include cultural factors that are difficult to understand correctly and to handle skilfully. The amount and length of the material was limited to 300 to 500 words, making it easy to sustain students' interest and giving them a sense of achievement. In addition, it was not made too difficult. We made a survey for this. From 23 books with contrastive materials on Cantonese and Putonghua, we drew some relevant materials and placed them into specific categories, and we made a statistical analysis of the frequency of occurrence of some specific items to get the main points of translation between Cantonese and Putonghua. We then relied on our own intuition and experience to draft up a list of the difficult areas. We consciously and systematically used the contents of this list in our own translation teaching in order to fine-tune and revise it, and which then formed the basis of our translation training. This shows how linguistic research can lend support to interpreter training.

Based on our many years of experience, we believe that from the point of view of linguistics, the focus of interpretation training is not to look for the lexisemantic or cultural equivalence between the source and target languages, but rather the internalization of syntactic fossilization so that this becomes a part of the translator's mental lexicon, which is stored in the brain, to be memorized wholly, extracted wholly and used wholly. In other words, the strengthening is realized in the syntactic distribution pattern on the sentential level so that it becomes a speech habit.

Teaching Format

From the distribution of sight-translation materials to the interpreting students, two parts are involved: group discussion and individual work. The former takes up 30% of the time in the entire process of preparation, concentrating on the solution of two problems. The first is to request the students to settle on a pattern of comprehension collectively, grasping entirely the information of the materials, then look for the typological asymmetries, such as collocational conventions, habitual expressions and syntactic framework, between the source and target languages.[4] The next is individual work which takes up 70% of the time in the process of preparation. Students have to complete three tasks: the first is to find the semantic approximation, the second is to find the syntactic realization, and the third is to find the optimal language in which to translate it. The entire knowledge package shall be realized in terms of smoothness, coherence and acceptability in expression.

Analysis of Examples

Cantonese-Putonghua sight translation consists of two kinds of essentially different training: Cantonese to Putonghua, and Putonghua to Cantonese. Due to the limitations of space, we can only give a few illustrative examples.

From Cantonese to Putonghua

Source of the text: *Oriental Daily*, 2 November 1998. Headline: "自己

友，手腳慢，惡搵食" (Fellow drivers who are slow in action will find it difficult to earn a living). The sample has 301 words.

Examples:

Source Text	*Target Text*	*Points Requiring Attention*
1. 係人都知香港 地路窄車多	人家都知道香港這 個地方路特別窄， 車又特別多	係人都……，香港地 (everybody…in Hong Kong)

[Everybody knows that Hong Kong is a small place with too many cars]

2. 而且道路仲 非常繁忙	而且交通還十分 繁忙	

[And the traffic is heavy]

3. 所以揸艇搵食嘅 司機	以開出租車為生的 司機	揸艇、搵食 (drive a taxi, to earn their living)

[That is why drivers who make their living driving]

4. 手腳快係基本嘅 條件	手腳靈敏是應該具備 的基本條件	手腳快 (quick in action)

[A basic requirement is being quick in action]

5. 哼！搵食嘅嘢手 腳慢就梗輸蝕嘅	喏，要掙錢，手腳慢 就不行	……嘅嘢，哼 (things, see)

[See! When it comes to making a living, slowness in action will put you at a disadvantage]

6. 尤其喺一啲繁忙 嘅街道裡面	尤其在交通比較擁擠 的街道上	

[This is especially the case when you get stuck in busy streets]

7. 如果你慢吞吞嘅 就分分鐘俾人砵 到你暈都似	如果你慢騰騰的話後 面的司機十有八九會 拼命地按喇叭	分分鐘、砵，……都似 (as the occasion demands, press the horns, …likely)

[If you are slow, drivers following you will press their horns, making you feel dizzy]

From Putonghua to Cantonese

Source of the text: *Beijing Evening News*, 29 July 1998, Headline: "查地圖" (looking at maps). The sample has 347 words.

Examples:

Source Text	*Target Text*	*Points Requiring Attention*
1. 這時，老王身邊的小劉探過頭來一看，	嗰陣，喺阿王隔籬嗰個劉仔哄個頭埋去一睇	探頭 (turned his head)

[At that time, Little Liu, who was sitting next to Old Wang, turned to take a look]

2. 問老王："你看的是甚麼地圖?	問阿王："你睇嘅係乜嘢地圖呀?"	

[He asked Old Wang: "What map are you looking at?"]

3. 老王一看地圖上側，嗐!	阿王一睇地圖上側，啤!	嗐 (oh my God!)

[Old Wang said "Oh, my God! as he looked at the upper corner of the map"]

4. 剛才著急，錯把洛陽地圖拽了出來	頭先心急得滯，攞鬼咗洛陽地圖出嚟㖭	著急，把字句，拽 (in a hurry, the *ba* sentence pattern, take out)

[He was in a hurry just now and had wrongly taken out a map of Luoyang]

Conclusion

In order to improve and enhance our work, we need to gradually expand the matching of Putonghua and Cantonese lexical equivalents on the list. In terms of quality, we focus on reproducibility so that it can be used repeatedly as a whole in most contexts. And in terms of quantity, it has to be large enough to cover the needs of the market.

Translated by Jennifer Eagleton

Notes

[1] The author holds the view that Putonghua training in Hong Kong tertiary institutions should consist of three parts: listening, speaking and translation. See the author's article given at the Sixth International Seminar on Bilingualism and Diglossia: "Whole Language Approach in Putonghua Teaching in the Tertiary Institutions of Hong Kong." In *Bilingualism and Diglossia,* Vol. 6, Hanxue Chubanshe (1999), pp. 421–25.

[2] See Lui Shu Ching (1984). *An Analysis of Error Types in the Compositions of Hong Kong Secondary School Students.* M.Phil. thesis, Faculty of Education, The Chinese University of Hong Kong. See also Ouyang Ruying's lecture on Putonghua training given at the Language Centre of the Hong Kong University of Science and Technology, November 1996.

[3] See a report on the course survey on "Cantonese Linguistics" offered by the Department of Chinese, Translation and Linguistics, The City University of Hong Kong. The report was entitled "A Study on the High-level and Low-level Written Language Used in Hong Kong as Shown by the Frequency of Occurrence of Cantonese Vocabulary in Different Sections of a Hong Kong Newspaper with a High Sales-volume." The language materials were taken from three Sunday newspapers that came out on 8, 15, and 22 March 1998.

[4] See Robin Setton (1998). "Meaning Assembly in Simultaneous Interpretation." *Interpreting*, Vol. 3, No. 2, pp. 163–99.

From One Convention to Another — Coming out of the SL Straitjacket into the TL Dancing Shoes: On Freeing the TL Text from the SL Syntax

Evangeline S. P. Almberg
Department of Translation
The Chinese University of Hong Kong

Kanpo, fangxia, zizai.   看破，放下，自在。

Say that in English.

This is not a matter of cultural specifics alone, or the solution here might well be Xuanzang's *wuzhongbufan*[1], conveying the concepts concerned through a long-term "naturalization" process by transliterating the words. Nor is this quite a question of spiritual enlightenment, for despite cultural divides, there are people East and West who *kanpo, fangxia* and *zizai*.[2] This tripartite when translated from Chinese into English presents a case of cohesion. For Chinese syntax does not involve such grammatical categories as verbal inflection and declension of nouns. To spell it out in English according to Xuanzang's principle of transliteration, one might have to say, "Once you have *kanpo*d, you can *fangxia* and then you attain *zizai*." *Kanpo*d is a past participle and *fangxia* is an infinitive while *zizai* is a noun as the object of "attain." All that which is implied in the Chinese gives rise to no fewer than nine words in the English, namely, "once you have," "you can" and "and then you attain." Or else, rendering the three words (yes, six characters, but three words) without adding the joints, i. e. saying "See through illusions, free from attachments, at ease with self," would turn out something quite incomprehensible. To make a text in English out of these isolated phrases, cohesion is necessary.

Cohesion is my topic today, but the "straitjacket" and the "dancing shoes" in the title of my paper could fit in, too, by trading places. They might well be the TL's straitjacket and the SL's dancing shoes, for the TL in this case is English and the SL Chinese. Even though the basic word order of Chinese is more rigid than that of English, sophisticated Chinese syntax offers relatively more room for dancing around; but such frolic is more for saying different things with the same words in various order (or, for that matter, in different measures) than for saying the same thing with the same words in different sequences. However, when it comes to cohesion, a Chinese text is often clad in an invisible jacket that holds the parts together in a definite relation, and any rendering of the text into English may call for shoes comfortable enough for the text-maker to trail the connection clearly but not clumsily, that is, to identify the gap, and fill it without making the joint stiff.

The gap is the thing.

Shou ba qing yang cha man tian	手把青秧插滿田
Ditou bian jian shui zhong tian	低頭便見水中天
Xindi qingjing fang wei dao	心地清淨方為道
Tuibu yuanlai shi xiangqian	退步原來是向前

The above is verse and poetry (traditionally ascribed to the legendary *Budai Heshang*[3]). Above all, it is a Chinese text. The gaps are not poetic license. They are Chinese and typical of the predominantly paratactic nature of the language, classical or modern. English cohesion could also be paratactic but to a much lesser degree. And it is pretty obvious that any attempt to translate these four lines into English, keeping the gaps, would make the TL text hardly a text but seemingly a disconnected sequence of sentences.

Now let us read the following:

Transplants the whole field with a handful of shoots,
Lowers head and sees the sky in water.
Only with clarity in mind is the way to Truth,
To take a step backward is in fact to move forward.

This is a real text generated by a former student of mine, who normally writes reasonable English. The horror now on show was not intended as any experiment or demonstration of possibilities. It was part of an attempt to complete a translation project for graduation and convey the *Zen* or *Chan* feeling of the original poem.

Let us for the time being overlook lexical items and brush aside peculiar features such as the absence of subjects, which is, of course, a Chinese and not English characteristic, which could create much ambiguity. Let us also forget about rhythm and rhymes. But what about the sense? Do please mind the gaps.

A text is a semantic unit, a unit in meaning, not, by definition, in form; it makes a whole not by virtue of any structural integration but through texture. If we regard the four lines in Chinese as a text, it is because we see texture in it. What then is the texture in the text above? We have to visualize the very activity of planting rice in the paddies. We have to see the farmer bending forward and wading backwards in the watery field. ("He" should move backwards in order to proceed with the work without trampling on the seedlings just planted). It is this picture that provides the cohesion and the texture. Then we grasp the semantic whole and bridge the gaps without seams. This requires imagination as well as knowledge. It may not be possible for an English version to rely on similar visualization on the part of the receptor (even though English poetry, as practically all poetry, lives, too, on such faculty, provided that certain linguistic require-ments are fulfilled). For one thing, one lexical item in the original is pivotal. The word *xindi*, a word made up of the characters for "heart" and "ground," involves very concrete images while denoting something very abstract (rather inadequately rendered as "state of mind") and thus links ingeniously the two sections of the quatrain. To make up for the cultural as well as linguistic difference, the texture of the English rendition may have to be re-created by other cohesive means, for example, grammatical or lexical cohesion. An attempt at paraphrasing has turned out the following:

> *While* planting green seedlings by hand all over the paddy,
> I bend *my* head and see the sky in the water.
> Only a clear and clean state of mind brings the Dao,
> *Showing* Stepping back to be really advancing.

The relative adverb "while" meets the largely hypotactic requirement of English and makes sense of the first two lines as a unit. (The "I" and "my" are there respectively to fill up the grammatical gap with a subject and as personal deixis.) To make a unit of the third and fourth lines, the participle "showing" is as much a grammatical connective as it is a seman-tic cohesive. Between the second and the third lines, however, is a leap from a particular concrete situation to a general statement of truth. But only if the receptor leaps along and it clicks, can the two units become one and form a text. We are aware that the paraphrase above has interpreted and thereby confined the meaning of the text to something less fuzzy and less suggestive than the Chinese original. But the point is to make sense out of the lines and the sense makes the text hold as a text with due semantic limitations.

Now, let us look back to the first of the "quatrains" in English from the point of view of cohesion. Regardless of the grammatical disaster and the hermeneutic muddle, it contains only one cohesive feature, and that is a comma between the last two lines, which makes the last line a clause in apposition to the noun at the end of the third line, namely "Truth." The anaphoric effect helps form a unit of the latter half of the "quatrain." whether we agree with the interpretation or not and whether the apparent interpretation as we see it was perceived by the translator or not. But what can we say about the first two lines? They hang in mid-air, separately. Even with the most generous of poetic license, and a touch of *Zen*, this sequence of words/lines does not provide a readable text, or any text at that. It contravenes the convention of the English tongue and thus leaves a "common reader" of the language without any textual clue. It becomes a rather forlorn scarecrow, tatters scattered here and there after a gatecrasher has visited the field. The teacher, like the farmer, is left to pick up the pieces.

To cut a long story short, the paratactic convention of Chinese syntax is so deeply ingrained in Chinese learners of English that it calls for special efforts to plant the seedlings of hypotaxis in their mind so as to help them see and hear when a text begins falling apart. They can then apply cohesive features as shown in the second "quatrain." I have picked a verse that happens to be poetry to illustrate my points, because even though parataxis occurs more frequently in poetry than in prose, hypotaxis is nevertheless the rule in English texts, poetic or otherwise, and the text-maker has to be competent and feel agile enough in the game of syntax to waltz between the two structures.

It is probably inevitable for foreign learners of Chinese to wrestle with the meaning of a text governed by paratactic syntax in order to translate its sense into English. If they are hardworking or perceptive enough, spiritual enlightenment may come and they may take the leap. On the other hand, a Chinese text could be strewn with traps for a native speaker under the illusion of freedom and they may forget to leave their invisible jacket at home before learning to dance in foreign shoes. The message comes "naturally" to them and naturally they fail to query if the reader/listener could receive anything close enough to the original. Of course, a thorough training in English grammar and a heightened awareness of cultural difference may help. Above all, the native speaker must understand how their own language works, especially in ways in which English would not work.

Further, what would then work instead in English? Knowledge of contrastive syntax is essential.

For cohesive purposes, what works in the SL text under discussion includes the absence of subject, the absence of punctuation and the near absence of conjunctions. However, there are also *xuci* (so-called empty words) in Chinese, roughly equivalent to English "function" words, which help convey, among other things, the tone of the text. In the text concerned, there are three such words playing such vital cohesive parts. They are *bian* in line 2, *fang* in line 3 and *yuanlai* in line 4. These words can hardly be translated without a context, and in context they perform highly versatile functions ranging from expressing the tone of the speech and the sequence of the events to implying the very attitude of the speaker. Since they are not "concrete" like nouns, adjectives and verbs (which are traditionally known as *shici*, i.e. "solid words" in Chinese grammar), it is "natural" for a native speaker without linguistic training, let alone language sensitivity, to be unaware of their presence and functions, which will have to be rendered in the foreign text.

Thus, granted we accept the interpretation of the original used above, we may express it in English with minimal change of syntax as in the text below:

> Planting green shoots to cover the paddy
> I bend down and see the sky in the water.
> Only a pure and clear heart can attain *dao*
> And see advancement in stepping backwards.

In verse, while neither the comma nor punctuation in general is indispensable, the participial phrase of the first line is instrumental to cohesion. The conjunction "and" is straightforward and appropriate in all cases, linking two verbs in line 2 and two adjectives in line 3 and making line 4 a result of line 3. The leap between lines 2 and 3 is kept and the task of cohesion is left to Zen. All other connections thus made are basic and simple English devices. The main point is to see that they are necessary – necessary because much in the SL text is invisible or taken for granted and the TL requires more explicit links to make the chain of thought possible.

So, beware, would-be translators, do not leave home without some legitimate striptease. Then, on with your dancing shoes and you can move backwards or forwards with ease.

> Xing ye budai　行也布袋
> Zuo ye budai　　坐也布袋

Fangxia budai   放下布袋
Ziyou zizai![4]   自由自在

A paratactic text for some hypotactic exercise.

Notes

[1]   Xuanzang, the Tang dynasty monk turned paramount translator of Buddhist scriptures into Chinese, maintains the principle of rendering five categories of untranslatable items by transliterating, one of which is SL cultural specifics non-existent in the TL culture.

[2]   A Buddhist tripartite of seeing through illusions, freeing oneself from attachments and finally being at ease as one is. The lexical items here, however, are Chinese translations and not transliterations from Sanskrit, but the concepts have become "naturalized" and adopted into Chinese culture.

[3]   *Budai Heshang*, literally "the cloth bag monk," (? – 916), was a Zen-Buddhist monk of the late Tang dynasty, of whom little is known. Legend goes that he had a dirty and untidy appearance, a rather disconcerting turn of phrase and a rather vagrant lifestyle. He went around carrying a cloth bag on a staff, begging for alms; hence the nickname "Budai Heshang." Traditional portraits of the monk feature a laughing figure baring his chest and carrying a cloth bag on his shoulder.

[4]   Another verse traditionally ascribed to *Budai Heshang* in praise of the freedom of non-attachment. Literally, the verse goes, "Walk also cloth bag/ sit also cloth bag/ put down cloth bag/ free and easy."

References

Berk, L. M. (1999). *English Syntax: From Word to Discourse*. New York: Oxford University Press.

Bryson, B. (1991). *Mother Tongue*. Harmondsworth: Penguin.

Chomsky, N. (1965). *Aspects of the Theory of Syntax*. Cambridge, Mass.: MIT Press.

Crystal, D. (1971). *Linguistics*. New York: Penguin.

Fries, C. C. (1957). *The Structure of English*. London: Longman.

Halliday, M. A. K. and R. Hasan (1976). *Cohesion in English*. London: Longman.

Hatim, B. and I. Mason (1997). *The Translator as Communicator*. London: Routledge.

Leech, G. N. (1969). *A Linguistic Guide to English Poetry*. London: Longman.

Leech, G. N. and J. Svartvik (1975). *A Communicative Grammar of English*. London: Longman.

Luo, Xinzhang, ed. (1984). 《翻譯論集》(*An Anthology of Translation Theory*). Beijing: The Commercial Press.

Lyons, J. (1992). *Language, Meaning and Context*. London: Cambridge University Press.

Neubert, A. and G. M. Shreve (1992). *Translation as Text*. Kent, Ohio: The Kent University Press.

Nida, E. A. (1975). *Language Structure and Translation*. Stanford: Stanford University Press.

Radford, A. (1997). *Syntax*. Cambridge: Cambridge University Press.

Wang, L. (1959). 《中國現代語法》 (*Modern Chinese Grammar*). Beijing: Zhonghua Shuju.

Wang, L. (1962).《古代漢語》(*Classical Chinese*). Beijing: Zhonghua Shuju.

Translation Studies in Hong Kong-China and the Impact of "New Translation Theories"

Leo Chan Tak-hung
Department of Translation
Lingnan University

> *Global capitalism has infiltrated China's cultural landscape not only with its commercial mass culture products but also with its academic, intellectual products, namely contemporary Western "theory."* (Liu Kang, 1996: 210)

In the West, the incursion of "new translation theories" into academia was begun over a decade ago. Evolving out of European and Anglo-American contexts, such theories have made, on their first appearance, a decisive break with the so-called linguistic approaches which found their earliest exponents in theorists like J. C. Catford and Peter Newmark, whose works on translation in the sixties can be said to have set the directions for the development of the discipline now referred to as translation studies. The difference between the "old" and the new has been articulated in an amazing variety of ways. For some, it was the evolution from a normative approach to a descriptive one; for others, a shift from a micro to a macro-level of study; for still others, it signaled a "cultural turn" in the field, with translation theorists turning increasingly to non-linguistic disciplines (like anthropology) for new insights.

Given such a state of affairs, those brought up on the older theories have no other alternative than learn to make adjustments, though these are by no means easy. For, after all, coming under fire in the new context are the age-old and sanctified notions of linguistic equivalence and fidelity to the source text, now replaced with new-fangled terms like *otherness, hegemony,* and *différance.* Some responded by noting how the meaning of the term "translation" has been broadened beyond recognition—even becoming almost synonymous with what the anthropologist Talal Asad calls "cultural translation" — and consequently lost its specificity. (Asad, 1988:141–64)

In the main, two theorists of the nineties must be said to have fueled the move in the new direction. Tejaswini Niranjana's *Siting Translation* (Niranjana, 1992) advanced the thesis that British civil servants during the Indian colonial era were engaged in translating Indian sacred texts so as to impose a definitive interpretation on them, grounded on the belief that English was a *purer* language and that the time was ripe for such texts to be reinterpreted. To this, Niranjana averred, the Indians in the post-Independence period have responded by providing their own re-translations of the same works in question. In his introduction to *Re-thinking Translation* (also published in 1992), Lawrence Venuti denounced the translator who covers up the violence often done to a text through the much sanctified method of translating "invisibly." While his arguments had appeared elsewhere earlier (Venuti, 1986: 179–212), it is in *Rethinking Translation* that they were made widely known for the first time, and it is also this anthology which made available views of some of the leading deconstructionist theorists of translation of our era. In its wake, it can fairly be said that an entire school of theorists of this persuasion have moved on stage, making themselves known through radicalizing translation studies. One can cite, for instance, the feminist approach of Sherry Simon and Louise von Flotow, the postcolonial approach of Douglas Robinson, and the deconstructive approach of Rosemary Arrojo.

Imports from the West

Viewed from a wider perspective, new translation theories are part and parcel of the body of ideas referred to in the West as *poststructuralist*. In the Chinese context these have been dubbed "New Theory," a term much bandied about in Chinese academic circles in the past decade. Among the first to introduce the term to Chinese readers is Zhao Yiheng, currently a professor of Chinese at the University of London. At the beginning of his article, "Post-isms and the New Chinese Conservatism," published in Chinese in 1995 and translated into English for *New Literary History* in 1997, Zhao discusses poststructuralism, postcolonialism and postmodernism as three strands of thought imported into China in the eighties, but he does note that a host of other "isms" popular in academic discourse at the time can be subsumed under poststructuralism. (Zhao,

1995: 4–15) It must be noted, of course, that the focus of his discussion was literary and cultural theories; translation theories were much slower to enter China.

Some even date the entrance of New Theory into China to 1985, when Fredric Jameson toured the country's major universities, giving a series of lectures which were later translated and published in an anthology. For some this initiated the period of China's "cultural fever" which ended with the government's crackdown on student protesters in Tiananmen Square in 1989. On the heels of Jameson, other Western scholars like Terry Eagleton, Ralph Cohen, and Gerald Gillespie also made their visits; in fact all of them came in 1995. The importation of ideas was also continued through a succession of efforts to translate seminal Western works in the field: Zhang Xudong translated Walter Benjamin; Zhou Ning translated Jauss and Holub; Xu Wenbo translated Harold Bloom; Tan Daming and Gong Jianming translated Robert Scholes; and Wang Fengzhen translated Terry Eagleton. Alongside these translations, anthologies of translated essays by Western theorists have appeared as well, including Zhang Jingyuan's *Contemporary Feminist Literary Criticism* (Zhang, 1992) and Wang Fengzhen, Sheng Ning and Li Zixiu's *A Selection of the Most Recent Critical Essays in the West.* (Wang, *et. al.*, 1991) Several series of translations of works in critical theory further fueled the craze, and these include those published by the Chinese Academy of Social Sciences (since 1986), the Liaoning People's Press (edited by Li Zehou, one of the most eminent of living Chinese philosophers), and Joint Publishing Company. The speed with which New Theory from the West was introduced is astounding. In fact, within the span of a decade or so, hundreds of works relating to Western theories on feminism, new historicism, deconstructionism, etc., were translated. The most remarkable thing about what happened is that, though these "new" concepts originated in various places in the West over the course of decades, in China they all appeared at roughly the same time. In 1991–92 alone, Toril Moi, Hans-Georg Gadamar, I. A. Richards, Jonathan Culler, E. D. Hirsch and Wolfgang Iser were introduced to the Chinese reader simultaneously.

While the general picture of the poststructuralist impact on China in the fields of literary and cultural studies, as given above, is clear, that of new translation theories is still rather murky. It may help to talk of their impact in two different areas, first in teaching and then as an object of intellectual inquiry. As regards the former, it seems that it is the translation teachers in Hong Kong, themselves witnesses to a flourishing of the discipline in the last two decades, who have taken up the challenge in introducing poststructuralist ideas of translation to their students.

In the past decade, translation programmes in Hong Kong (as in the West) have borne witness to a massive invasion of poststructuralist ideas, and the teaching of translation theory has undergone drastic changes. Courses on theory offered at tertiary institutions there used to be dominated by the "fathers of translation theory" — Newmark and Nida, but today it is virtually impossible to leave out of the syllabuses such names as Derrida, de Man and Venuti. Venuti's *Rethinking Translation* has almost become a must-read for translation students of today and that is the case in Hong Kong as elsewhere. A look at the reading list of the M.A. course on translation theory at Dublin City University, described in a recent issue of *The Translator,* is perhaps most revealing: Venuti is to be read alongside representatives of the linguistic and non-linguistic schools — Catford, Baker, Mounin, Reiss, Vermeer, Holmes, Bassnett and Snell-Hornby. With the exception of Mounin, all these names figure prominently in the sylla-buses of the six translation programs in Hong Kong — those of the Chinese University of Hong Kong, Lingnan University, the University of Hong Kong, City University, the Polytechnic University and Baptist University. This state of affairs testifies to the way in which more traditional theorists have lost ground to an entirely new generation of theorists from continental Europe. One is indeed very far from the days when one did not need to bother with Walter Benjamin. (In fact his "Task of the Translator" was written as early as 1923, though he remained largely in limbo till his rediscovery by the deconstructionists in the eighties.) The advocates of "new translation theories" are a force to be reckoned with.

As for the "intellectual" reception of new translation theories, a con-venient starting point for our discussion is the Bookman Translation Li-brary Series, which is a sampling of representative texts in translation theory published in the Mainland, Taiwan and Hong Kong in the last thirty years or so. Bookman Publishers, a leading publisher of academic books in Taiwan, began the series in the late eighties. Not only does it publish new translation scholarship; it also reissues significant Chinese works on trans-lation that have gone out of print. For that reason it becomes for present purposes one useful indicator of the "state of the art" in translation theoriz-ing in China as well. Below is a list of ten books on translation theory in the series (out of some twenty-three titles published by 1998), each accompa-nied by a brief description of the content from the publisher:

1. Xiao Liming (C=China). *New Explorations in Translation.* 1992. Discusses both Western and Chinese translation theories, illustrating them with ample examples.

2. Huang Bangjie (T=Taiwan). *On the Art of Translation.* 1988 [1985].
   Explicates translation theories and techniques through the contrastive analysis of the two languages involved. Proceeds from the easy to the difficult.

3. Liu Jingzhi (H=Hong Kong). *Affinity-in-spirit and Affinity-in-form.* 1996.
   Considers affinity-in-spirit to be of paramount importance in literary and music translations.

4. He Weijie (H). *Translating Revisited.* 1989.
   Touches on various aspects of translation, including how to raise the standards of translation theorizing.

5. Liu Miqing (C). *Contemporary Translation Theories.* 1993 [1990].
   Attempts to develop a theory of translation based on a linguistic analysis of Chinese-English translations.

6. Hu Gongze (T). *Changes and Development in Translation Theory.* 1994.
   Views translation as an act of communication, and seeks to theorizes translation from a "communicative" perspective.

7. Ke Ping (C). *Chinese-English and English-Chinese Translation.* 1994.
   Introduces Western translation theories and discusses central issues in Chinese-English translation from a "semiotic" perspective.

8. Jin Shenghua and Huang Guobin (H). *Artistry in Encountering Difficulty.* 1996.
   Collects essays by leading translators in the Mainland, Taiwan and Hong Kong on their personal experiences in translating Western classics and what they learn in the process.

9. Jin Di (C). *An Investigation into Equivalence-in-effect.* 1998.
   Continues the work begun with Nida and discusses the many facets of the theory of equivalent effect, illustrating with examples from translations of works like *Ulysses.*

10. Peng Jingxi (T). *Touching the Elephant*. 1997.
    Comments critically on some literary translations and offers some
    personal views of translation. ("Touching the elephant" is a Bud-
    dhist allusion, referring to how a blind man mistook the part of the
    elephant that he touched to be the whole elephant).

Even from the most cursory purview, one can see that the majority of
these "key" Chinese texts on translation theory are written in a traditional
(impressionistic or experience-based) vein. Most notably, Liu's *Contemporary Translation Theories* and Huang's *On the Art of Translation* show
some linguistic background, while Jin's *An Investigation into
Equivalence-in-Effect* and Ke's *Chinese-English and English-Chinese
Translation* evince some awareness of recent linguistic and semiotic
trends. Given this strong overall tendency, it is no wonder that theory often
co-exists with criticism, and theoretical insights are thought to derive,
ultimately, from practical translation experience. In practically all the texts
listed, equivalence is upheld as the golden rule; artistry, particularly in
literary translations, is valorized above everything else; a good command
of the source and target languages is considered an essential prerequisite
for success. It would perhaps not be inaccurate to say that concern for the
cultural underpinnings of translation, and for the ideological maneuvering
to which translations can be subject, is very much absent from these
examples of Chinese theorizing, some of which appeared just a few years ago.

In contrast to this assemblage of Chinese translation theory in a traditional mode, new translation theories have made their presence felt in a
small way, in particular through scholars connected to universities in the
Mainland and Hong Kong. As in many areas of investigation in the
humanities, then, the revolution begins silently in academia. For some
years, *A Short History of Western Translation Theories* (Tan, 1991), by a
professor of foreign languages at Shenzhen University, has been instrumental in bringing Chinese scholars into contact with translation theories
from the outside world, from St. Jerome and the Bible translators down to
Nida and Steiner of the present century. It was on the basis of Tan's
description of Western translation theories that a couple of introductions to
descriptive translation theories and deconstructionist theories of translation
have been written for academic journals like *Chinese Translators Journal*
(Beijing-based, founded in 1950 under a different name), *Foreign Language Teaching and Research* (also Beijing-based, founded in 1977),
Language and Translation (Urumqi-based, founded in 1985), *Foreign*

Languages and Translation (Changsha-based, founded in 1994) and *Foreign Languages* (Shanghai-based, founded in 1978) in the past few years (Liu, 1997: 51–57; Jiang, 1995: 64–67; Zhao, 1996: 46–47, 50). The appearance of these introductions may well be a phenomenon parallel to the introduction of New Theory in general, or they might have been connected with the "cultural fever" that has been prevalent since the mid-eighties. There is also the possibility that China is taking her own "cultural turn" in translation studies. Whatever the reason, the couple of essays do signal an interest in the cultural contexts of translation, and perhaps this interest will increase to a point where substantial research along the lines set out by Western poststructuralists will be undertaken in universities in Mainland China.

Several books complement these introductory articles. While not directly applying new translation theories, they must still be viewed as symptomatic of where the wind is blowing. One can begin by looking at the translation of Western translation theories first. A very recent publication is *Masterpieces in Western Translation Theory* (2000) by Chan Tak-hung and Chang Nam-fung, both of Lingnan University, Hong Kong. In this anthology the seminal pieces on translation theory by Benjamin, Derrida, de Man and Venuti—key texts for the poststructuralist theorists of translation—are themselves translated for the first time into Chinese. Since as early as the fifties, Western translation theories have been imported into China through a series of translations, though most of these theories are in the traditional vein, with a predominance of works by linguists. As can also be expected, there is a greater percentage of works by Russians at first, superseded later by works from Western Europe and the States. Quite a few also pertain to the teaching of interpreting, spiced with only a smattering of theory. Roughly speaking, judging from the publication dates of the translations in Mainland China, Western translation theorists were presented to the Chinese readers in the following order:

1955	Andrei Fedorov (Soviet Union)
1959	Mikhail Morozov (Soviet Union)
1959	Pavel Toper (Soviet Union)
1972	Danica Seleskovitch (France) (translated also in 1990 and 1992)
1982	Herbert Jean (Switzerland)
1984	Eugene Nida (U.S.)
1985	Leonid Barkhudarov (Russian)

1987   George Steiner (Switzerland)
1988   Wolfram Wilss (Germany)
1988   Jean Delisle (Canada)
1991   J.C. Catford (England)

While *Masterpieces in Western Translation Theory* does not deal in depth with new theories in translation, it aims at playing a role in disseminating poststructuralist approaches to translation through highlighting their differences from the traditional and the linguistic approaches. Since most translators in this anthology are professors at universities, there is ample reason to expect the tertiary institutions to continue to be responsible for taking "new translation theory" into the next millennium.

But has there been no application of new translation theories in China at all? Were there not even mere traces of these theories being used? Deserving special mention in this context are two recent publications, one from Mainland China and one from Taiwan, which study translations in the context of their target culture, paying special attention to the distortions (leading to a lack of "transparency") that texts undergo when crossing linguistic borders. The authors in both cases are in fact Mainlanders. Zou Zhenhuan's *One Hundred Translations That Had an Impact on Modern Chinese Society,* published by the Chinese Translation Company of Beijing in 1996, reviews (in separate sections) translations of works by Freud, Goethe, Edgar Snow, etc., which have influenced the way the Chinese looked at the world in the past century. Of special interest is the fact that for a Chinese study of translation, it is one of those rare instances where the focus is placed upon the target cultural context rather than the linguistic elements involved in translation. *The Chinese Language and the Modern Chinese Cultural Enlightenment,* also published (in Taibei) in 1996, was authored by two professors from Central China Normal University — Zhou Guangqing and Liu Wei. It is also a sign of the application of the new approach in which historical as well as cultural concerns supersede those of language. In roughly a third of the book, the authors deal microscopically with language change in the first two decades of the twentieth century, in the context of the translation of terms signifying new concepts and objects imported from the West.

Perhaps even more important than either of these books are attempts made in an article and an M.A. thesis to theorize about translation that confront head-on the "lie" often expressed about using translation as a means of building bridges and enhancing understanding between nations.

After all, it can be argued that the monographs mentioned in the above paragraph embody nothing more than a new awareness of the cultural implications of translation. They may even reflect a historical awareness of the background against which translations were carried out, and it must be remembered that Liu Wei is after all a professor of history. But there is no doubt at all that deconstructionist theory did set foot in China in 1994, with an article in the Taiwanese journal *Chung-Wai Literary Monthly* by the Hong Kong-born scholar-translator Wai-lim Yip, who teaches at the University of California, San Diego. This article antedates all the works discussed above which contain a modicum of information about "new translation theories," though it lags far behind the first introductions of New Theory into China, which can be located in the mid-eighties.

Yip's "Debunking Faithfulness, Comprehensibility and Elegance: The Afterlife of Translations" starts off by quoting from Walter Benjamin's "The Task of the Translator," the essay generally believed to contain the "seeds" of the deconstructionist translation theory later adumbrated by Venuti and others (Yip, 1994: 74–84). By way of Benjamin, Yip discusses at length the impossibility of achieving the two supreme Chinese principles of translation first enunciated by Yan Fu — *faithfulness* and *comprehensibility* (the third principle he subsumes under the latter). For him

> translation is a linguistic event, a voice from another time and another space being played out before us; through it we are allowed to enter into dialogue with each other. It is the dialectical interaction between two histories and two cultures. The "realm" displayed by this voice is often similar to (i.e. showing points of intersection), and yet also different from, that imagined by the translator (who is simultaneously the reader, critic and creative artist) due to historical, cultural and educational constraints. There is absolutely no possibility of equivalence. (Yip, 1994: 76)

Yip notes the recent debunking of the illusion of a "common humanity," which provides the basis for the search for equivalence, by Western scholars of comparative literature and cultural studies, as well as deconstructionists and feminists. For them, in our time and age, neither the belief in truly objective interpretations (by hermeneuticians like Schleiermacher, Dilthey and E.D. Hirsch), nor the Kantian faith in scientific and instrumental reason, has any validity. That being the case, it is pure folly to expect the translator to be able to reconstruct the original author's "world" in translation. He succeeds better, in fact, in "demythologizing and dehistoricizing" the original through his manipulation of language, and in the process allows the original to fit comfortably in the new context.

Unlike his Mainland counterparts, Yip does not stop short at a descriptive account of these theories; he elaborates the concept of *difference*, with examples of Pound's translation of Chinese poems ("jeweled staircase" is more appropriate than "jade staircase," though the latter is more "faithful") and Chinese translations of Andrew Marvell and William Wordsworth (in which elements of intertextuality create insurmountable obstacles for translation). Nevertheless, Yip reiterates that his is only a preliminary attempt at using deconstructionist ideas to understand the impact of translation on Chinese literary expression. At the end of his article, quoting a line from a poem by Shang Qin which contains some Europeanized structures showing the influence of Chinese translations of English works (but which, ironically, are not translatable back into English), he illustrates Walter Benjamin's idea of the "afterlife" of translations. For him, though, the intention is simply to say a few words about this phenomenon he calls the "fertilization of the flower from abroad" and the "reproduction of seeds from abroad," and on this note he ends the first discussion (at the time) of Benjamin in Chinese. Brilliant use of Benjamin also appeared elsewhere, but since it was published in English, it falls outside the scope of the present discussion. (Chow, 1995: 173–202)

The last example of a Chinese translation scholar's active deployment of Western poststructuralist ideas in understanding a body of translated texts is found in Xiao Peifei's "Orientalism and Self-orientalizing: The Translation of Western Sinological Works in China in the Eighties and Nineties," (Xiao, 1999) a Master's thesis with a focus of attention on the third peak of translation activity in twentieth-century China — in the past two decades (the first peak occurred at the beginning of the century, the second during the May Fourth period immediately after 1919). Translations were undertaken with feverish intensity: counting non-literary works alone, at least 1,500 were published in the ten-year period since 1979, the year that marks the beginning of the Deng Xiaoping era (Siu, 1999: 111–227). Among these an interesting category consists of works by Western sinologists, especially those that deal with China's history, politics and culture in traditional times as well as the present century, by noted scholars like Jacques Gernet, Max Weber, Benjamin Schwartz, Thomas Metzger and so on. Specimens of Orientalizing by scholars in the West, these works were avidly translated and published in several well-known series, most notably the "Overseas Research on China" series from the Nanjing-based

Jiangsu People's Press. Apparently innocuous and transparent translations, for Xiao they were underlined by the ideological maneuvering of a generation of intellectuals in China.

In contrast to what, according to Niranjana, was an oppositional strategy adopted by the post-Independence Indian translators to retranslate much of what was previously translated by the British colonizers, for Xiao the Chinese translators of the eighties and early nineties were, deliberately or otherwise, perpetuating images of China fabricated by Western scholars through their translations of sinological works (mostly carried out in the United States). This Xiao calls a "self-Orientalizing" strategy, in which Chinese intellectuals can be seen as being complicit with Western sinologists. Through the close analysis of a translation of Benjamin Schwartz's *In Search of Wealth and Power: Yen Fu and the West* (and the Chinese readers' response to it), Xiao reveals that Orientalizing and self-Orientalizing are mutually reinforcing strategies, and the so-called complicity takes place on two levels:

> Firstly, there is theoretical complicity, or complicity on the level of image building. Self-Orientalizing discourse directly appropriates the China image constructed by Orientalism and duplicates it. In other words, Chinese readers and critics endorse Schwartz's Orientalist discourse, which is taken over and used to construct China versus the West: the latter is governed by democracy, liberty and legal rule, and also "wealthy and strong," while the former is a society that suppresses potentials, one which is "poor and weak." Secondly, there is methodological complicity. Whether they accept or reject the image of China projected by Western sinologists, Chinese scholars aim at using the binary opposition of China and the West to construct an ontologically unified and unvarying discourse on China. (Xiao, 1999: 205)

Thus translations of this kind transmit back to China a message urging the need for change (or "modernization"), and Xiao might have even gone one step further speculating on the possible connection that these translations had with the championing of political reforms at the time. Many reasons have been adduced for the outbreak of demonstrations leading to the Tiananmen Square Incident, but perhaps it ought to be mentioned that the proliferation of translations of Western scholarship in general, and of works of Western sinology in particular, added fuel to the fire of discontent. To conclude, in view of the absence of research in this area as a whole, Xiao's thesis can be said to have broken new ground and is a brilliant example of the deployment of new translation theories for research in China.

Problems in Reception

In contrast to the relative ease with which new translation theories become incorporated as part of translation studies in the West, it must be said that their introduction into China has met with more than a little resistance. Charges of impracticality have often been made against these theories especially by students of translation. Some even have doubts whether they are really theories *of* translation and not theories *about* translation—in other words, whether they are extrinsic, and not intrinsic to translation as a human activity. The essential question, then, becomes one of how it is possible to *translate* translation theories of a poststructuralist bent for a Chinese audience. In what follows, I will seek to explore the issue of reception from the multiple perspectives of the translator, the scholar, and the theorist, and conclude with suggestions about ways in which new translation theories can be made meaningful and therefore acceptable.

Indeed, after over a decade since they were first introduced, the intellectual reaction to "New Theory," at least as far as Mainland China is concerned, must be characterized as rather "mixed." Voices of repudiation are in fact still heard years after Jameson made his epoch-making trip. Recently Xin Xiaozheng and Guo Yinxing concluded their critique of New Theory by wryly noting that its influence is "weak," its future "foggy and unclear." (Xin and Guo, 1988: 10; Meng, 1990: 36–39) In the case of new translation theories, as the above discussion shows, the reception is certainly lukewarm. Given the differences in cultural climate, it is conceivable that ideas like postmodernism and postcolonialism, whether applied to translation or not, should be viewed in China with some suspicion. (Lu, 1996: 139–64; Wang, 1993:49–61; Tang, 1993: 278–300; Zhang, 1993) That raises hopes that new translation theories can find a congenial home in Hong Kong, whose readiness to accept things Western is often noted, and whose receptivity to postcolonialist theories in particular might be enhanced by the fact that it has entered a unique post-colonial phase upon China's takeover in 1997. That, unfortunately, does not seem to be the case; there is a paucity of research utilizing the insights of the new theories, whether translation-related or non-translation-related, and this in spite of the fact that poststructuralist theories like those mentioned in the present article are usually taught in translation programmes. Whether the efforts of someone like Siu Pui-fei will be followed up still remains to be seen. As for the situation of universities in the Mainland, at this very moment none of them runs a full-fledged programme on translation, not even one at the B.A.

level — though a couple are being anticipated for the near future. This means that it will be premature to speak of the contribution of a younger generation of scholars from the Mainland. The best that one can say is that some breakthrough may be in sight; with the growing influence of new translation theories, one can reasonably expect to see — eventually — a total "immersion" in poststructuralist translation theorizing.

The importance of poststructuralist translation theories to China is bedeviled primarily by two related problems: first, Chinese cultural attitudes towards the meaning and significance of translation theorizing; and second, the divorce of these theories from the reality of translation in the Chinese context.

Probably even more than in the West, for China, translation theory has always served to provide norms that can assist the translator in translating. (Here you have the eternal bone of contention between the translation teacher and the translation scholar.) The prescriptive nature of the three principles of translation, as advocated by the foremost Chinese translation theorist of the century, Yan Fu, has been pointed out time and again by scholars in the field: faults in translation are as a rule seen as deviations from those principles, incontestable and true for all time. Theory is not distinguishable from principles, which are normative. Another prevalent belief is the inseparability of translation theory from criticism; for that reason evaluative statements almost invariably pass for "theory" in China. The privileging of practice over theory, and the virtual non-existence of a tradition of philosophical reflection on the processes and products of translation, means that when new translation theories are introduced, they need a great deal of adjusting to. It would be worth remarking, at this point, that the issue of the accountability of the translation theorist to the practitioner of translation is a perennial one that even Western theorists have had to confront in the first place, and it does not seem that such die-hard thinking can be easily eradicated. In China, however, the tendency to denounce theorizing that is not made relevant to practice as empty talk has been particularly strong.

Furthermore, the merits of poststructuralist translation theories notwithstanding, it still cannot be denied that they need to pass the test of immediate applicability when transplanted to foreign soil. Even granting that, in principle, they allow us to understand translation as a means whereby cultures are re-interpreted, as an exemplary case of how language can be manipulated as a significative system, the true worth of such theories needs to be verified through detailed textual study. Apparently, new translation theories, by some curious freak in their nature, have always had a tendency to move ahead of practice. Borrowing terms from disciplines outside of translation studies, theorists have evolved within a short time-span an elaborate framework for a poststructuralist discourse on translation. It is only after the theories have been established that Western translation scholars began reexamining translated texts already published on the one hand, while translators started experimenting with new strategies (one thinks here of Philip Lewis's "abusive translation" [Lewis, 1985: 31–62]) for rendering their source texts on the other. An example of the former is that of André Lefevere's re-reading of the translations of Aristophanes's *Lysrstrata* by Wheelwright (1837), Hickie (1902) and Housman (1911). As examples of the latter, there are Suzanne Jill Levine's rendition of Guillermo Cabrera Infante's *Infante's Inferno* using what she calls her own subversive translation methods, and the Canadian (English) translators' inventive translations of contemporary Quebecois texts, as examined by Sherry Simon.

In the Chinese context, however, few translation studies in the "new mode" — and perhaps not even single translations purposely deploying the new strategies — seem to have made their appearance as yet. We can only look forward to mature translation research in the future applying the new theories to existent translations. After all, an entire generation of translation scholars have emerged since translation courses were first introduced into tertiary institutions in Hong Kong two decades ago. And with the inauguration of M.A. and Ph.D. programmes in several universities in Hong Kong, we can fairly assume that "new" readings of translated texts will be forthcoming. However, it may be a while before *retroactive* translation research (*retroactive* because it deals with translated texts already in existence) ceases to be the only kind of activity that the translation scholars can engage in, and new translation theories become directly relevant and "operative" for practicing translators and their translations.

At the same time, from the difficulty new translation theories had in establishing themselves in China, one can easily see the shortcomings of a rather narrow approach to theorizing that does more harm than good. A look at the reaction on the part of linguists to the challenge of poststructuralist translation theories in recent years is highly instructive. In fact the response of several translation theorists with a strong linguistic background shows some of our artificial demarcations to be more limiting than real. And the gap between what we have almost characterized as two opposed camps in translation theorizing, if it does exist, is not as wide as it seems. Cultural components in translation have engaged the attention of trained linguists: Mary Snell-Hornby is a case in point. Breaking through the narrow theoretical confines of her predecessors of a previous generation, she advocates the view that translation is more a case of *cross-cultural* transfer than *interlingual* transfer, and she hopes to enhance understanding of translation by incorporating knowledge from fields as diverse as psychology, philosophy and ethnography; yet few can surpass her linguistic analyses of translated textual features. The word "integrated" in what is her best book to date is most telling here. (Snell-Hornby, 1988: 31–62)

Other linguists, perhaps reacting unconsciously to the "new" theories, have sought to make up for the deficiencies of traditional linguistic approaches, especially the much criticized, fragmentary study of small linguistic units like the sentence, by proposing ever-expanding units for analysis — from de Beaugrande's "text" to Hatim and Mason's "discourse." (Mason and Hatim, 1989; Mason, 1997) They can be said to have continued the exploration of the possibilities of the new linguistic science called "text linguistics," championed as early as 1972 by none other than Wolfgang Dressler and de Beaugrande, who were among the first proponents of "beyond-the-sentence" analysis of translations. The German functionalist school (represented by Vermeer, Reiss, Nord and Holz-Mänttäri), convinced that translation theories should not only be linguistically based, have drawn on a general theory of action to account for the multiple facets of translation as an act of human communication.

For one with a strong sense of history, in particular of the relatedness of ideas in time, two points would be obvious if one were to sum up what has been happening to linguistics-based translation theory in the West in the past three decades, since the forefathers of the sixties began writing about translation as an independent field of inquiry: there has been decline and there has been rejuvenation. Furthermore, considering the fact that the reshaping of linguistic theories of translation occurred at roughly the same time as re-readings of Benjamin's essay were undertaken by Derrida and de Man (these were later followed by re-readings of Derrida's and de Man's essays by Venuti and Niranjana), one may be tempted to think of both camps, the linguistic and the non-linguistic, as vying with each other and yet playing complementary roles. Of course one explanation for what has transpired is that they were both responding to either some "crisis in consciousness" experienced by the Western world at large, to the oft-repeated "cultural turn," or to disciplinary/institutional reconfigurations in Western academia in the last few decades of the twentieth century.

It seems inevitable, in fact, that in translation theorizing one has to persistently struggle with the micro-level of the text and the macro-level of culture (which includes ideology, history, philosophy, law, customs, and so on). The two, however, are related "metonymically" (Tymoscsko, 1999: 41–62), though translation theories have always had a tendency to emphasize either one of the two. For some time now, the school that focuses on the latter has been on the ascendancy, though such theories do not translate well, as in the case of its transplantation to Chinese soil. Yet should we give up hope? Still granting the apparent difference between the new theories and the old, it remains true that poststructuralist theories of translation do open up opportunities for novel reflections on translation, as well as usher in a new set of tools for methodological analysis. To theorize on the basis of untranslatability, to view translation as being inscribed within the power contests between cultures, to debunk translation as mimesis — these have given new life to translation studies in the West. For that reason, we too would like to see new translation theories reinvigorating the theoretical (if not yet the practical) study of translation in China. In the meantime, one needs to keep an eye open for these theories to demonstrate their practical utility by encouraging bold and daring Chinese translators to indulge in translation experimentation of a kind yet unseen.

References

Asad, Talal (1988). "The Concept of Cultural Translation in British Social Anthropology." In James Clifford and George E. Marcus, eds., *Writing Culture: The Poetics and Politics of Ethnography*. Berkeley: University of California Press, pp.141–64.

Chan, Tak-hung and Chang Nam-fung (2000). *Masterpieces in Western Translation Theory*. Hong Kong: Lingnan University.

Chow, Rey (1995). *Primitive Passions: Visuality, Sexuality, Ethnography, and Contemporary Chinese Cinema*. New York: Columbia University Press.

Hatim, B. (1997). *Translation across Cultures: Translation Theory and Contrastive Text Linguistics*. Exeter: University of Exeter Press.

He, Weijie (1989). *Translating Revisited*. Taibei: Bookman Publishers.

Hu, Gongze (1994). *Changes and Development in Translation Theory*. Taibei: Bookman Publishers.

Huang, Bangjie (1988). *On the Art of Translation*. Taibei: Bookman Publishers.

Jiang, Xiaohua (1995). "Exploring Deconstructionist Theories on Translation." *Foreign Language Teaching and Research,* No. 4, pp. 64–7.

Jin, Di (1988). *An Investigation into Equivalence-in-effect.* Taibei: Bookman Publishers.

Jin, Shenghua and Huang Guobin (1996). *Artistry in Encountering Difficulty.* Taibei: Bookman Publishers.

Ke, Ping (1994). *Chinese-English and English-Chinese Translation.* Taibei: Bookman Publishers.

Levine, S. J. (1991). *The Subversive Scribe: Translating Latin-American Fiction.* Saint Paul, Minnesota: Graywolf Press.

Lewis, Philip (1985). "The Measure of Translation Effects." In Joseph F. Graham, ed., *Difference in Translation.* Ithaca: Cornell University Press, pp. 31–62.

Liu, Jingzhi (1996). *Affinity-in-spirit and Affinity-in-form.* Taibei: Bookman Publishers.

Liu, Junping (1997). "The Deconstructionist Approach to Translation." *Foreign Languages,* 2, pp. 51–54.

Liu, Kang (1996). "Is There an Alternative to (Capitalist) Globalization?" *Boundary 2,* Vol. 23, No. 3, p. 210.

Liu, Miqing (1993). *Contemporary Translation Theories.* Taibei: Bookman Publishers.

Lu, Hsiao-peng (1996). "Postmodernity, Popular Culture, and the Intellectual: A Report on Post-Tiananmen China." *Boundary 2,* Vol. 23, No. 3, pp. 139–64.

Mason, I. and B. Hatim (1989). *Discourse and the Translator.* London: Longman.

Meng, Fanhua (1990). "The Advocacy of Third World Cultural Theory, and the Problems It Faces." *Wenyi zhengming,* No. 6, pp. 36–39.

Peng, Jingxi (1997). *Touching the Elephant.* Taibei: Bookman Publishers.

Schwartz, B. (1964). *In Search of Wealth and Power: Yen Fu and the West.* Cambridge, Mass.: Harvard University Press.

Snell-Hornby, Mary (1988). *Translation Studies: An Integrated Approach.* Amsterdam: John Benjamins.

Tan, Zaixi (1991). *A Short History of Translation in the West.* Beijing: The Commercial Press.

Tang, Xiaobing (1993). "The Function of New Theory: What Does It Mean to Talk about Postmodernism in China?" In Liu Kang and Tang Xiaobing, eds., *Politics, Ideology, and Literary Discourse in Modern China: Theoretical Interventions and Cultural Critique.* Durham: Duke University Press. pp. 278–300.

Tymoczko, Mary (1999). *Translation in a Postcolonial Context: Early Irish Literature in English Translation.* Manchester: St. Jerome Publishing, pp. 41–61.

Venuti, Lawrence, ed. (1992). *Rethinking Translation: Discourse, Subjectivity, Ideology.* New York: Routledge.

Venuti, Lawrence, ed. (1986). "The Translator's Invisibility." *Criticism,* Vol. 28, No. 2, pp. 179–212.

Wang, Fengzhen, *et al.* (1991). *A Selection of the Most Recent Critical Essays in the West.* Guilin: Lijiang Publishing Company.

Wang, Ning (1993). "Constructing Postmodernism: The Chinese Case and Its Different Versions." *Canadian Review of Comparative Literature,* No. 2, pp. 49–61.

Xiao, Liming (1992). *New Explorations in Translation.* Taibei: Bookman Publishers.

Xiao, Peifei (1999). "Orientalism and Self-Orientalizing: The Translation of Western Sinological Works in China in the Eighties and Nineties." Unpublished M.Phil. Thesis, Lingnan University, Hong Kong.

Xin, Xiaozheng and Guo Yinxing (1988). "The Situation of New Theory." *Dangdai zuojia pinglun,* No. 6, p. 10.

Yip, Wai-lim (1994). "Debunking Faithfulness, Comprehensibility and Elegance: The Afterlife of Translations." *Zhongwai wenxue,* Vol. 22, No. 4, pp. 74–84.

Zhang, Jingyuan (1995). *Contemporary Feminist Criticism.* Beijing: Beijing University Press.

Zhang, Yiheng (1995). "'Post-isms' and the New Chinese Conservatism." *Twenty-first Century,* Vol. 27, pp. 4–15.

Zhang, Yiwu (1993). *Searching beyond the Edge.* Beijing: The Times Publishing Company.

Zhao, Jiajin (1996). "A Brief Introduction to Contemporary Schools of Translation." *Chinese Translators Journal,* No. 5, pp. 46–47, 50.

Zhou, Guangqing and Liu Wei (1996). *The Chinese Language and the Modern Chinese Cultural Enlightenment.* Taibei: Dongda Press.

Zou, Zhenhuan (1996). *One Hundred Translations That Had an Impact on Modern Chinese Society.* Beijing: Chinese Translation Company.

Demythologizing Translation Theories

Alan Tse Chung
Division of Language Studies
City University of Hong Kong

There are two major points I would like to make in this short paper. First I wish to stress at the very outset that I am not against theory or theories, as the title of this paper may suggest. You can rest assured that no teaching job is being threatened. It seems that Translation Theories, or course titles to this effect, has become a standard, and to many a translation aspirant, a haunting feature of any decent translation programme. At the same time, we, as teachers of translation, are too familiar with the perennial complaint of our students that they fail to see the practical value of many of these theories, that they are hard put to apply many of them. Have we somewhere along the line misled our students, and even ourselves, to believe that there is always and necessarily an operational link between translation theories and the practice of translation? Let us start off with an oft-quoted cliché. Peter Newmark conveniently assigns an omniscient and omnipresent role to translation theories:

> Translation theory's main concern is to determine appropriate translation methods for the widest possible range of texts or text-categories. Further, it provides a framework of principles, restricted rules and hints for translating texts and criticizing translations, a background for problem-solving. (Newmark, 1988: 19)

The proposition seems to assume that the ultimate mission of translation theories is that they will be applied in some real translation context at the end of the day. This is one of the greatest and tenaciously enshrined myths about translation theory which have generated the utter disappointment of many a translation student as they finally discover that much of what has been taught in a translation theory course has nothing to do with the profession of translation. My position here is simple and straightforward: there are theories which are not supposed to be applied while others may have a more visible applicational nature, or what Gideon

Toury has called the "operational norms." (Toury, 1995) The former, which we may call "theoretical theories," aim at explicating the nature of translation rather than providing practising and prospective professional translators with hard and fast rules. In other words, they exist and are pursued to satisfy our inborn curiosity to unravel the unexplained. We may honestly ask ourselves how many of the theories described in Edwin Gentzler's *Contemporary Translation Theories* (1993) can be readily applied, if they are meant to be applied at all. Compared with the "prescriptive theories" proposed by Etienne Dolet, Tytler, Nida, Yan Fu and the like, which seem to be more application-friendly and application-ready, can we really see any application potential in the so-called polysystem theory or in the comparison of the relationship between the source text and translation to the power relationship between man and woman (Bassnett, 1996: 17), or in Eugene Eoyang's classification of translation into "surrogate translation," "contingent translation" and "coeval translation" (Eoyang, 1993: 144–45), to name but a few examples? In all fairness, Newmark does not confine the identity of translation theory to application. He has actually observed that "…translation theory attempts to give some insight into the relation between thought, meaning and language; the universal, cultural and individual aspects of language and behaviour, the understanding of cultures; the interpretation of texts that may be clarified and even supplemented by way of translation." (Newmark, 1988: 19) All this is of course a truism to most of us. But the real problem is that very few of us go out of our way to tell our students what is obvious to us, so much so that our students have unrealistic expectations about translation theory. By "deconstructing" the myth that there is necessarily an operational link between theory and practice, we can certainly clear the cobwebs and hopefully make our students more receptive and responsive to translation theories.

There is another observation I would like to make on this occasion. And this is directly related to the applicability of operational or methodological translation theories. A theory, and here I have operational theories in mind, being a set of generalizations, is very likely to suffer from its inability of being related or applied to concrete situations. There is always some discrepancy between theory and reality. Having said that, generalizations, despite all their defects and failures, appear to be a necessary evil that any viable society has to live with, not least because: (a) generalization is what the promulgation of human knowledge is all about; any book on any subject, any lecture delivered at a university, is an instance of generalization, a prototypical theory; (b) the very nature of language encourages and facilitates generalization. We have to accept that a theory will, in all probability, collapse in some way when it comes to concrete settings. Most of the time, when we say a certain theory does apply or has been applied to a concrete translation task, we are actually "modifying" the theory and using our own interpretation to suit the circumstances. The discrepancy between theory and practice can be accounted for in terms of the semiotic paradigm of Charles Peirce, the father of modern semiotics. In the first triad of his paradigm, Peirce draws a distinction between the "sign," "interpretant" and the "object." This is how Peirce delimits the sign and the interpretant:

> A sign…is something which stands to somebody for something in some respect or capacity. It addresses somebody, that is, creates in the mind of that person an equivalent sign, or perhaps a more developed sign. That sign which it creates I call the interpretant of the first sign. (Peirce, 1931 II: 135)

The most relevant point in Peirce's postulation is that the interpretant is attributed the quality of endless commutability. In other words, the interpretant can become a sign that produces a new interpretant, and the same operation can occur with each subsequent interpretant. (Silverman, 1983: 15) In other words, in an endless chain of signification, signs always lead to other signs, and every sign is an evolution or translation of another sign. Language, as a set of signs, is open and subject to different interpretations. That is to say, new interpretants keep coming up to cover the old ones. Translation theories, like any other verbal account of any human experience, are every bit encoded in language. Despite their putative mission to give universal guidance to the translator, translation theories are formulated in linguistic signs and as such they have to enter into an interpretive interaction with whoever applies the theory. We may claim, if not to fool our students, that we have applied a certain translation theory in a particular translation task, but most of us will be hard put to give the evidence. The interpretation of translation theory is both essentially and ultimately discursive. In discharging her duties in a given context, the translator is more likely to be guided along or rather, coerced along, by a host or pyramid of contextual factors peculiar to the given translation task. In particular, she will be subjected to what are referred to by Toury as the "matricial norms" and the "textual-linguistic norms," (Toury, 1995) which are long established in a particular field, for example, the translation of documents in a government setting. She will also take into account such factors as the poetics of the time and patronage, the two constraints which André Lefevere expounds in *Translation, Rewriting and the Manipulation of Literary Fame*. (Levevere, 1992) Among these, patronage may, in many cases of professional translation, take precedence over other considerations, not least because "the proof of the pudding is in the eating"! More importantly, all of these contextual factors bear on the translator's interpretation of a theory if he starts off with one. Whether it is a theory or a norm, the translator will anyway mould them, redefine them according to his universe, his model of the world. In the final analysis, in the extreme, and I know this is controversial, there is no theory left except the translator's own.

References

Bassnett, S. (1996). "The Meek or the Mighty: Reappraising the Role of the Translator." In R. Alvarez and M. Carmen-Africa Vidal, eds., *Translation, Power, Subversion*. Clevedon: Multilingual Matters Ltd.

Gentzler, E. (1993). *Contemporary Translation Theories*. London: Routledge.

Lefevere, A. (1992). *Translation, Rewriting, and the Manipulation of Literary Fame*. London: Rouledge.

Neubert, A. and G. M. Shreve (1992). *Translation as Text*. Kent: Kent University Press.

Newmark, P. (1988). *Approaches to Translation*. London: Prentice Hall.

Peirce, C. S. (1931). *The Collected Papers of Charles Sanders Peirce*, eds., Charles Hartshorne and Paul Weiss. Cambridge, Mass.: Harvard University Press.

Silverman, K. (1983). *The Subject of Semiotics*. New York: Oxford University Press.

Translating: It Does Not Matter Whether You Are a Formalist or a Functionalist

He Yuanjian
Department of Translation
The Chinese University of Hong Kong

Introduction

As is well known, modern Translation Studies makes a distinction between the production and the characterization of translation. (Lefevere, 1978, 1992; Holmes, 1972, 1978, 1988 amongst others) *Production* refers to the *translating process* through which an end product, i.e. a piece of translated work, is produced. *Characterization* refers to the description of that end product, no matter from what angle the description may be conducted. Most often, the description falls in either the formalist, i.e. text-based, premises, or the functionalist realm, i.e. a communication-purpose-defined description of translation.

In this paper I make two tentative claims regarding the nature of the translating process. First, the formalist-and-functionalist watershed is justifiable only from the *product* point of view. From the point of view of *translating process*, there is no such a thing as "a formal process" or "a functional process." Secondly, the translating process is one governed by universal cross-linguistic and cross-cultural principles as well as by parameterized factors rooted in individual languages and cultures. I will elaborate on these claims in the following. As a priori to the discussions that follow, it is necessary to reiterate the nomenclature that *translation* is a term that traditionally refers to either *product* or *process*; *translating* the term that refers to *process* only. (cf. Bell, 1990)

Process vs. Product

Holmes (1972), who pioneered the establishment of Translation Studies as an independent discipline, sets off the process-oriented study of translation as one of the three major areas of Translation Studies (the other two areas being product-oriented and function-oriented studies. But, as He (1999) argues, the function-oriented study can be subsumed in the product-oriented study itself). Many authors have so far offered their versions of the mental process involved in the act of translating. (see, for example, Nida and Taber, 1969; Holmes, 1988; Bell, 1990; Honig, 1991; Lorscher, 1986, 1991; Cheung, 1993; Liu, 1998; He, 1999) In particular, Holmes's (1988) "Mapping Theory" has been an inspiration for works reported in Honig (1991) in the area of examining the translation-induced mental process, delivering a better understanding of the process itself. Also, he suggested that introspective methods from psychological studies such as the technique of thinking-aloud could be adopted for investigating the translating process. This suggestion has further prompted the development of more sophisticated methods such as the dialogue protocol by House (1988) and Kußmaul (1991). However, at the current stage of research, our understanding of the process that directly influences our meta-linguistic modeling of it is still rather limited, so are the empirical methods that gain us access to the process.

Conceptually, the actual mental process induced by translation is a "black box," which as Holmes (1988) suggested can be accessed to, more traditionally, by prediction on the basis of analyzing source language text (SLT) in the manner of contrastive linguistics, or by speculative retrospection on the basis of analyzing target language text (TLT) in the manner of translation criticism. (also see Kußmaul 1991) I will assume such approaches here, looking specifically at how the characterization of a piece of TLT *might* reflect the translating process. Pertinent to our discussion, the actual translating process can be very roughly illustrated in (1):

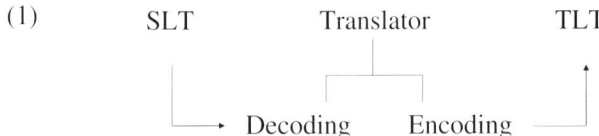

(1)   SLT   Translator   TLT

The end of the process is the TLT, which can be characterized in different ways. For instance:

(2) No Thoroughfare. (i.e. There is no thoroughfare here.)
Through Translation (TT): (這裡) 沒有通路．
(TT is based on sentence constructions.)
Functional Translation (FT): 此路不通．
(FT, as said above, is translation defined by communication purposes.)

(3) No Unauthorized Entry. (i.e. There is no unauthorized entry here.)
Semi-TT: (此地) 不可擅入．
FT: 非請勿進．

(4) Overhead Live Wires. (i.e. There are overhead live wires here.)
TT: 頭上有電線．
FT: 小心懸空高壓電纜．

(5) Exact Fares. (i.e. Please pay exact fares.)
Semi-TT: 付車資請用輔幣．
FT: 自備輔幣，方便快趣．

(6) Please wave for the bus to stop.
TT: 請招手讓司機停車．
FT: 要乘車，揮揮手．

(7) Please do not obstruct the aisle.
TT: 請勿阻塞通道．
FT: 通道無阻，利己利人．

(8) No pets and animals are allowed on bus.
Semi-TT: 請勿攜帶寵物動物上車．
FT: 雞犬不寧，騷擾他人．

(9) We preserve the right to prevent overloading.
TT: 司機有權防止超載．
FT: 超載危險，安全要緊．

In (2)–(9), where the Chinese is the TLT, we have chosen TT (Through Translation), Semi-TT (Semi-through Translation) and FT (Functional Translation) as particular ways to characterize a piece of TLT. Which characterization represents a better TLT depends on the purpose a TLT serves. In the view of some authors (e.g. Nord 1995, 1997a, b), FT should be preferred, at least for TLTs such as (2)–(9) that have a conspicuous utility purpose. But this is not our concern here. Our concern is whether the characterization of a piece of TLT reflects the translating process. If it does, to what extent?

In theory, the possible number of characterizations for a TLT is numerous, and we can illustrate this by representing the characterizations on a continuum:

(10)   TT ... 3/Quarters-TT ... Semi-TT ... Quarter-TT ... FT

Each point, i.e. TT, 3/quarters TT, semi-TT, quarter-TT, and FT, represents a piece of TLT of relevant characterization. To answer the question of whether these characterizations would reflect the translating process, we have to ask further what these characterizations mean in respect to the translating process.

The nature of such characterizations is in my view no more than to serve as indicators that the translator has made a decision to use one type of sentence construction rather than another. If the type of sentence construction that is used in the TLT turns out to be the same as that in the SLT (source language text), then we characterize the translation as Through Translation. If not, we then characterize the translation by way of Semantic or Functional Translation and so on. But bear in mind that in most cases the translator makes a decision without realizing, or caring about, what characterization of his translation would later be. In other words, the decision-making process is one of psycholinguistic nature. (cf. Honig, 1991; Lorscher, 1991) If the characterization of a piece of TLT indicates no more than the translator has (consciously or unconsciously) made a decision in using particular types of sentence construction, then the next question to ask is to what extent such decision-making process affects the translating process as a whole.

Principles vs. Parameters

Unfortunately, the factors that play a role in the decision-making process in question are largely unknown and remain to be better understood in the course of future research. This is exactly part of the reason why we know so little at the moment about the translating process as a whole. This is virtually an untouched ground in Translation Studies in the sense of conducting solid empirical researches (though there has been a tradition of "talking about" the translating process by translators and scholars). However, we may make reasonable assumptions when engaged in the study of this process.

The basic assumption is, as I advocated elsewhere (He and Wei, 1998; He, 1999), that the translating process is one governed by universal principles that apply across languages and across cultures, as well as by parameterized factors that are rooted in individual languages and cultures. The universal principles are not subject to change with the source language and target language pairs, but the parameters will. The principles are likely to be identified in the areas of (1) cognition, (2) linguistic processing, and (3) human cultural and social fundamentals, which intersect with deposits of human languages.

Parameters vary across languages and cultures. If we identify individuals to be unit-elements of their cultures, then the translator represents a parameter that dynamically influences the translating process. This brings us back to the issue of how the decisions made by the translator may affect the translating process. Let us assume that decisions to use one type of sentence construction instead of another are made in the Conceptual-intentional System (a term from Chomsky, 1995), which is part of the cognitive system of the brain. Then the C-I system gives instructions to the mental grammar to process a particular type of construction. But the linguistic processing remains independent of the C-I system. Its job simply is to implement the instructions from the latter. This means that the translator's decisions related to decoding are limited to the C-I system, and have little to do with linguistic processing. In this sense, the way we characterize a piece of translation, such as TT or FT (see (2)–(9)), also has little bearing on the linguistic processing that produces a piece of translation. Of course, linguistic processing is only one part of the translating process, which in my view can be understood only when we have established the system of principles and parameters for translating, a task to be accomplished in the years to come.

References

Bell, R. (1990). *Translation and Translating: Theory and Practice*. London: Longman.

Cheung, M. (1993). 〈《哈姆雷特》疾病比喻的漢譯－翻譯過程的多系統制約探討〉(Translating Disease Metaphors from *Hamlet* into Chinese — An Inquiry into the Multi-system Restraints on the Translation Process: A Comment on Translation by Different Translation Schools). In Eva W. Y. Hung 孔慧怡 and Chu Kwok Fan 朱國藩, eds.,《各師各法談翻譯》(*Views on Translation*). Hong Kong: Ng Tor-tai Chinese Language Research Centre, The Chinese University of Hong Kong, pp. 107–22.

Chomsky, N. (1995). *The Minimalist Program*. Cambridge, Mass.: MIT Press.

He, Y. (1999). "Translating: Toward a Principles-and-parameters Theory." *Journal of Translation Studies*, No. 3, pp. 97–114.

He, Y. and Wei Z. (1998). 〈描寫譯學的研究與運用〉(Descriptive Translation Studies: Theory and Practice).《外語與翻譯》(*Journal of Foreign Languages and Translation*), No. 1, pp. 1–9.

Holmes, James S. (1972). *The Name and Nature of Translation Studies.* Amsterdam: Translation Studies Section, University of Amsterdam.

Holmes, James S. (1978). "Describing Literary Translations: Models and Methods." In J. Holmes *et. al.*, eds., *Literature and Translation: New Perspectives in Literary Studies.* Leuven: Acco, pp. 69–82.

Holmes, James S. (1988) "Translation Theory, Translation Theories, Translation Studies, and the Translator." In J. Holmes (1988). *Translated! Papers on Literary Translation and Translation Studies.* Amsterdam: Rodopi, pp. 93–8.

Honig, H. G. (1991). " Holmes' 'Mapping Theory' and the Landscape of Mental Translation Process." In K. M. van Leuven-Zwart and T. Naaikens, eds., *Translation Studies: The State of the Art.* Amsterdam: Rodopi, pp. 77–90.

House, J. (1988). "Talking to Oneself or Thinking with Others." *Fremdsprachen Lehren und Lernen, FluL,* pp. 84–98.

Kußmaul, P. (1991). "Creativity in the Translation Process: Empirical Approaches." In K. M. van Leuven-Zwart and T. Naaikens, eds., *Translation Studies: The State of the Art.* Amsterdam: Rodopi, pp. 91–101.

Lefevere, A. (1978). "Translation Studies: The Goal of the Discipline." In J. Holmes *et. al.* eds., *Literature and Translation: New Perspectives in Literary Studies.* Leuven: Acco, pp. 234–35.

Lefevere, A., ed. (1992). *Translation/History/Culture: A Sourcebook.* London: Routledge.

Liu, Miqing (1998). 〈文化翻譯探索－兼評 David Hawkes 譯屈原「天問」〉(Explorations into Cultural Translation—On David Hawkes's Translation of Qu Yuan's *Tian Wen*). *Humanity Journal*, No. 5, pp. 24–40.

Lorscher, Wolfgang (1986). "Linguistic Aspects of the Translation Process." In J. House and S. Blum-Kulka, eds., *Interlingual and Intercultural Communication: Discourse and Cognition in Translation and Second Language Acquisition Studies.* Tubingen: Gunther Narr.

Lorscher, Wolfgang (1991). *Translation Performance, Translation Process and Translation Strategies: A Psycholinguistic Investigation.* Tubingen: Gunther Narr.

Nida, E. and C. Taber (1969). *The Theory and Practice of Translation.* Leiden: E. J. Brill.

Nord, C. (1995). "Text Functions in Translation: Titles and Headings as a Case in Point." *Target,* Vol. 7, pp. 261–84.

Nord, C. (1997a). *Translating as a Purposeful Activity.* Manchester: St. Jerome.

Nord, C. (1997b). "A Functional Typology of Translations." In A. Trosborg, ed., *Scope and Skopos in Translation.* Amsterdam: John Benjamins.

Translating for the Financial Market in Hong Kong

Kenneth Au Kim-lung
Department of Chinese, Translation and Linguistics
City University of Hong Kong

Introduction

The financial market in Hong Kong, to begin with, has enjoyed a period of rapid growth in recent years and a sophisticated network of financial institutions has evolved offering a wide range of products and services. The success of Hong Kong as a financial centre is evident in the following impressive statement on the achievement of Hong Kong in the "Welcome Message" on the homepage of Financial Services Bureau of the Hong Kong SAR Government:

> Hong Kong is now the ninth largest banking centre in the world in terms of external transactions, tenth largest stock market in terms of market capitalization, and seventh largest financial centre in terms of foreign exchange turnover and sixteenth largest in terms of interest rate and foreign exchange derivatives turnover. (Financial Services Bureau, 1999a: 1)

English is generally adopted as the medium of business and finance in Hong Kong, an international financial centre. But the majority of the people here are Chinese, and the Chinese language has become another official language in Hong Kong, in addition to English. So in order to facilitate communication with the general public, it is essential for the companies concerned to produce both Chinese and English versions of these financial texts. For instance, it is stipulated in *Rules Governing the Official Listing of Securities* by the Stock Exchange of Hong Kong that "prospectuses must be printed in sufficient numbers and must be duly advertised in one leading English newspaper and in one leading Chinese newspaper in Hong Kong." (Hong Kong Stock Exchange, 1986: 8)

The prosperous growth of the financial market in Hong Kong creates a huge demand for translating services which are indispensable in the process of producing a diversity of bilingual financial documents, such as annual reports, interim reports, prospectuses, financial circulars, public announcements. The trend is even more evident as more and more "red chip" companies and Chinese state-owned enterprises have sought listings in the local bourse ever since the milestone issue of H-shares by Tsingtao Brewery in Hong Kong in July 1993.

The recent boom of the cyber business and e-commerce also has boosted the demand for translating services of financial texts as many bilingual financial writers, editors and translators are needed for the financial websites and internet content providers.

This paper outlines the scenario of the profession of financial translation in Hong Kong with some brief descriptions of the opportunities and challenges faced by financial translators. Efficiency and accuracy are the keywords of the industry, as financial translators have to rush through large piles of source texts to meet tight deadlines on the one hand, and struggle with specialized terminology and complicated sentence structures on the other. With the advancement of modern information technology, financial translators can gain access to the vast ocean of related information on the Internet, and communicate with other practitioners in cyberspace, thus their pain in translating is alleviated to some extent. Finally, some suggestions on the training of financial translators in tertiary institutions are made with the aim of helping translators to face the keen competition in the local translation market and the market in Mainland China, where the labour cost is relatively lower.

Financial Translation: A Profitable Business?

Financial translation is a broad term for the translation tasks of a variety of financial documents including annual reports and interim reports of listed companies, prospectuses for the exercise of initial public offerings (IPO), investment reports, public announcements and financial circulars issued by the listed companies, memoranda and articles of associations, and investment reports. The huge volume of these documents creates an enormous market for financial translation services. According to the webpage of the Financial Services Bureau, by the end of August 1999, for instance, there were 688 companies listed on the Stock Exchange of Hong Kong with a total market capitalization of HK$3,587 billion, making Hong Kong the second largest stock market in Asia in terms of market capitalization. Each of these listed companies produces an annual report and an interim report in both Chinese and English every year. A steady source of income is thus generated for the translation agencies specialising in financial translation.

In addition, there are statutory requirements for listed companies to disclose price-sensitive information related to certain categories of transactions. Since the disclosure must be in the form of public announcements in both Chinese and English local newspapers, there is a strong demand for the translation of these announcements, and hence another steady source of income for financial translators.

Perhaps it is the production of a bilingual prospectus for the initial public offerings (IPO) of a company at the Stock Exchange of Hong Kong that generates the greatest income for financial translators in a single piece of work. It usually takes months of preparation work before the details of the prospectus can be finalized and translated into Chinese. Ever since the milestone issue of H-shares by Tsingtao Brewery in Hong Kong in July 1993, the local bourse has been playing its role of a capital-formation centre for Chinese enterprises. By the end of March 1998, there were 43 Chinese state-owned enterprises that had raised a total of more than HK$60 billion through their initial public offerings. In addition, there were 45 "red chip" companies incorporated and listed in Hong Kong that are controlled by PRC interests. So the close economic ties between Hong Kong and China have greatly boosted the demand for financial translation services.

In addition, the growth of the dotcom business and the resultant proliferation of e-commerce in recent years also boosted the demand for translating services of financial texts. In order to build up a bilingual financial websites and update them later, either the dotcoms themselves or the internet content providers (ICP) recruit a large number of bilingual translators or bilingual financial writers to translate or re-write Chinese and English financial information. The strong demand provides a very good prospect for the financial translation practitioners and attracts many people to join the profession of financial translation.

Challenges Faced by Financial Translators

Financial texts are factual in nature. They aim at providing accurate and updated information in the financial market to the investors. As long as the information is accurately transmitted, the translation task is successful. Given their pragmatic function, they tend to pose fewer difficulties than literary texts to translators.

However, financial translators have to face other challenges which translators of literary texts might not have. Firstly, financial translators have to meet stringent deadlines. As many financial documents are either prepared in a hurry, or revised frequently, translators are given very limited time to complete their task. So a competent financial translator must also be an efficient translator. He has to rush through large piles of source texts in order to meet the tight deadlines. The situation is aggravated during the peak season from April to August when most companies are busy preparing their annual reports to be sent to their shareholders for consideration before the annual general meeting.

As for the dotcom business and e-commerce, keen competition among the financial websites rules out the possibility of allowing the translators sufficient time to finish the work. As a result, the quality of the translation might be affected, as Aubert voices out a concern of the profession: "the relevance of the time factor i.e., of cut-throat deadlines, as a major conditioning factor of performance in professional translation." (Aubert, 1995: 122)

Accuracy is another challenge for financial translators. In the process of preparation, financial texts are subject to frequent revisions and updating. More often than not, some parts of the translation are rendered useless and the efforts of the translator are drained. The translator will also be easily confused with the different versions given at various points of time as he is already working under great time constraint. An inadvertent mistake would cost millions of dollars. For example, in one case, the currency "US dollar (US$)" was mistranslated as "Hong Kong dollar (HK$)," and in another, the quantity "one billion" (1,000,000,000) was mistranslated as "一億" (100,000,000).

Financial terminology and syntactical structures are the major linguistic challenges a financial translator has to face. Different domains of subject have different sets of terminology. The financial translator should be sensitive enough to apply the right set of terminology to the text in question. For example, the term "margin" can be rendered differently under different contexts. In the stock market, the word "margin" refers to the "money or securities deposited by a client with a stockbroker as security against the client's failure to pay for deals about to be made for him by the stockbroker." (Adam, 1995: 518) It can be rendered as "保證金," or is even more commonly known as "孖展" in Hong Kong. But the term "profit margin" has often been mistranslated into "邊際利潤," which actually means "marginal profit," an economic concept referring to the additional profit derived from an additional input of resources. A more appropriate translation for "profit margin" should be "利潤率，盈利率," or "利潤幅度," which is "the relationship between profit and selling price." (Adam, 1995: 517)

Another hurdle for the financial translator to overcome is the long and complex syntactical structures in financial documents. It is not uncommon to find long sentences in financial texts, which are usually formed by the use of passive voice and multiple negatives ("No adjustments shall be made to the sale consideration if the net asset value difference does not exceed 5% of the deemed net asset value"), or excessive definitions ("The Stock Exchange of Hong Kong Limited (the 'Stock Exchange')"). While the complexity and subtlety of financial transactions might dictate the use of lengthy structures, the readers (including the translator) easily get lost after the twist and turn of the sentences. The following example was cited in a report by Securities and Futures Commission of Hong Kong, the regulating body overseeing the operation of the stock market and futures market, to illustrate how the clumsy structure of the long sentence hinders comprehension. It is made up of 83 words, posing considerable difficulties for the financial translator:

> The rights shares to which overseas shareholders would otherwise have been entitled and any rights shares arising from the aggregation of fractional entitlements to the rights shares and which, in each case, are not sold as described herein, and any rights shares allotted provisionally but not accepted, will be made available for application on the form of application for excess rights shares by qualifying shareholders and will be allocated on an equitable basis to be decided by the directors at their sole discretion.
>
> 原應配發予海外股東而未經以本文所指的方式出售的供股股份及任何因彙集零碎供股股份所得而未經以本文所指的方式出售的供股股份，以及任何已暫定配發而未獲接納的供股股份，將可供合資格股束以額外供股股份申請表格申請認購，並將按董事以全權酌情決定之公平基準予以分配。(Securities and Futures Commission, 1999: 6)

In order to promote the use of simple sentences in financial documents, Securities and Futures Commission had set up a working group to conduct a project on the use of plain language. Two on-line documents were released in July 1997 and January 1998 respectively, suggesting ways to write announcements and prospectuses in plain language. It is hoped that the project will foster the use of a simpler and clearer language in financial documents, thus facilitating a smoother translation process and a more readable translation.

The greatest challenge of the financial translators perhaps comes from the keen competition of their counterparts in Mainland China, where translation fee is much lower than that in Hong Kong. With the widespread use of information technology, such as the Internet and emails, outsourcing of translation jobs in China becomes possible as the dispatch of work and delivery of completed job can be conducted within seconds. In order to stay competitive, local translators have to lower their translation charges on the one hand, and develop their competitive edge on the other.

Pedagogical Implications

Nearly all tertiary institutions in Hong Kong offer translation programmes with various characteristics. Financial translation is an integral part of these programmes as it serves the purpose of meeting the genuine needs of the financial markets and the business environment of Hong Kong.

Given the great opportunities offered by the business boom and the development of E-commerce, and in response to the various challenges mentioned above, appropriate approaches should be adopted for financial translation.

First, financial translation courses should be designed to increase students' awareness and understanding of the actual operation of the financial world. Teaching materials should be updated frequently which should provide students "with a well-designed and succinct introduction to the procedures and operations involved in business and trade activities." (Li, 1999: 200)

Second, both local and overseas translation scholars agree that authentic tasks, instead of didactic translation, should be designed in translation classes, because the translation exercises done in classroom will be totally different from what professional translators are doing in the real world. The complexities of real-life translation therefore will be apparent in the teaching materials. (Li, 1999; Zeng and Lu-Chen, 2000) Students will be given some timed assignments in order to have some training in working under great pressure. With the joint efforts of teachers and professional translators, appropriate teaching materials can be incorporated into the course, whereby financial terminology and the structural features of financial publications can be studied in detail.

Thirdly, given the broad range of subject areas in commercial and financial translation, despite the hard work of teachers, students are still not able to learn everything. So there is a growing awareness of the inclusion of a top-down approach in curriculum design. (Almberg, 1997; Zeng and Lu-Chen, 2000) Students will be able to expand "not only from the word to the text but from skills to visions." (Almberg, 1997: 37)

Lastly, the use of information technology should also be incorporated into the curriculum so that the students can gain access to the vast ocean of related information on the Internet and work more efficiently. With sufficient exposure to the IT industry, students might also be more confident when translating for the financial dotcoms.

Conclusion

Financial translation is a rewarding but challenging profession that offers both opportunities and challenges. The steady growth of the financial market of Hong Kong, the increasing fund-raising activities in the local bourse and the gradual integration of Hong Kong with the Chinese financial market have generated a stronger demand for financial translation than before. The tight deadlines, the technicality of the financial subject matter, and the terminological/syntactical problems in translating are all but a few hurdles for the translators to overcome.

With the advancement of modern information technology, financial translators can easily search for useful information on the Internet, and communicate more closely with other practitioners in cyberspace, thus facilitating a smoother translation process. It is hoped that a well-designed curriculum and good teaching materials can improve the training of financial translators in tertiary institutions. Our graduates will thus be more adequately equipped with financial knowledge and the translation skills so as to meet the keen competition in the local translation market and the market in Mainland China, where the labour cost is relatively lower.

References

Adam, J. H. (1995). *Longman English-Chinese Dictionary of Business English.* Hong Kong: Longman.

Almberg, E. S. P. (1997). "Where to Begin: Top-down or Bottom-up." *Proceedings of the Conference on Translation Teaching,* 2–4 December. Hong Kong: The Chinese University of Hong Kong, pp. 32–39.

Aubert, Francis Henrik (1995). "Translation Theory, Teaching and the Profession." *Perspectives: Studies in Translatology,* Vol. 3, No. 1, pp. 121–31.

Financial Services Bureau, Hong Kong SAR Government (2000a). "Welcome Message." http://www.info.gov.hk/welcome/index.htm. 15 June.

Financial Services Bureau, Hong Kong SAR Government (2000b). "Fact Sheet on Financial Services." 15 June. http://www.info.gov.hk/fsb/fs/index.htm.

Li, Defeng (1999). "The Teaching of Commercial Translation in Hong Kong: Problems and Perspectives." *Babel*, Vol. 45, No. 3, pp. 193–204.

Securities and Futures Commission. "Project on the Use of Plain Language." 15 June. http://www.hksfc.org.hk/eng/reg/issuer.htm.

Stock Exchange of Hong Kong Ltd. (1986). *Rules Governing the Official Listing of Securities*. Second Edition.

Zeng, Suzanne M. and Jung Ying Lu-Chen (2000). "Task-based Translator Training, Quality Assessment, and the WWW." 8 June. http://nts.lll.hawaii.edu/lu/TBTT/Default.htm.

Subtitling in Hong Kong

Yiu Po Kwong
Ming Pao Daily News

For years scholars have laid so great a stress on the translation of literature, such as novels, drama, prose and poems, that the rendition of movie subtitles has been neglected. In fact, subtitling translation should not be overlooked, because ninety-five per cent of moviegoers cannot understand the English dialogue. They count on reading the Chinese subtitles to understand the storyline of the movie. Such being the case, it is generally known that no cinema, or television series for that matter, would dare show an English language programme without Chinese subtitles.

We all know that a popular television episode in Hong Kong will be seen by millions of viewers at the same time and the majority will need Chinese subtitles. Subtitles can also be a useful medium by which they can learn the norms of spoken English. Movies and television programmes, which are full of colloquialisms, provide a practical and interesting way of making language-learning fun. Therefore, subtitling translation should not be any less important than the translation of literature.

Thirty years ago, there was no translation department at any university in Hong Kong; so the motion picture companies and television stations were hard pressed to find anyone with the expertise needed to translate movie dialogue. Translators in those years were not very familiar with American colloquial expressions so many amusing and alarming mistakes occurred when they subtitled. Let's look at some specific examples:

1. *Get it off your chest.* This line was rendered into "take off your bra." In a certain children's movie, this meant "just say it."
2. *John is <u>having a cow</u>.* He said that we were short the other night. "Having a cow" was rendered into "in possession of a cow." That was a big mistake as well. This idiom means "angry and upset." This sort of mistake can confuse television viewers.
3. *If you think you are near enough, <u>draw</u>.* In a duel between two cowboys, one of them challenged the other to pull out their gun. The word "draw" was wrongly translated into "paint a picture."

4. *Her mother is a <u>sister</u> in a Melbourne hospital.* In this line it does not indicate a family relationship. It only means a senior nurse in a hospital.

5. *He's unhappy now, because he had a <u>blue</u> with his girlfriend just now.* In this line, "blue" means an argument, fight or quarrel. It has nothing to do with colour.

6. *Last evening I went to a <u>do</u>.* Here "do" means social function.

7. *The See of Finding.* Here the word "See" means the official seat of a bishop.

8. *You can say that again.* This is an American expression. It means, "You are entirely correct."

9. *You don't say.* It is often wrongly rendered into "Stop talking." Actually, this expression means, "Really?"

10. *I don't <u>buy</u> that.* In this line "buy" doesn't mean to purchase something. It actually means, "believe."

11. *I thought that I could <u>crash with</u> you.* The idiomatic expression "crash with" means, "stay at someone's place." It is often mistakenly translated into "Collide with."

12. *The drinks are on the house.* It doesn't mean that the drinks are on top of the house. So when you hear this expression don't bring your friends to the penthouse for drinks. This line only means the drinks are free.

13. *You bet.* It doesn't mean that you do the gambling. It means "of course."

14. *Take care of him.* This is a tricky line that has two entirely different meanings. It can mean, "look after him" or "kill him" simply depending on the mood and tone of the actor who delivers it.

15. *I'm from Missouri.* This is a typical American expression. The actor who says that may not actually come from this state. It actually means, "I won't believe it until I see it."

The above examples only show a small portion of the mistakes made in the subtitling translation process from English into Chinese in the 1960s and 1970s.

In the 1990s, translators have made great progress in subtitling translation because they have improved their understanding of both British and American expressions. However there are still not enough good translators working in television stations or film distribution companies.

As Hong Kong is still in a period of recession and underemployment, I would like to suggest that universities in the city should consider providing subtitling translation courses. This can serve a dual purpose: help students improve their bilingual capabilities and offer them more job opportunities.

The Internet and Translation Studies in Hong Kong

Lai Swee Fo
Department of Translation
The Chinese University of Hong Kong.

I would like to discuss several aspects of the connection between the Internet and translation studies. On the most basic level, there are many kinds of websites on the Internet these days that can help the translator or a researcher in translation studies to find a great deal of useful material, and help them to solve simple problems relatively quickly. All those who have used the Internet should be aware of this function.

For example, a few days ago, I consulted the *Dissertation Abstract International* to find out the title and thesis of a Ph.D. dissertation written by a professor in the English Department at the University of Hong Kong. All I had to do was to enter the Professor's name in English, and all the essential information I need, especially the abstract of the dissertation, appeared on my computer screen in less than a minute. In addition to the *Dissertation Abstract International,* quite a number of major bibliographies, like the *MLA International Bibliography,* and standard reference books like the *Encyclopedia Britannica,* are already available on the Internet. Searching on the web is much quicker than if I went to the library myself. Speed and convenience are the two most important aspects of the Internet. It provides some of the most basic assistance to modern scholarly research. (Bynum, 1998; Ferrante-Wallace, 1998; Hall, 1998; Kurland, 1997; O'Donnell, 1997)

But the Internet does much more than this. Most people haven't realized that there are more and more electronic texts on the Internet, and they are getting better and better all the time. When the Internet began to gain popularity, around 1993 and 1994, some of the most important works of western literature, such as Homer's *Odyssey* and the Greek tragedies, were made into electronic texts and were placed on the web. However, the quality of those early electronic texts was not good, since the best texts were often not selected mainly for copyright reasons. The *Odyssey,* for example, was made available in an outdated English translation done in the nineteenth century or the early twentieth century, since the copyright of these early translations has expired. The latest and the best English translations, such as those of Richard Lattimore and Robert Fagles, are still not available on the Internet, for copyright reasons.

In the last two years, however, I have discovered more and more electronic texts of a much higher quality on the Internet. We should take note of this. For example, a few weeks ago, I was surprised to find that someone had put James Joyce's monumental work *Ulysses,* in its entire English original, on the Internet, along with the Chinese translation by Xiao Qian 蕭乾 and Wen Jieruo 文潔若. These parallel texts contain some seven to eight hundred pages. Electronic texts, especially in bilingual editions, are very useful for translation studies, since they are what we call "machine readable" texts. The computer is able to read it and allows us to do a variety of searches and comparisons. (Baker, 1993, 1995, 1996; Far, 1996; Flowerdew, 1994; Lindquist, 1984; Sinclair, 1987 and 1991; Svartvik, 1996)

This brings to mind the research project "Theory and Practice in Descriptive Translation Studies," (He and Wei, 1998) in which Professor He Yuanjian of The Chinese University and Professor Wei Zhiqiang of the Chinese Academy of Social Sciences, make a comparative study of the two Chinese versions of the Japanese classic novel *Genji Monogatari* 《源氏物語》 (*The Tale of Genji),* as translated by Lin Wenyue 林文月 and Feng Zikai 豐子愷. They have analysed and compared the frequency and distribution of certain syntactic structures used in the two Chinese translations. After talking to Professor Wei when he recently visited Hong Kong, I realized that much time and energy was spent in counting such syntactic structures manually. I think if someone had already put these translations into electronic form on the Internet at that time, then it would have saved the researchers a lot of time and trouble in statistics gathering.

Therefore, I think the most immediate impact of electronic texts on translation studies will be seen in descriptive translation studies. Descriptive translation studies is a relatively new field that has risen in recent years, especially after the publication of *Descriptive Translation Studies and Beyond* by Gideon Toury in 1995.

In the three papers on descriptive translation studies by Mona Baker of the University of Manchester that first appeared in 1993, 1995 and 1996, she makes the point that corpora will have a great impact on descriptive translation studies, on the making of bilingual dictionaries and on the compilation and management of specialist terminologies. But when Baker published her papers in 1993, 1995 and 1996, there were not as many electronic texts on the web as now, so she did not mention electronic texts. What she had in mind are the more traditional "corpora." Since then, what is available on the Internet is more and more advanced than what Baker has anticipated at that time. (Laviosa, 1998; Tymoczko, 1998)

These electronic texts will open up many areas of research. As to how they are to be used, it is entirely up to one's imagination. (Laviosa, 1998; McEnery, 1993; Thomas, 1996, Aijmer, 1991; Ljung, 1997) For the sake of brevity let me give an example to illustrate how electronic texts could be put to good use.

As we all know, the Hong Kong Government is the biggest employer of Chinese-English translators in the territory. It is also probably the organization responsible for putting the largest amount of bilingual Chinese-English electronic texts on the web. For instance, the most recent financial budget and the seven-volume report on the new airport are now freely available on the Internet. Not only are they bilingual, but they can also be downloaded to one's personal computer, making it ideal for further research and the creation of translation teaching materials. (Ebeling, 1998; Bowker, 1998; Munday, 1998; Zanettin, 1998)

I am very interested in the Hong Kong Government's two electronic databases: the *Bilingual Laws Information System* on the Department of Justice website and the *Chinese-English Bilingual Legislative Records (Hansard)*. These two databases are huge. The *Bilingual Laws Information System,* for example, contains the entire set of Hong Kong ordinances and other legal documents in both Chinese and English. According to a statement in its home page, it has as many as "95,000 pages." If a book has 200 pages, then "95,000 pages" is equivalent to more than 400 volumes.

By my calculations, there are probably about 5 million Chinese characters and 3 million English words in the bilingual *Hansard,* and it is getting larger and larger all the time, since the Legislative Council sits nearly every week. Every time they meet, they produce about 150 pages of Chinese and 100 pages of English transcript, so the amount that accumulates after a year is staggering. As Mona Baker in her 1993 paper points out, there are many monolingual databases in the world (a fairly well-known example in Chinese is the *Twenty-four Dynastic Histories* full-text database developed by the Academia Sinica in Taipei). But there are very few bilingual full-text databases. She cites the Canadian parliamentary *Hansard* in English and French as an example. Now we can of course add Hong Kong *Hansard* in Chinese and English.

How are these two Hong Kong databases useful to our translation studies? What comes to my mind are the latest software tools in computer-aided translation (CAT). Using these software tools in conjunction with the bilingual databases, perhaps we could create a large-scale translation database called *translation memory*. This then can be used in translation studies, and in the translation of government documents.

The principle behind translation-memory databases is really very simple. First we have to break up the whole *Hansard* database into individual sentences, and link up the original and translated sentences, one by one. Technically, this is called "alignment," a somewhat tedious and time-consuming process that can now be handled by CAT software tools. In this way, a huge database of translation memory can be built up, readily available for retrieval as the occasion demands. (Kay, 1993; Ker, 1997) In other words, such a database is like a memory. It collects the valuable translation experience of countless translators in the legislature and stores it in the computer's memory, all ready for immediate recall. (Clark, 1994)

After such a translation-memory database has been set up, when we encounter a new sentence in translating official government documents, the computer system is able to search its translation memory, to see if that sentence has been previously translated or not. If it has, the original and the translated sentence will appear side by side on the screen. The translator's task then is to decide whether the previously translated sentence is acceptable or not. If it is, then all it takes is a click of the mouse, without having to translate that sentence again.

If there is no exact 100% match, the computer will find a nearly identical or similar sentence, and the translator can use it for reference or modification. After modifying it, this new sentence will also be stored in the translation-memory database. Therefore, the more you use this translation system, the richer its translation memory will be. It will thus become more and more "intelligent," amounting to a kind of artificial intelligence (Trados, 1999).

This system can even put into its memory many of the tricky problems of English-Chinese translation as discussed by Cai Siguo 蔡思果 in his numerous articles and books. It can also store those frequently made errors in translating government documents as mentioned by Professor Serena Jin, so that future translators using this memory will not repeat the same errors.

This system will also be able to help us to make proper use of specialized technical terms that have been translated before, saving a lot of the translator's time in consulting dictionaries. We can even use what the CAT system calls "automatic terminology management software tools," such as *MultiTerm* and *StarTerm,* to compile a series of standard Hong Kong glossaries and specialized terminologies, extracting terms from the two government databases. This kind of terminology management will be corpus-based, thus avoiding many of the problems encountered when manually compiling glossaries and terminologies as in the past. With the aid of translation memory, coverage will be complete and thorough, selection will no longer be arbitrary, compilation will be less time-consuming, and computer searches can be easily performed. (Ahmad, 1992; Pearson, 1998; Sager, 1994)

Since computer memory is "perfect," it would be best to entrust such a tedious and repetitive task to the computer. And we as human translators could have more time to do more creative and stimulating work.

Since government documents, especially legal contracts, tend to be rather repetitive in nature, sentences that have been translated in the past can be used over and over again, without the need for new translators to re-translate them every time they occur. This kind of computer-aided translation system is especially suitable for the translation of government documents, legal contracts, commercial, scientific and technical papers. But it would not be useful when it comes to literary texts, since such texts are seldom repetitive.

As I was writing this paper, thoughts of IBM's famous computer Deep Blue came to mind, because of the stir it created when it defeated world chess Grand Master Gary Kasparov in May 1997. Some might say that a computer has defeated the human mind. But I am afraid this is not so. Deep Blue was able to defeat Kasparov because it could store a huge number of brilliant chess moves made by the past grand masters in its memory. After every move made by Kasparov, it was able to search its memory for many brilliant moves that had been used in the past and come up with the best solution. In other words, it was actually drawing on human experience accumulated in the past.

That is why our translation-memory database has much to learn from Deep Blue. We should be prepared to store in this translation memory not only existing translated documents from the Hong Kong government, but also some of the most brilliant and ingenious solutions in this field of translation. In the future, when a novice translator encounters a new sentence, he would have a "secret weapon" to use and become almost like a professional.

I have seen demonstrations of this technology. I am aware that some of the biggest translation companies in the world, especially those in Europe, are using this translation-memory database to translate business, scientific, technical and legal documents (Trados, 1999), so I am confident that it will work in the English-Chinese context as well. Perhaps in the next few years, after our translation-memory database has been built up, we will have a "secret weapon" with which to improve the quality as well as the speed in the translation of government, business, scientific and technical documents in Hong Kong.

Translated by Jennifer Eagleton

References

Ahmad, K., A. Davies, H. Fulford and M. Rogers (1994). "What Is a Term? The Semi-automatic Extraction of Terms from Text." In Mary Snell Hornby *et al.*, eds., *Translation Studies: An Interdiscipline.* Amsterdam/Philadelphia: John Benjamins.

Aijmer, Karin and Bengt Altenberg, eds. (1991). *English Corpus Linguistics: Studies in Honour of Jan Svartvik.* London: Longman.

Baker, Mona (1995). "Corpora in Translation Studies: An Overview and Some Suggestions for Future Research." *Target,* Vol. 7, No. 2, pp. 223–43.

Baker, Mona (1993). "Corpus Linguistics and Translation Studies: Implications and Applications." In Mona Baker, Gill Francis and Elena Tognini-Bonelli, eds. *Text and Technology: In Honour of John Sinclair.* Amsterdam/Philadelphia: John Benjamins, pp. 233–50.

Baker, Mona (1996). "Corpus-based Translation Studies: The Challenges that Lie Ahead." In Harold Somers, ed., *Terminology, LSP and Translation: Studies in Language Engineering, in Honour of Juan C. Sager.* Amsterdam/Philadelphia: John Benjamins, pp. 175–86.

Bowker, Lynne (1998). "Using Specialized Monolingual Native-Language Corpora as a Translation Resource: A Pilot Study." *Meta,* Vol. 43, No. 4, pp. 631–50.

Bynum, Terrell Ward and James H. Moor, eds. (1998). *The Digital Phoenix: How Computers Are Changing Philosophy.* Oxford: Blackwell.

Clark, Robert (1994). "Computer-assisted Translation: The State of the Art." In Cay Dollerup and Annette Lindegaard, eds., *Teaching Translation and Interpreting 2: Insights, Aims, Visions.* Amsterdam/Philadelphia: John Benjamins, pp. 301–8.

Ebeling, Jarle (1998). "Contrastive Linguistics, Translation, and Parallel Corpora." *Meta,* Vol. 43, No. 4, pp. 602–15.

Far, Ali Khazaee (1996). "Towards a Corpus-based, Decoding Translation Dictionary." *Babel,* Vol. 42, No. 3, pp.129–40.

Ferrante-Wallace, Joan (1998). *Let's Go Anthropology: Travels on the Internet.* Belmont, California: Wadsworth Publishing.

Flowerdew, Lynne and K. K. Tong, eds. (1994). *Entering Text.* Hong Kong: Language Centre, The Hong Kong University of Science and Technology.

Hall, Georganna (1998). *The Internet Guide for Accounting.* Cincinnati, Ohio: South-Western College Publishing.

He, Yuanjian and Wei Zhiqiang 何元建，衛志強 (1998).〈描寫譯學的理論和實踐：《源氏物語》兩個中譯本中轉折句的對比分析〉(Theory and Practice in Descriptive Translation Studies). 《中國翻譯》(*Chinese Translators Journal*), No. 2, pp. 17–20.

Kay, M. and M. Roscheisen (1993). "Text-translation Alignment." *Computational Linguistics,* Vol. 19, No. 1, pp. 121–42.

Ker, S. J. and J. S. Chang (1997). "A Class-based Approach to Word Alignment." *Computational Linguistics,* Vol. 23, No. 2, pp. 313–43.

Kurland, Daniel J. (1997). *Internet Guide for Sociology: For the Practice of Social Research.* Belmont, California: Wadsworth Publishing.

Laviosa, Sara (1998). "The Corpus-based Approach: A New Paradigm in Translation Studies." *Meta,* Vol. 43, No. 4, pp. 474–79.

Lindquist, Hans (1984). "The Use of Corpus-based Studies in the Preparation of Handbooks for Translators." Wolfram Wilss and Gisela Thome, eds., *Translation Theory and Its Implementation in the Teaching of Translating and Interpreting.* Tubingen: Narr, pp. 260–70.

Ljung, Magnus, ed. (1997). *Corpus-based Studies in English.* Amsterdam: Rodopi.

McEnery, T. and A. Wilson (1993). *Corpora and Translation: Uses and Future Prospects.* Lancaster: Unit for Computer Research on the English Language Technical Paper 2.

Munday, Jeremy (1998). "A Computer-assisted Approach to the Analysis of Translation Studies." *Meta,* Vol. 43, No. 4, pp. 542–56.

O'Donnell, K. and L. Winger (1997). *The Internet for Scientists.* Melbourne: Harwood Academic Publishers.

Pearson, Jennifer (1998). *Terms in Context.* Amsterdam: John Benjamins.

Sager, J. C. (1994). *Language Engineering and Translation: Consequences of Automation.* Amsterdam/Philadelphia: John Benjamins.

Sinclair, John (1987). *Looking Up: An Account of the COBUILD Project in Lexical Computing.* London: Collins.

Sinclair, John (1991). *Corpus, Concordance, Collocation.* Oxford: Oxford University Press.

Svartvik, Jan (1996). "Corpora Are Becoming Mainstream." In Thomas *et al,* 1996, pp. 3–13.

Thomas, Jenny and Mick Short, eds. (1996). *Using Corpora for Language Research: Studies in the Honour of Geoffrey Leech.* London: Longman.

Toury, G. (1995). *Descriptive Translation Studies and Beyond.* Amsterdam/ Philadelphia: John Benjamins.

Trados (1999). *Translator's Workbench for Windows: Workflow Manual.* Stuttgart: Trados.

Tymoczko, Maria (1998). "Computerized Corpora and the Future of Translation Studies." *Meta,* Vol. 43, No. 4, pp. 652–59.

Zanettin, Federico (1998). "Bilingual Comparable Corpora and the Training of Translators." *Meta,* Vol. 43, No. 4, pp. 616–30.

Machine Translation in Hong Kong

Chan Sin-wai
Department of Translation
The Chinese University of Hong Kong

Machine translation is rapidly becoming one of the most important areas of development in recent decades in the field of translation. As knowledge explosion becomes acute, the translation of a large amount of information in different domains and through various channels is a daily headache. In a recent lecture given by Eugene A. Nida, we were told that in Europe, nearly 30% of official documents are now translated by computers alone. And it is hoped that the percentage can be raised to 50% in a few years' time. This is a clear indication that machine translation will take up more and more of the work originally handled by a human translator. It is against this background that we look back on what has been achieved so far and what needs to be done in future.

In Hong Kong, early efforts were made at The Chinese University in the late 1960s and there is strong indication that with the rapid advances made in the areas of computer science and computational linguistics, and aided by the government's promotion of technology, interest in machine translation will be rekindled and it is also very likely that more and more effort will be devoted to the teaching of computer-related courses in the various tertiary institutions in Hong Kong, and that interdepartmental and inter-faculty and even inter-collegiate collaborative research projects will be launched to put machine translation between Chinese and English on a more solid ground. In the following discussion, focus will be placed on the teaching and study of machine translation in Hong Kong.

Teaching

The teaching of courses in the area of machine translation is a fairly recent development. With the coming of the Age of Technology in the new millennium, it can be predicted that translation departments in Hong Kong will increase the computer literacy of their students and familiarize them with the use of the Internet as well as other computer softwares in translation. This is likely to be the trend in the years to come. Some of the translation departments in Hong Kong began to offer courses in information science and translation several years ago, while others have planned to introduce computer-related courses in the near future.

Department of Chinese, Translation and Linguistics
The City University of Hong Kong

When they later offered a BATI programme (Bachelor of Arts in Translation and Interpretation) as a separate programme, BAAL was re-structured and renamed BALIS (Bachelor of Arts in Language Information Science), which has since become one of the three programmes offered by the Department of Chinese, Translation and Linguistics. The aim of this programme, according to the departmental brochure, is to train students who are proficient in both Chinese and English and also in the computational processing of both English and Chinese texts. The following is quoted from their Website:

> The programme is designed to meet the language information needs of Hong Kong and is unique in its focus on the computerized processing of language in Chinese contexts. By applying current theoretical and methodological insights from the discipline of linguistics to the study of language and computers, it aims to produce graduates with expertise in languages and linguistics who are familiar with language-related applications of computers such as text indexing and retrieval and machine translation, in both English and Chinese. They will also participate in the ongoing development of systems capable of natural language understanding and generation.

> There is also a Website Management Programme which provides students with the opportunity to gain hands-on experience in managing a web server dedicated to publishing information on the Chinese Language and topics in Chinese Linguistics.

Students majoring in this programme have to take some required "Programme Core" courses such as:

CTL2205 Computers and Language
CTL2207 Introduction to Linguistic Computing
CTL3217 Computational Linguistics
CTL4208 Advanced Linguistic Computing

In addition, they have to choose 3 of the following courses:

CTL3210 Text Processing and Information Retrieval
CTL3220 Corpus Linguistics
CTL3221 Natural Language Parsing
CTL3222 Machine Translation
CTL3224 Computational Lexicography
CTL3225 Computer Assisted Language Learning
CTL4218 Advanced Topics in Computational Linguistics
CTL4223 Instrumental Phonetics

Department of Chinese and Bilingual Studies
Hong Kong Polytechnic University

At the Hong Kong Polytechnic University, the Department of Chinese and Bilingual Studies offers two computer-related courses to their students:

Introduction to Information Technology
Information Technology for Chinese and Translation

Department of Translation
The Chinese University of Hong Kong

This year, a new course, entitled "Machine Translation," has been offered as a Special Topic course (TRA4710) to students interested in this branch of knowledge in the field of translation. In 1999–2000, two computer-related courses will be introduced, as there is, within the department, a shared view among colleagues that additional resources should be sought to encourage a more technologically advanced learning environment.

TRA3610 Computers and Translation
TRA3620 Machine Translation

The first course aims at teaching students how to apply computer knowledge to translating, while the second introduces the general development of machine translation in the last fifty years, paying special attention to the translation systems designed for automatic translation between English and Chinese.

Translation Unit, Department of English
Hong Kong Baptist University

The Translation Course, which is a unit in the English Department in the Faculty of Arts, Hong Kong Baptist University, does not offer any courses related to the use of computer in translation work. All students majoring in translation, however, have to take one course from the "Complementary Studies Subjects" (9 units), one of which is computer-related.

COMP1110 Computer Literacy

Department of Translation
Lingnan University

As far as we can gather from the information provided by the department, there is one computer-related course on its curriculum.

Computing for Translators

As for the Department of Chinese of the University of Hong Kong and the Translation Programme of the Open University, no machine translation courses have been offered to their students.

Research

The Language Information Sciences Research Centre
The City University of Hong Kong

As far as the study of machine translation is concerned, The City University is most active, and has succeeded in getting a large sum of funds to support their research into various aspects of machine translation. They established, several years ago, a CityU Linguists, "to conduct research into the Chinese language with a view to achieving a better understanding of the Chinese language and to enchancing the development and application of linguistic science." Some of the projects carried out in the CityU Linguists are in the area of machine translation, such as *A Workstation Environment for Chinese Text Analysis and Processing, An Automated Chinese Full-text Abstraction System, Computer-aided Text Processing,* and *Corpus-based Linguistic Knowledge Acquisition for Noun Phrase Extraction.*

More important, it occurs to me, is the Language Information Sciences

Research Centre that was established in 1996 to conduct research into computer-related language studies and translation. To promote its image and academic standing, the centre has published *Newsletter* and, in partnership with John Benjamins, a reputable publishing house, the *International Review of Chinese Linguistics* in 1997. A number of projects in different areas have been reported in the *LISRC Newsletter* (Language Information Science Research Centre, 1966–1988). They include:

3.1999–2000
Proect Diatran: Voice Translation among Chinese Dialects

William S. Y. Wang, Kenneth K. Mei and H. Y. Huang
(City University Central Fund)

12.1998–5.2000
A Computational Approach to Analyzing Lexical Cohesion in Chinese Discourse Structure 〈應用計算模式分析中文文章結構中的詞匯凝聚性〉

Samuel W. K. Chan and B. K. Tsou
(City University Strategic Research Grant)

10.1998 — 9.2001
Computerized Database of Synchronous Chinese Newspaper Corpus from Different Chinese Speech Countries: Research into Sociolinguistic Variation and Distribution through the World Wide Web 〈各華語地區中文報紙電腦語料庫：社會語言學之變異研究與於互聯網分佈〉

B. K. Tsou and Jerome P. H. Hu
(UGC, RGC, CERG)

3.1998 — 12.1998
Active Management of Student Records in Teaching Cantonese Jyutping and Putonghua Pinyin on the Internet 〈網際網絡粵語拼音及漢語拼音學習歷程自動化管理〉

B. K. Tsou, Samuel W. K. Chan, C.C. Cheng, Tom B. Y. Lai (Teaching Development Grants, City University)

1.1998 — 9.1998
Course Material on Chinese Computing〈中文計算機運算教材〉

Samuel W. K. Chan, Terence Y. W. Chan, C. C. Cheng, Tom B. Y. Lai,
Huang Changning and Sun Maosong
(Division of Computer Studies, City University)

6.1997 — 5.1999
Implementation of Legal Bilingualism in Hong Kong and Jurilinguistic
Engineering (continuation)〈法律雙語化的施行和法律語言工程, 續〉

B. K. Tsou, K. K. Sin, Chief Justice P. Chan, and Caeser S. Lun
(UGC, RGC, CERG)

6.1997 — 12.1997
Common Chinese IT Terminology〈常用中文計算機術語〉

B. K. Tsou and Sun Maosong
(Hong Kong Computer Society and LISRC)

3.1997 — 12.1998
Design and Promotion of "Hanyu Pinyin" and "Jyutping" Computer
Software (Phase I) ; (2) Internet-based Jyutping and Pinyin Teaching
Programme,〈漢語拼音和「粵拼」電腦學習軟件 (第一期) 互聯網上「粵
拼」〉; (2)「漢語拼音」教學課程

B. K. Tsou , B. Y. Lai, P. K. Wong, and M. Leung ((1) Language Fund,
$700,000; (2) City University Central Fund $400,000 and City U Technology Development Grant $125,000).

1.1997 — 12.1997
Practical Implementation of Automatic Abstraction〈自動文摘實踐研究〉

B. K. Tsou, B. Y. Lai, H. L. Lin and R. Mitkov (Wolverhampton)
(RGC)

12.1996 — 11.1998
A Syntactic Marker-based Multi-level Discourse Analyzer with
Application to Chinese Full-text Abstraction〈基於語法標記的多層次
篇章分析器與自動化中文撮要〉

B. K. Tsou, T. Y.W. Chan, B. Y. Lai and H. C. Ho
($1,064,500, UGC, RGC, CERG)

12.1996 — 9.1998
Endangered Languages of South China〈中國南方的瀕危語言〉

William S-Y Wang, B. K. Tsou and Shi Feng ($690,300, RGC, CERG)

7.1996 — 6.1998
Computer Recognition of Cantonese with Intense Variable Noise 〈可變
噪音下的粵語電腦識別〉

W.S-Y. Wang and S. H. Leung
($282,860, CityU Strategic Research Grant)

9.1996 — 4.1998
*A Cross-cultural Comparison Study of the Use of Vocabulary Items
among Secondary and Tertiary Students in Four Asian Cities — Setting
Banchmarks for Language Education in Hong Kong (Phase 1)*〈中文詞
匯知識的跨文化研究：探討語文水平設定，英語教學及語文教育政
策的製定〉第一期)

B. K. Tsou, Godfrey K. F. Liu, Anna S. F. Kwan, and C. K. Leong
($1,386,000 Language Fund)

6.1996 — 12.1996
Readings in Chinese Natural Language Processing

K. J. Chen, C. R. Huang and B. K. Tsou
(Computational Linguistics Ass. (ROCLING))

6.1995 — 11.1997
*Implementation of Legal Bilingualism in Hong Kong: A Study in
Jurilinguistic Engineering.* 〈法律雙語化的施行：法律語言工程學的研
究〉

B. K. Tsou, K. K. Sin, T. A. Cheng and Caesar S. Lun
($383,000 UGC, RGC, CERG)

5.1995 — 8.1996
*Promoting the Use of Chinese among Hong Kong Students: How a
Cantonese Romanization Input Method can Facilitate Bilingual Word
Processing.*

Peter Tung, Raymond Lam (HKU), Carol Sin, and Priscilla Sum.
($642,000, Language Fund)

7.1994 — 12.1996
Training in Morphophonological Awareness Makes a Difference in
Speech Perception and Reading Comprehension 〈增強英語音素音節與
英語形態的潛識可增強識別口語音位的技能及閱讀〉

S. Hsia and C. K. Leong
($460,200, UGC, RGC, CERG)

11.1992 — 6.1997
Language Variation in Chinese Communities: Database and
Comparative Study 〈華語社會中的語言變化：資料庫與比較研究〉

B.K. Tsou, C.H. Chew, J. Tse, G. Liu, H.L. Lin, J. Hu,, and T. Chan
(C.K. Chiang $1,085,944, UGC, RGC, CERG $800,000)

12.1992 — 11.1996
An Automated Chinese Full-text Abstraction System

B. K. Tsou, H. C. Ho, B. Y. Lai, T. Y. W. Chan, H. L. Lin, T. Woo and C. S. Lun

The above information, all publicized in the Centre's *LISRC Newsletter,* shows that under the leadership of Professor Benjamin K. Tsou, a number of collaborative projects in the area of machine translation have been conducted since 1992. A total of nineteen projects have been recorded and $8,523,944 has been granted by various sources to conduct nine of its projects. The findings of these projects should make considerable contribution to the field of machine translation.

Human Language Technology Centre (HLTC)
The Hong Kong University of Science and Technology

The Hong Kong University of Science and Technology is the only tertiary institution in Hong Kong that does not offer a translation programme. However considerable research on language and speech technology, including machine translation, has been conducted by teaching staff of the Department of Computer Science and Department of Electrical and Electronic Engineering.

At HKUST, a Human Language Technology Centre (HLTC) was founded several years ago. The following was found on its webpage:

Human Language Technology Centre (HLTC) is an Emerging High Impact Area research centre at HKUST specializing in speech and signal processing, statistical and corpus-based NLP, machine translation, information extraction, Chinese language processing, and related fields.

With the efforts of four teaching staff from the Department of Computer Science –Professors Wu Dekai, Brian Mak, Gan Kok Wee, and Roland Chin and three from the Department of Electrical and Electronic Engineering — Professors Pascale Fung, Oscar Au and Bertrand Shi, the Centre was established "to lead new state-of-the-art research directions that drive the development of new applications in the area of language and speech technology." Also, "special emphasis is given to machine processing of Chinese language and Chinese information." With the servers and workstations set up in the Main Laboratory, a number of systems have been built at HLTC, including automated language translation for the Internet, speech-based web browsing, and speech recognition for the telephone. An on-going project is "The SILC (Statistical Interlingual Conversion) Research Project on Machine Translation Learning."

A quick glance at the publications put out by members of the HLTC shows they have written extensively on computational lexicography, speech processing, dialog modelling, speech characterization, Chinese computing, and computer-aided instruction.

The Hung On-To Research Laboratory for Machine Translation (60s–70s) and Machine Translation Laboratory, Department of Translation (1999), The Chinese University of Hong Kong

The Chinese University of Hong Kong should be regarded as the first tertiary institution to conduct research into machine translation. As early as 1969, a team of researchers at the Hung On-To Research Laboratory for Machine Translation, led by Professor Loh Shiu-chang, began work on a practical machine translation system known as *The Chinese University Language Translator* 中文大學語言翻譯器, abbreviated as CULT (Loh, 1997). Professor Loh and his colleagues, such as Kong Luan and Hung Hing-sum, worked on the IBM 1130 system in 1969 and the ICL1904A system in 1972. The system had been used to translate ten short pieces of Chinese scientific writings, mainly papers on mathematics, into English. By means of some pre-editing techniques, the machine could produce results that were found to be satisfactory by the designers. Later, with the construction of a new Chinese keyboard, it was redesigned as an interactive on-line machine translation system that could also translate from English into Chinese.

To continue the work of our predecessors, the Department of Translation has now set up a new research centre on machine translation. The centre, known as "Machine Translation Laboratory," has five goals to achieve in the coming few years:

(1) MTL will serve as a centre for the collection of computer-related materials. Apart from printed materials such as books and journals, MTL will actively acquire translation softwares to serve as basic teaching materials for the running of computer-related and machine-translation courses. The acquisition of softwares is costly as most can only be used by a single user on a single machine and protective devices have been built in to prevent infringement on copyrights. In the last five months, some forty thousand dollars have been spent on software purchases and maintenance. To acquire one copy of the full version of the Systran System with all the language pairs included, for example, would need a sum of one hundred thousand dollars.

As Hong Kong has yet to produce machine translation softwares to be used and studied in classrooms, most of the teaching materials have to be acquired from companies in Mainland China and Taiwan. The following is a breakdown of translation softwares into three main categories:

(I)   On-line Dictionary 線上字典

    (1)   新人類超速網典 (*High Traffic Newtype*) (Taiwan)
    (2)   網際金點 (Taiwan)
    (3)   譯典通98 (*Dr. Eye 98*) (Taiwan)
    (4)   通譯 (Taiwan)
    (5)   網際譯典 (Taiwan)

(II) Computer Screen Translation Software 漢化軟件

    (1)   國際護照 (*Passport for Windows*) (Taiwan)
    (2)   東方快車 (*Oriental Express*) (China)
    (3)   大革命 (Taiwan)
    (4)   地球村英漢詞典 (*Earth Village English-Chinese Dictionary*) (Taiwan)

(III) Text Translation Software 全文翻譯軟件

    English into Chinese

(1) 譯經 (*TransWhiz English-to-Chinese Translation System*) (Taiwan)
(2) 新航線線上全頁英譯中系統 (Taiwan)
(3) 譯橋全功能翻譯系統 (*Transbridge Instant English to Chinese Translator (Taiwan)*
(4) 翻譯小精靈 (Taiwan)
(5) 靈譯世界 (*Key Trans World*) (Taiwan)
(6) 網際譯 (Taiwan)
(7) 大譯家 (*Wonderful Translator*) (Taiwan)
(8) 譯典通豪華版 (*Dr. Eye*) (Taiwan)
(9) 漢神 (*Hansbridge*) (China)
(10) 東方快車 2000 (*Oriental Express*) (China)

Chinese to English

(11) 亞歷山大漢譯英翻譯軟件(*Alexander Chinese-English Translation System* (Taiwan)
(12) 寰宇通漢英翻譯系統〉(China)
(13) *Systran: Chinese-English Translation System* (USA)

(2) MTL will serve as a centre for the study of the application and analysis of the existing softwares available in the market. Emphasis will be placed on the adequacy of the following translation functions of software on a comparative basis:

Sentence Translation 單句翻譯
Text Translation 全文翻譯
Instant Screen Translation 即時屏幕漢化
Web Page Translation 網頁翻譯
Mouse-trailing Word-translation 即拖即譯
Highlight and Translate 標式翻譯
Instant Transliteration 即時音譯
Address Translation 地址翻譯
Dictionary Modification 字典修改
Text Reading 譯文音讀
Professional Dictionaries 專業字典
Automatic Multi-code Identification 多內碼自動識別
Download Update 下載更新

(3) MTL will gradually build up a communication network of machine translation centres throughout the world and of active researchers in the

field through membership affiliation. Educational institutions and business companies, for example, can join MTL as corporate members, while specialists and people interested in machine translation can serve as individual members. This will facilitate the flow of information in the area of machine translation, which is one of the major goals that MTL hopes to achieve.

(4) MTL will propose some interdepartmental, interfaculty, or even intercollegiate projects that will contribute significantly to the scholarship in the field or meet the needs of the local community.

(5) MTL will build up terminological databases for various subjects or professions that will help to achieve standardization in the translation of specialized vocabularies. This will be a long-term project involving a large number of scholars and experts and possibly the tolerance and even cooperation of the governments concerned in order to standardize the regional variant translations of terms and expressions used in Mainland China, Taiwan, Hong Kong and other Chinese communities in different parts of the world.

The above is a list of objectives that we hope to be able to achieve in the near future. Like other sister institutions, we will match our research efforts with pedagogical needs, but certainly we would be more interested in breaking new paths than following the beaten track.

Conclusion

Thirty years have elapsed since the pioneer researchers in Hong Kong invented the first machine translation system at The Chinese University. What we have achieved so far is hard to assess. What has been produced from machine translation between Chinese and English, two major languages in the world, is still viewed with suspicion. It is high time that barriers should be torn down to allow a more effective use of the resources available to us. For an institution strong in research on machine translation but without a translation programme to help with the assessment of its findings, intercollegiate collaboration should be encouraged. Large projects that need the expertise not found in the funded institution should have support from other departments or institutions. Interdepartmental cooperation across institutions can benefit the academic world much more than isolated efforts. The cost factor that has been discussed earlier should serve to illustrate the need to remove duplication of expenses and spend our resources on the more important and significant issues in the realm of machine translation.

References

Language Information Sciences Research Centre 語言資訊科學研究中心 (1966–1988). *LISRC Newsletter*, Nos. 1–4.

Loh, Shiu-chang (1972). "Machine Translation at The Chinese University of Hong Kong." In J. Matthias, ed., *Proceedings of the CETA Workshop on Chinese Language and Chinese Research Materials*, 24–25 March, Washington, D. C.

Translating for the "New Age": Theoretical, Professional and Pedagogic Implications

Simon S. C. Chau
Department of English
Hong Kong Baptist University

Our Era of Change

As the old millennium draws to a close (292 days to go at the time I am writing this paper), the entire human civilization is undergoing a sea change. Worldviews, perceptions, values, as well as modes of operation are turning upside down and inside out, as decades if not centuries of deviations and off-balances are getting redressed. It looks as if in the face of global calamity, our race will find a new direction in time. The scope of this paradigm shift, as well as its consequences, could very well be unmatched since the beginning of time. Nothing will remain untouched, and no one will emerge without changing quite drastically on various levels of existence. And this is happening right before our eyes every moment now.

This global transformation is sometimes conveniently referred to as the "New Age." Historically, it could have been an outgrowth of the hippie movement in North America in the 1960s, which itself was a reaction against the post World War Two Western materialistic worldview and lifestyle.

The New Age, once a fringe movement, is taking on the role of a major swing in world thinking. This thinking is being changed and reshaped. It would not be quite correct to say that it is based on new ideas, for it is in fact the "not new ideas" that are shaping the New Age. The New Age should be called the revival of old age, since it has a pre-occupation with and a tendency to return to the skills and beliefs of a past era.

The pre-occupation that is occurring is more orientated toward the physical skills of those past times. But there is a larger movement that is occurring underneath this layer of "new discoveries." This movement is a powerful awakening of the spirit. This awakening is returning to the individual, the power to control their own direction in spiritual beliefs and removing the power from controlling bodies and external individuals. It is a spiritualism of "self." (Pickering, n.d.: 1).

What Is the "New Age"?

As it is commonly understood here and now[1], the term "New Age"[2] is used in at least three different ways, referring to separate but related phenomena:

(1) *The somewhat universal end-of-the-century/millennium hype,* fuelled by the media and commercial sector, as people yearn for a new beginning and deliverance from the frustration, anxiety and despair brought about by the technology, materialism, commercialism and social changes, etc., of recent decades.

(2) *The commercial fad exploited by marketing forces* to sell products (e.g. crystals, "health foods," essential oil, and music CDs), services (e.g. massaging, clairvoyance, and *fengshui* consultations), and courses (e.g. Neurolinguistic Programming, Healer training, and Transcendental Meditation classes). With its occultist and commercial flavour, this facet is invariably the one exploited by the popular media for its sensationalist effect.

(3) *The spiritual revival on personal, social and human levels* that is taking place during the last quarter of the twentieth century, resulting in a general paradigm shift in terms of values, visions and directions, as well as changes in lifestyle, beliefs, social structures, and relationships.[3]

It is the last of these areas that is the focus of the present discussion.

Essence of the Phenomenon: Humans Being Once More

Based on the essence of teachings common to many epochs and cultures, but adapted for a world that has changed drastically, this New Age thinking proposes an entirely different attitude towards ourselves, the earth, and all aspects of our life while on this planet. (St. Aubyn, 1990: 1)

But what is this "thinking" about?

The New Age movement means different things to different people. However, I feel that most New Age topics have one basic underlying theme: personal spiritual development. Every day there are thousands upon thousands of people around the world who are waking up to the knowledge, understanding and realization of who they really are, where they came from, and why they are here.

The New Age Movement itself is somewhat of a paradox, since to organize into some kind of "movement" could be considered contrary to the fundamentals of *individual* spiritual development.

The New Age is strongly related to some of the concepts defined in the branch of philosophy commonly referred to as *metaphysics*. Although the academic branch of metaphysics is mostly concerned about the nature of ultimate reality, popular metaphysics often include discussion and analysis of subjects beyond the physical third dimension. Some examples of metaphysical topics include: free energy, out of body experiences, UFOs, psychic phenomenon, alternative healing, and other topics that our conventional sciences find difficult to explain. (Lutts, n.d.: 1)

Jack Clarke, a leading figure in this "movement," made a long list of statements in respond to the question "What is New Age, anyway?" The following is a selection from the list that could be particularly relevant to translating:

— It's people who search for strength from the universe by going inside themselves.

— It's people who see others as not better than nor less than, but rather different from themselves, yet part of the same whole.

— It's people who realize that now is all we have, since yesterday is just a thought and so is tomorrow.

— The New Age is not a movement based on guilt, anger, fear or hurt. It is a journey toward the love that is God.

— New Age is not just human doing, it is humans being (quoted in Tang, n.d.: 73–7).

He made other statements in response to the question "Why a New Age, anyway?" Here are those that should concern the translator:

— Because this millennium is giving way to an unnamed new era.

— Because old methods aren't working as well as they have in the past.

— Because a better way to treat our planet and those living on it must be found.

— Because fear has too long diminished the love within us.

— Because it is a time to learn from the masters, not worship them.
— Because we have powers within us that can no longer be suppressed.
— Because our intuition knows what is best, and we have begun to listen.
— Because we are learning to sense for ourselves those other realities which mystics describe and scientists are beginning to verity.
— Because religion, metaphysics and science are blending together.
— Because values are shifting away from material goals.
— Because belief in ourselves leads to a belief in a higher power.
— Because our gift of spirituality can no longer be denied.
— Because people know more and more that we are on a journey back home to the source, known to many as God.
— Because we are entering an era when spirituality has a more personal meaning to each individual.
— Because it is time to believe in miracles again.
— Because we are who we are. (quoted in Tang, n.d.: 69-72)

Andrew Lutts, another writer on the topic, gave an unofficial list of beliefs that some individuals in New Age may have in common:

— You create your own reality and destiny. This is a planet of free choice, and you have your own free will.
— You have certain challenges to face and overcome in this lifetime. If you don't learn your lessons this time, you'll get them again.
— There is no such thing as coincidence.
— There is more to life than meets the eye, much more.
— Nothing really matters in this life unless it is done for the benefit of others.
— We are not alone.
— We are multidimensional beings currently having a human experience.
— We are all receiving more help than we know, from angels, spirit guides, ascended masters and others.
— We can heal ourselves, our society, and our world.
— The ultimate transformation for mankind is ascension. (Lutts, n.d.: 2)

Implications for Translation Theorizing

As indicated in the statements cited above, "New Age thinking" is in a number of ways a direct challenge to the mainstream "world order" that is taken for granted by the typical member of "modern" society. With its new (or revived) paradigm centering on individual spirituality and inter-connected cosmic consciousness, it somehow obliges the translation theorist to critically re-examine the very grounds on which twentieth-century theories are built, and perhaps expand his vision by accepting ideas that are not always compatible with time-honoured presuppositions. For example,

1. The role of linguistics in translatology — Can we *really* assess, ascertain, or define the meaning or any utterance/text/communicative event by utilizing scientific tools? If the twentieth century provided the arena for the linguistic sciences to flourish, would not the following one require a new generation of ideas for practitioners to open their *mystic* files, to *download* inspiration obtained through spiritual communications, or to account for if not justify their *paranormal* understanding?

2. The role of equivalence in practice and criticism — Are we *actually* supposed to reproduce a text that is "faithful" to the original, however this is understood and measured?

3. The role of objectivity in handling meaning — Is the "transparency" of the translation that important after all, even if that is possible at all?

These considerations would, in all probability, not render the efforts of the twentieth century theorists obsolete. There is, however, an increasing demand for new-paradigm translation scholarship and modes of operations to cater for New Age needs.

Implications for Translation Practice

With the popularization of the Internet and the dawning of the cyber world, translating will have to enter into a further stage of evolution to catch up with the times. New global languages, inter-languages, and meta-languages will gain increasing currency. Ideas, experiences and visions will travel around the world in a manner and speed unimaginable before. Market demands will follow new trends, some of which would, to say the least, appear bizarre to the conventionally minded practitioner today. In the light of these drastic changes, it is only reasonable to predict that translators of the coming era will operate somewhat differently. For example:

1. The role of intuition further recognized —
    Rather than adhering to "orthodox" translation methods or techniques, the New Age translator will feel much more at home "following his heart." By surrendering his own conscious mind to the "guidance" from above, he is thus able to tap his own inner resources more or less at will. Far from being metaphysical or far-fetched, this is exactly what conference interpreters do when they perform beautifully. On the one hand, knowledge, experiences, and skills are effectively internalized and retrieved for proper use. On the other, divine guidance or the innate abilities and sensitivities come into play and facilitate the process of trans-ference/re-creation.

2. The emphasis on holistic understanding —
    Instead of dissecting the original text like a biologist does with his laboratory specimen to determine the "reality," the New Age translator gets the "feel"/"spirit"/"essence" of the original directly through his identification with the situation.

3. Catering for new market needs —
    Instead of one-to-one text transference requiring reverence to the author, there will be an increase in the proportion of spiritual, "mystical," and "religious" text that defy scientific analysis and require the translator to "follow his heart."[4] The resulting re-creations are "consumed" in ways and for purposes unlike most translations in the twentieth century.

4. The emphasis on meaning and purpose —
    Apart from making a living and serving clients in the mercenary sense, the New Age translator finds himself compelled to look for the value of, or "calling" in his service. Just as the twentieth century required the translating profession to work mostly on political, commercial, academic and journalistic texts, the New Age calls for the "re-channeling" of ideas, experiences, inspirations, paradigms, and worldviews across cultures and communities. The "translating" of such materials requires more than art, craft and technology: it is the *heart* that plays the para-mount role. Only those practitioners with a *Why* will be best endowed with the *How*.

Implications for Translation Education

If the translation educator allows the impact of the ideas outlined above to sink in, he will realize that the making of a competent translator for this new era requires more than bilingual mastery, professional skills and bi-cultural awareness, indispensable as they are in the training curriculum. In addition to these basic elements, there could well be a place for "extra-academic" and "extra-professional" nutrition in the trainees' diet, such as:

— Holistic health — How to function as a positive, sociable and happy being, well-balanced on the physical, emotional, psychological, social, mental and spiritual levels.
— Holistic sensibility — How to develop, maintain, and fully utilize the power of understanding, including what is commonly understood as intuition, inspiration, empathy, extra-sensual perception, enlightenment, and divine guidance.
— Cosmic consciousness — How to communicate with the macro-environment (the universe, other sentient beings, the ultimate power, etc.) and the microenvironment (one's self, the divine sparkle within, the sub-conscious world, etc.), and be aware of the bonding with all these.
— Ultimate concerns — How to find meaning in life and one's work.

How can the translation educator "translate" such knowledge into action? Can or should this be done formally in class? To me, these are non-questions. Every sincere teacher will be given the answer to serve his purpose. Nevertheless, I found this saying useful: "Children never listen to their parents. They just copy them."

Notes

1   While the *New Age Movement* is considered an imported novelty (or disease, according to some Christian churches) by this community, a full spectrum of its practices, together with the very spirit behind them, has already gained recognition in various degrees since the beginning of the 1990s. Among these are environmentalism, equality of the sexes, simple living, EQ, keeping fit, healthy diets, *qigong, fengshui,* divining, astrology, massaging, bodywork, fire walking, neuro-linguistic programming, rebirthing, palm reading, aromatherapy, acupuncture, herbal medicine, meditation, healing, fasting, animal rights, and vegetarianism.

2   It is known as 新世紀 ("New Century") in Mainland China, and 新紀元 ("New

Era") in Taiwan and Hong Kong. Apparently, the latter translation carries a heavier occultist connotation to some people.

3 A fair description of the scene can be found in Cheng 1995, Chapter 1.

4 The author is speaking from personal experience. A casual visit to popular bookstores in Chinese communities will confirm this: an increasing proportion of translated works into Chinese are original texts with a "New Age" flavour.

References

Cheng, C. S. (1995). *Alternative Green Brochure: New Millennium Primary Analysis and the Green Movement.* Hong Kong: Cheuk Yuk Publishing House.

Lutts, Andrew (n.d.). *New Age FAQ: Frequently Asked Questions.* www.salemctr. com/newage/centerl.htm.

Pickering, Clive (n.d.). *The New Age.* www.sd.com.au/db/newage.htm.

St. Aubyn, Lorna (1990). *The New Age in a Nutshell: A Guide to Living in New Times.* Bath: Gateway Books.

Tang, Tang (n.d.). *The Benefits of Vegetarianism.* Taibei: Tang Tang Vegetarian Foods.

Back to the Future[1]:
The Future Development of
Translation Studies in Hong Kong[2]

Elsie Chan Kit-ying
Division of Language Studies
City University of Hong Kong

This paper attempts to trace recent translation research that cross-examines the Chinese translation tradition with applicable Western theories and to suggest it as a future trend of translation studies in Hong Kong. The writer is optimistic that Hong Kong, given its specific socio-political development as a once alienated and now unalienable part of China, can be pivoted as both a window, fostering perception of and exchange with the non-Chinese world, and a centre, pulling together high-level research expertise, of Chinese translation studies.

Interpretation

It is important to define the key terms in the title before proceeding with my argument. The core term is "translation studies." It is beyond the intention of this paper to dwell on the painstaking history of establishing translation studies as a discipline. I shall stick to the century-end consensus that translation studies "has now come to mean something like anything that (claims) to have 'anything to do with translation'. Twenty years ago it meant: training translators. It is amazing to see, with hindsight, how preposterous some of the questions that were asked twenty years ago seem to us now." (Bassnett and Lefevere, 1998: 1) Earlier on, it was already noted that the field had been cleared in the Lutheran sense for translation studies which has grown rapidly as a separate interdiscipline over the last few decades. (Snell-Hornby, 1995: 131–35) This obviously involves concerted research efforts in linguistics, literary studies, cultural studies, philosophy, anthropology and other disciplines. Like any other universal discipline, be it economics, history, geography, it has to be ontological, epistemological and well-structured, aiming at producing "a comprehensive theory which can be used as a guideline for the production of translations." (Lefevere, 1978)

In this light, I would like to draw an analogy between translation studies and other academic disciplines, say, economics. Economics is studied all over the world as a university discipline, seen as a lucrative profession, with the objectives of describing economic phenomena as they manifest themselves in the world of our experience. It establishes general principles by means of which these phenomena can be explained and predicted, and makes use of such knowledge in the practice of economic planning and economic training. The same logic is embodied in James Holmes' explication on the objectives of translation studies. Holmes' vision of the scope of translation studies comprises an applied branch embracing translator training, translation aids and translation criticism and a pure branch embracing all types of theoretical and descriptive studies (Holmes, 1998: 67–80), including area-restricted studies on, for example, translation between language and culture pairs. Suffice it to say that labels like British economics or American economics sound grotesquely preposterous (albeit Adam Smith is regarded as the founder of classical economics and Milton Friedman won the Nobel Prize for economics). But there are virtually many research scholars and institutes dedicated to the intensive study of specific economic issues, of specific time and space frame, or contrastive study of the economic phenomena of two or more areas, through which general principles can be proved or disproved, new insights gained.

It is along the same line of reasoning that I mention "Chinese" translation studies. Chinese scholars who have suggested that translation theory ought to be language and culture-pair specific include Jin Di 金隄 (Jin, 1998), Tan Zaixi 譚載喜 (Tan, 1998a) and Liu Miqing 劉宓慶 (Liu, 1990). Liu elucidates his construction of Chinese translation studies in his landmark treatise *Studies on Translation Today* 《現代翻譯理論》[3] and states that translation studies should be contrastive, multi-dimensional and based on the Chinese tradition (Liu, 1990: 8–14). Although I am at times perplexed by Liu and Tan's call for "the construction of a translation theory with Chinese characteristics" and assertions like "Chinese translation studies must acquire a Chinese flavour,"[4] I totally agree to the need for intensive study into China-specific or Chinese-specific translation and translating (referred to as "Chinese translation studies" in this paper) alongside general, theoretical and applied studies, to substantiate the literature of the discipline. And this provides the backbone of my catch phrase in the title: back to the future.

By "back," I mean historical study of the Chinese tradition, though not confined to translation tradition. It involves the entire Chinese macrocosm and cross-examination of the many facets of any single translation phenomenon from various perspectives, at once cultural, historical, literary, philosophical, ideological, in a nutshell, interdisciplinary and multidimensional. This will provide the broader framework that Chinese translation studies well deserve, since the process of translation manifests probably the most complicated yet fundamental issues in human activity. Working in the present to re-read our legacy is the pivot where we shall move toward the future.

"Future" here inevitably points at the twenty-first century, and the reader will feel such labels as "globalization" or "internationalization" as large as life. I will trace recent attempts at the invigorating and internationalization of Chinese translation studies. Presumably one may question why and how a culture and language-specific study should go international. It is not my intention to display rhetoric here, let alone paradox. I believe that Chinese translation studies must be rooted in the Chinese tradition and intrinsically differ in many respects with studies in the other traditions. But as no single system is perfect, in-depth contrastive studies between the Chinese and other traditions should shed light on the universal and specific features of each system. Concerted efforts ought to be taken to place this under the limelight, to draw wider attention on how findings in one system can be complementary to another. This is one display of internationalization. And Chinese translation studies need not be limited to a Chinese audience. Given the curse of Babel and the intrinsic subtlety and complexity of Chinese in relation to other languages, a broader audience can be reached if local research findings get written or translated into a language with more international currency, such as English, or discussed and published in open channels, such as international journals and conferences. This is another display of internationalization.

The joint forces of looking back at the Chinese macrocosm and forward to the international playing field equal, in my humble summation, interface of East and West. Mediation of two starkly different worldviews, not just two languages or cultures, that have shaped two independent translation traditions. That mediation, to be reciprocal and constructive, must be selective, discriminatory, progressive and multi-dimensional. The internationalization of Chinese translation studies can be best conducted in post-colonial Hong Kong, where its close bond to its Chinese roots and exposure to the outside world never cease. Such is my vision of the "future development of translation studies in Hong Kong."

The Chinese Tradition

Chinese translation theory evolves out of the specificity of the Chinese language and mode of thinking. In the first instance, Chinese characters are monosyllabic and mainly phono-ideographic, which enables the coining of new words by direct compounding of ideographic morphemes or blending them with phonetic and referential morphemes. Similarly, juxtaposing existing words and phrases conveniently forms new phrases and expressions. In terms of signification and expression, this unique paratactic and composite nature of the Chinese language allows fascinating flexibility and creativity on the one hand, but leads to equivocal and imprecise clustering thus hindering perception on the other hand. This is not necessarily bad, at least from the appreciation point of view. Lovers of Chinese poetry, painting and calligraphy, for instance, have long marvelled at the myriad of interpretations possible and plausible, as the traditional Chinese text allows or, to be more precise, requires subtle and intuitive understanding, a feature epitomised by Chinese poetry.[5] It sets a world totally different from that moulded by the multi-syllabic, hypotactic and inflectional Indo-European languages.

The abstract expression mode of classical Chinese texts more often than not poses annotation problems, let alone stark translation problems, especially for the conventional translator who believes that a classical text should possess standard, canonical meaning and thus feels obliged to transcode it into an equivalent foreign version. Refraining from arguing against this pre-supposition, I just want to suggest here that certain foreign concepts can be applicable in the appreciation of Chinese art. One example is the classical Chinese poem, which calls for the interpreter's intuitive understanding and participation, not unlike the deconstructionist claim for double activity and close reading. Attempts to prescribe a standard meaning are often futile; the translator is left, on the contrary, to appreciate the plurality of words, ideograms and images that weave the text.

> Let us first posit the image of a triumphant plural, unimpoverished by any constraint of representation (of imitation). In this ideal text, the networks are many and interact, without any one of them being able to surpass the rest; this text is a galaxy of signifiers, not a structure of signifieds; it has no beginning;

it is reversible; we gain access to it by several entrances, none of which can be authoritatively declared to be the main one; the codes it mobilizes extend *as far as the eye can reach*, they are indeterminable (meaning here is never subject to a principle of determination, unless by throwing dice); the systems of meaning is never closed, based as it is on the infinity of language. (Barthes, 1974: 5–6)

If we consider a classical Chinese ink and wash painting, the connoisseur will agree that

Necessary assertion is difficult, however, for as nothing exists outside the text, there is never a *whole* of the text…there cannot be a narrative structure, a grammar, or a logic; thus, if one or another of these are sometimes permitted to come forward, it is *in proportion* (giving this expression its full quantitative value) as we are dealing with incompletely plural texts, texts whose plural is more or less parsimonious. (Barthes, 1974: 6)

One will recall the Chinese philosopher Laozi's 老子 (C. 570 B.C.) view on the limited function of speech and writing and the indetermination of text meaning, as well as Chinese philosophical tenets which fall upon transcendental metaphysics, at once different from the Western tradition of theoretical reasoning and sensible intuition.

The way that can be spoken of is not the constant way;
The name that can be named is not the constant name.
The nameless was the beginning of heaven and earth;
The named was the mother of the myriad creatures.
Hence always rid yourself of desires in order to observe its secrets;
But always allow yourself to have desires in order to observe its manifestations. (Lau, 1963: 3)

Thus, since the words are the means to explain the images, once one gets the images, he forgets the words, and, since the images are the means to allow us to concentrate on the ideas, once one gets the ideas, he forgets the images…. Therefore someone who stays fixed on the words will not be one to get the image; and someone who stays fixed on the images will not be one to get the ideas….Getting the ideas is in fact a matter of forgetting the images, and getting the images is in fact a matter of forgetting the words. (Lynn, 1984: 31–32)

The post-structuralist translator, regardless of race or nationality, can benefit from participating in the deconstructionist game of signification, legitimizing the endless interplay between the text and the reader, and come up with multiple justifiable translations. Deconstruction asks the reader to go beyond the constraint of representation by intruding the textual galaxy at blindspots at the signifier level; Taoism and Confucianism require the reader to do the same by contemplating the indefinite signified hidden behind the aesthetics of manifestation. Both stress the importance of letting the text to speak for itself, which is conceptually beneficial to the translator of Chinese classics. This proves one viable way of rereading the Chinese tradition and invigorating it with applicable western models.

Equivocal clustering and subtle expression in Chinese aesthetics undoubtedly allow immense creativity. Yet this has resulted in an "impressionistic" tendency in nomenclature and terminology and poses a flaw in representation[6], heightened by the proneness of Chinese philosophy to evaluative intuition, loose representation and moral subjectivity, quite the opposite of that of Western philosophy to deductive perception, definitive rhetoric and theoretical objectivity.[7] The interpretation of many Chinese terms does not rest on distinctive and dialectical definition, but rather on fuzzy consensus based on canonized classics and commentaries. This poses an obstacle to Chinese translation studies since we lack a scientific and differentiating locution for internal verification and external dialogue with other traditions.

The same impressionistic tendency exists in traditional Chinese art and literary criticism, as well as translation theory which, according to Tan, remains largely philological and hermeneutic (Tan, 1998a: 14). From ancient translators of Buddhist scriptures like Zhi Qian 支謙 (c. third century), Dao'an 道安 (314–385), Kumarajiva 鳩摩羅什 (350–409) and Xuanzang 玄奘 (602–664), to modern translators of Western works like Yan Fu 嚴復 (1854–1921), Fu Lei 傅雷 (1908–66) and Qian Zhongshu 錢鍾書 (1910–98), translation discourse is centered round the debate over form/rhetoric 文 vs. content/substance 質, the origin of which can be traced back to Laozi and Confucian stylistics. Similar to other indigenous classics, their style of writing is terse and aphoristic, without strict dialectical distinction between rhetoric and substance, their definition and norms, and thus demands from the learner more spontaneous enlightenment than deductive reasoning. Thus is formed the lineage of translation theory in China traced in existing anthologies[8], and Luo Xinzhang puts it straight that China has its own system of translation theory: evolving from Dao'an's notion of "original purport" 案本, to Yan's "faithfulness" 求信, then Fu's "spiritual resemblance" 神似 and consequently Qian's "sublime consummation" 化境. (Luo, 1984: 1–19) Another illustration of the Chinese' preference for crisp and epigrammatic representation. These notions, stemming from empirical study on translation of religious and literary texts in the traditional context, should be illuminating for future studies as long as they are not fossilized as the sole canons for verification and sole subjects of study on translation; otherwise, they may be dismissed as "pre-scientific." In recent years, more and more Chinese scholars have re-examined these catchphrases drawing complementary reference from other areas, for instance, linguistic, cultural, communication and functional studies. Many also recognize the rise of translatology 翻譯學 or translation studies 翻譯研究 as a discipline.

Such a turn is witnessed in multifarious publications, among them the *New Anthology on Translation.* (Yang and Liu, 1994) The articles in the book are grouped under three headings: Studies on Translation 翻譯研究, Studies on Translatology 譯學研究, and Interdisciplinary Approaches to Translation 跨學科研究 (sic). The distinction between the first two may perhaps confound the meticulous reader, who would naturally have assumed that the three categories represent three different branches of study under the same broad subject "Translation." If "Studies on Translation" is meant to differ from "Studies on Translatology," does the former examine translation as an art while the latter translation as a science? The reader may also recall that translatology, or science of translation, derived from the German term *übersetzungswissenschaft,* could be better termed "translation studies," (Holmes, 1988: 68–70) which has more or less replaced "translatology" as the name of the discipline in Western discourse (Shuttleworth and Cowie, 1997: 148–149, 188). Even the original Chinese terms offer no clue. "Studies on Translatology" here is meant to represent the English equivalent of "譯" (translation) "學" (discipline) "研究" (study), while "Studies on Translation" to represent that of "翻譯" (translation) "研究" (study). From the Chinese perspective then, the baffled reader may also wonder whether "Studies on Translation" 翻譯研究 concerns applied translation more and "Studies on Translatology" 譯學研究 the scientific study of translation. If so, then why is it loosely represented as "譯學" (translation discipline) here instead of "翻譯科學" (translation science), the proper Chinese rendering of "science" being "科學" instead of merely "學" (discipline)?

A closer look at the articles under each heading unfortunately does not offer clarification. The "Studies on Translation" part includes titles which should otherwise be grouped under "translation science": "Sci-Tech

Translation", "Enterprise Translatology is Wanted in China" and "JFY-V Machine Translation System," while the "Studies on Translatology" part comprises such papers as "How to Appreciate Good Translation," "A Word for Criticism on Literary Translation" and "Skill Consciousness in Translation," which should be classified as anything but "science." If anything, this portrays the problem of indiscreet terminology in Chinese translation studies[9], reminding us of the impressionistic Chinese tradition of representation. This ought to be fine-tuned, though it ought not to dwarf the significance of this and similar volumes. To start with, it is totally legitimate to say that any study about translation naturally falls within the realm of and contributes to the discipline as a whole. Second, the present volume undoubtedly charts major recent explication in the field and helps to expand the scope of Chinese translation studies as an interdisciplinary and multi-dimensional discipline.

Globalization

The above example illustrates that a more scientific and analytic discourse or system of representation can be beneficial to internal verification of Chinese translation studies. It also opens a channel for complementary dialogue with other traditions. Moving toward the next millenium, we need strategic planning for translation studies in this part of the world, an integral part yet of the larger global village. To this end, let me reiterate my former proposition, internationalization of Chinese translation studies. This is not a one-way traffic, because while we are reaching out, the outside world is eyeing us also for mutual exchange and complementation. In fact, more Western scholars now show an interest in contrastive studies embracing Chinese translation studies. And a few scholars have admitted a hegemonic Eurocentric basis in anthropology, culture, translation and other disciplines in the past.[10] They are calling for more interface between the Orient and the Occident through contrastive studies, reinforcing the existing effort of their Chinese colleagues.[11] My view is that engagement is often better than containment, and would help substantiate the construction and literature of Translation Studies as a universal discipline.

Yet this prospect is not cleared of obstacles. Orient-sceptics and Occident-sceptics are bound to exist, if I may ironically exercise a little liberty with terminology here. They see each other as the "other," the Orient, for example, being seen as unscientific and inscrutable, probably stemming from a worldview based on hegemonic research and reasoning accompanying Western colonial expansion in the past few centuries. In turn, the Occident is at times seen as alien and intimidating to home conventions in the East. There are Chinese who dismiss Western theories as inapplicable and, in the post-colonial sense, strict interpellation, as betraying our inherent Chinese tradition. They feel subjugated when their own country is labeled as "developing" and culture as "subordinate." (Venuti, 1998: 158–89) This myth is sometimes fostered unfortunately by attempts of indiscriminate transplantation of Western theories, which, as a matter of course, fail to enter the mainstream of Chinese translation studies.

I would like to argue that this kind of xenophobia is unnecessary. First, dialogue with the West — not confined to translation theory since translation studies should be multi-dimensional — is constructive, provided that the introduction of ideas is selective and complementary. At times, this may result in the betrayal of certain home conventions (on a playful note, aren't translators traitors after all?) and hybridity of certain concepts on both sides (logically, as well as dialectically, is translation not a kind of hybrid?), but the same phenomenon has always existed in various domains everywhere in history. The forerunner of modern Chinese literature Zhou Shuren 周樹人, pen-named Lu Xun 魯迅, also a translator himself, thought the introduction of Indo-European syntax through foreignizing in translation could help to render more precisely the representation of the newly developed vernacular *baihua* 白話 to suit the needs of the mass modern readers. This goes in line with the Roman view that translation is a channel to enrich the language and literature of the target system. Fu Lei's analogy between translating and painting and "spiritual resemblance" as a translation norm is similar to the seventeenth-century metaphor of the translator as "portrait painter,"[12] attempting to reach the spirit and imitate the style and manner of the source text. It is also interesting to note that notions like reader reception and domesticating translating approach are already embodied in the exposition of some translators of Buddhist sutras. For instance, as early as the second century, An Shigao 安世高 (c. second century) drew association with Taoist terminology and concepts, which are essentially Chinese, in his translation of foreign Buddhist concepts. Kumarajiva insisted on readability through massive textual adaptation and trimming of the tautological source poetics. (Ma, 1984: 28–35) And the fact that the appeal of the most distinguished Chinese translator of Buddhist scriptures Xuanzang might have been swelled by the throne and aristocracy (Ma, 1984: 51–52) illustrates the influence of institution and patronage on translation, a topic that has gained increasing currency in translation research in the West.

Such contrastive studies strike us that there are indeed universal principles in translation through inductive self-study and deductive cross-referencing, alongside every system's own specificity. To cite one more example, Liang Qichao's 梁啟超 (1873–1929) casual remark that Buddhist sutras were the first foreign texts to be accepted and treated with modesty in China since Buddhist culture at that time attained a status "comparable" to that of China[13] amazingly affirms the claim that the "other" was not considered very important in ancient China. (Bassnett and Lefevere, 1988: 13)

The fact that scripture translators tended to uphold faithfulness to the original sutras, though more in principle than in practice, also interestingly testifies to the opposite of Lefevere's hypothesis: when a high culture "considers itself central with regard to other cultures, it is likely to treat the texts produced by those cultures in a rather cavalier manner." (Lefevere, 1992: 70)[14] Albeit from hindsight, it is my conviction that historical study drawing upon both the indigenous and foreign traditions has proved and will remain heuristic and nourishing to both entities. More importantly, I see this as a means to rediscover indigenous voices that have hitherto been silenced or marginalized by mainstream canons, to revitalize immature or discursive insights that have yet to be expanded and systematized, and feasibly to spark off another renaissance in Chinese studies. We must not forget that the pinnacle of translation in ancient China came during the Tang Dynasty (618–907), a period of cosmopolitan grandeur, territorial expansion and proliferation of the arts, receptive to foreign cultures, notably Buddhist culture from the West. It is worth reflecting that in those days, India was literally the only remarkable Western "other" on the map when China saw itself as the "Middle Kingdom" 中國 of the world. It is also absorbing to note that Buddhism in China has now become more Chinese than Indian, let alone Mauryan or Guptan, reflecting the strikingly successful mediation, or hybridization, between the extraneous Buddhism and indigenous Confucianism and Taoism.

Thus the Roman view on translation as nourishment holds also for translation studies as a whole. Translating another tradition can produce a vigorous and productive hybridity to strengthen the native tradition. It must be reiterated that this presupposes anything but promiscuity. Rather, it calls for reflective meditation, scrupulous assimilation and selective transplantation. Some scholars have done this on a more colossal scale, a telling paragon being the neo-Confucian guru Mou Zongsan 牟宗三[15], albeit beyond the scope of this paper.

Strategic Position of Hong Kong

Alongside our interest in comparative and contrastive studies involving the West, there is no lack of Western scholars who share a genuine interest in Chinese studies. To this end, most of them can only consult existing Western works on Sinology, oriental and contrastive studies, which are comparatively scanty and at times skewed. This is sometimes due to ideological differences, if not for epistemological reasons. The telling fact is that the Translators' Association of China joined the Féderation Internationale des Traducteurs only in 1987. The *International Bibliography of Translations* published by UNESCO does not include China among its 60 member countries, a fact in fact not extraordinary, considering that China is not yet on the bandwagon of the World Trade Organization. But we can see a slight change from recent Western publications like *Translators through History* (Delisle and Woodsworth, 1995), recognizing the contribution of Chinese translators, *Bibliography of Translation Studies* (Lynne, 1998), featuring an entry on "Translating Chinese Literature"[16] and *Routledge Encyclopedia of Translation Studies* (Baker, 1998) with an entry on "Chinese Translation Tradition."[17] There are surely multifarious works on Chinese translation studies that Westerners can check with but, given the ghastly intervening linguistic and cultural gaps, not many of them can seriously read paratactic Chinese. Chances are they might bump into amateur translation and commentary, running the risk of capricious interpretation or even manipulation of secondary sources, such as what Ezra Pound did to the classical Chinese poet Li Bai 李白 (701–762)[18], or Edward Fitzgerald to Omar Khayam.

It is the genuine wish of the writer that Westerners can get an unveiled whole picture of research conducted in this part of the world, through and perhaps better through scholarly contact and writing in English, which has become the de facto international language of communication. Many Chinese scholars, from Chinese Mainland, Hong Kong and Taiwan have extended great efforts in this regard, not least in the realm of translation studies. There are quite a number of Chinese translations and commentaries on Western translation theory, with Eugene Nida and Peter Newmark being the most discussed[19], with their frequent visit to the Far East. Two major examples of recent publications are *An Encyclopaedia of Translation*

(Chan and Pollard, 1995) and *A Topical Bibliography of Translation and Interpretation* (Chan, 1995), assembling essays by Chinese and Western translation scholars, published in Hong Kong.[20] I wish to argue that Hong Kong naturally serves as a window of Chinese translation studies for Western translation scholars. A hundred years of colonial subjugation has effected here an intimate and sobering understanding of and reflection on the reference frame of the Western world, yet it has never detached itself from its matrix, nor has it ever lost its Chinese identity. As far as translation studies is concerned, this Special Administrative Region of the People's Republic of China brags an arresting array of publications, translation associations, research centres, as well as university translation departments offering translation programmes at all levels (Liu Ching-chih, 1998b). The strategic position of Hong Kong interestingly confirms the observation made by Bassnett and Lefevere:

> It is no accident that so much exciting work in translation studies is coming from those cultures who are presently in a phase of post-colonial development. As the world reassesses its relationship to the European "original," so concepts of translation are inevitably re-evaluated and canons of excellence based on Eurocentric models are revised. (Bassnett and Lefevere, 1998: 10)

Returning to the constitution and internationalization of Chinese translation studies, my conviction is shared also by mainland scholars.[21] Actually Chinese scholars have recognized the need for and possibility of establishing a systematized framework for the study of Chinese translation, for example, Dong Qiusi 董秋斯 as early as 1951. He has drawn no few successors, as already mentioned above. Two recent reference tools, *A Companion for Chinese Translators* 《中國翻譯詞典》 (Lin *et al.*, 1997) and *Dictionary of Chinese Translators* 《中國翻譯家辭典》 (Lin *et al.*, 1998), should suit Dong's criterion of large-scale study projects. The former, apart from general entries, features a section on commentaries of one hundred translation scholars and an appended index on translation thesis from 1914 to 1995. On the level of individual and specific critique, one illuminating view comes from Zhang Borang 張柏然, who criticized past studies speculating the translator's experience, the translated text and the reader as the thing-in-itself, which should, in his view, be perceived as the form of existence to be determined by translation as a pure concept. His stance that the study of translation should be ontological echoes, for instance, the Low Countries School of translation scholars who believe translation studies should be ontological, epistemological and a priori. We again trace another manifestation of universality here. Recent re-examination of the translated works and notes of Yan Fu reveal that the most influential translator-theorist in modern China actually attempted a century ago, consciously or otherwise, a very functional and reader-oriented approach to translation[22], and can be studied and interpreted as such, in spite of Yan's explication himself on faithfulness, expressiveness and elegance as the norms of translating.[23]

I see such efforts as yet another illustration of consolidation of Chinese heritage through self-reflection and cross-referencing, which can simultaneously provide insights to Western studies on, say, functional approaches, cultural and post-colonial studies.[24] I also see them as another form of internationalization of translation studies, which should not be limited to any medium (e.g. English) or channel (e.g. "international" journal) of discourse. I am optimistic that this will chart a healthy course in the development of Chinese translation studies, free from the danger of blind allegiance to home traditions or indiscriminate pursuit of Western models. This is afterall a post-structuralist world devoid of simplistic parameters, in which fuzzy logic may be better than conventional wisdom, hybridity preferred to narcissism. Of course, such studies can become truly reciprocal and mutually beneficial if concerted efforts can be made to translate more works on Chinese translation studies and to discuss and write about Chinese translation studies in European languages, as well as in major international venues. This, in my opinion, can serve to foster interface, clarify obscurities and soften differences.[25]

To this end eventually, Hong Kong can be pivoted as a centre of Chinese translation studies. Indeed Hong Kong has thrived as the window of China to the Western world. In my opinion, this one-time British colony enjoys a coveted position in working out what and how Chinese and Western elements can and cannot be mediated, especially now that it is endowed with a more transparent eye affixed by an unequivocal Chinese identity after a hundred years of colonial interpellation. So with our own tradition, we need consolidation, re-reading. With the West, we need positive engagement, not containment. Suffice it to remember the unprecedented boom in Buddhist culture and translation theory we once enjoyed through translating our Indian West. I would like to end here on a slightly philosophical note: What is East and what is West? Or more specifically, where is the East and where is the West. The planet in which we are living is round after all.

Notes

1. Titled after a Hollywood movie, directed by Robert Zemeckis and starring Michael J. Fox.
2. The writer wishes to thank Professor Susan Bassnett and Dr. Jane Stevenson for their invaluable post-conference comments on this paper.
3. Liu's blueprint of Modern Translation Studies comprises two organic constructions: an internal scheme embracing the study of translation history, translation theory and information engineering; an external scheme embracing thought and philosophy, linguistics and semiotics, and culture and sociology. (Liu, 1990: 18–22) Liu expounds upon his perspective of translation studies in his later volumes, notably 1991 and 1995.
4. See Preface in Zhang and Xu, 1997, pp. 1–2.
5. See, for example, Yip, on the syntactic problems in translating Chinese poems and how this is tackled by Pound, pp. 8–33.
6. See also Liu Miqing, 1990, pp. 12–3; Tan, 1998a, p. 16.
7. On the essential distinction between Chinese and Western philosophy, I am basically drawing from Mou Zongsan; Xu Siyuan and Feng Yu-lan.
8. See Chen Fukang, 1992; Chen Yugang, 1989; Liu Ching-chih, 1981; Luo Xinzhang, 1984; Ma, 1984.
9. There are other publications which use the term "translatology" and "translation studies" quite loosely, e.g. employing "translatology" when they mean translation theory, and "translation studies" to mean translation techniques. It is beside the point to make a list out of them and it should be noted that such works also offer valuable insights to both translation and translating.
10. See Venuti, 1998, Robinson, 1997, Bhabha, 1994, Alvarez and Vidal, 1996, Niranjana, 1992, and Cheyfitz, 1991. One confession is that, in cultural anthropology, "for many Europeans, any non-European cultures were automatically 'anthropologized' and their cultures studied and evaluated as 'other'. The norm was European." (Bassnett and Lefevere, 1998:130)
11. On the importance of comparative studies in language, culture and society, see for example, Liu Zhongde, 1998; Luo and She, 1997; Liu Miqing, 1991; Yang and Li, 1990; Deng and Liu, 1989.
12. See Dryden, in Robinson, 1997, p. 174.
13. See Liang, 1988, p. 85. The translation of Buddhist scriptures into Chinese in fact embodies many notions central to the tenets of modern translation studies, discussed in my paper titled "Translation of Buddhist Scriptures into Chinese: A Power-governed Discourse" presented at the Conference on Translation and Power, University of Warwick, 1997 and forthcoming in *Translation Perspectives*.
14. In fact, the two golden eras of translation in China occurred when the source culture being translated achieved a high status in the target system. As the translation of Buddhist scriptures boomed from the fourth to the seventh centuries, Buddhist culture was esteemed and contemporary Indian economy was flourishing. Starting from the middle of the nineteenth-century, volumi-

nous works on Western learning and thoughts were introduced when Western economic and political power imposed upon the antiquated target culture as progressive and intimidating.

[15] Mou Zongsan (1909–1995), most influential figure of "the third movement of Confucianism," is noted for rejuvenating Chinese culture and philosophy by reflecting on the Chinese tradition and cross-referencing with Western traditions.

[16] Eugene Eoyang and Lin Yao-fu, eds.

[17] Eva Hung and David E. Pollard.

[18] Curiously enough, though, Pound's interpretation of Chinese poetry has contributed significantly to the development of Modern English poetry. Yet such "whimsical" enterprise might be the least necessary, if not the least tolerated, in the globalized twenty-first century.

[19] See, for example, Jin, 1998; Jin and Nida, 1984; Tan, 1993, 1984 and Chang, 1996.

[20] Liu Ching-chih, 1998a, in his review of the two works, remarks that translation studies dealing with Chinese and English should be "rooted in Hong Kong, contributing to China and fronting the world" and Hong Kong has played a leading role in this respect.

[21] See Xu Jun, 1998, pp. 463–584 on "Translation Theory Polemics." One of the essays directly calls for the establishment of translation departments and research centres in major universities, writing of high quality research papers, preferably in an international language like English and French, and targeted to international journals, like *Target, Perspectives* and *Babel.* (Wang Ning, "My Views on the Internationalization of Translation Studies," pp. 554–57)

[22] See, for example, Huang, 1998; Wong, 1997.

[23] See Yan's article in Luo, 1984 and Liu, 1981. Yan discussed the three norms in his famous and often quoted preface to his translation of Huxley. In terms of esteem and coverage, Yan is probably the most significant translation theorist in China hitherto. Resulting from his three norms is a basically philological debate dominating Chinese translation theory over the past century; this can be attributed partly to the Chinese tradition of respect for authority and canonized texts.

[24] Responding to the cultural turn in translation studies, there are publications like Wang, 1997, Luo and She, 1997. As for post-colonial studies, a number of scholars based in Hong Kong have done refreshing case studies on the role and policy of translators and interpreters serving Western governments and institutions in China, including Hong Kong, during the period of Western imperialism; some case studies were presented at this Conference.

[25] I agree totally with Bassnett's eloquence in this regard, "...both cultural studies and translation studies have tended to move in the direction of the collaborative approach, with the establishment of research teams and groups, and with more international networks and increased communication...in these multifaceted interdisciplines, isolation is counterproductive. Translation is, after all, dialogic in its very nature, involving as it does more than one voice. The study of translation, like the study of culture, needs a plurality of voices." (Bassnett and Lefevere, 1998, p. 138)

References

Works in Chinese

Chen, Fukang (1992).《中國翻譯理論史稿》(*A History of Chinese Translation Theory*). Shanghai: Shanghai Foreign Languages Educational Press.

Chen, Yugang (1989).《中國翻譯文學史稿》(*A History of Chinese Translation Literature*). Beijing: Foreign Translation Press.

Deng, Yanchang and Liu Runqing (1989).《語言與文化》(*Language and Culture*). Beijing: Foreign Languages Teaching and Studies Press.

Dong, Qiusi (1984).〈論翻譯理論的建設〉(On the Construction of Translation Theory). In Luo Xinzhang, ed.,《翻譯論集》(*Anthology of Translation Theory*). Beijing: The Commercial Press, pp. 536–44.

Huang, Zhonglian (1998).〈重識嚴復的翻譯思想〉(Re-reading Yan Fu's Thoughts on Translation),《中國翻譯》(*Chinese Translators Journal*), Vol. 2, No. 12, pp. 6–8.

Jin, Di (1998).《等效翻譯探索》(*Explorations on Equivalent-effect Translation*). Taibei: Shulin Publishing.

Liang, Qichao (1988).《中國佛教研究史》(*History of Chinese Buddhist Studies*). Shanghai: Joint Publishing Press.

Lin, Hui *et al.*, eds. (1998).《中國翻譯家辭典》(*A Dictionary of Chinese Translators*). Beijing: Foreign Translation Press.

Lin, Huangtian *et al.*, eds. (1997).《中國翻譯詞典》(*A Companion for Chinese Translators*). Wuhan: Hubei Educational Press.

Liu, Ching-chih (1998a). "Review of *An Encyclopaedia of Translation* and *A Topical Bibliography of Translation and Interpretation*." *Translation Quarterly,* Nos. 7–8, pp.161–66.

Liu, Ching-chih, ed. (1981).《翻譯論集》(*Essays on Translation*). Hong Kong: Joint Publishing.

Liu, Miqing (1995).《翻譯美學導論》(*Introduction to Translation Aesthetics*). Taibei: Shulin Press.

Liu, Miqing (1991).《漢英對比研究與翻譯》(*Chinese/English-English/Chinese Contrastive Studies and Translation*). Nanchang: Jiangxi Education Publishing House.

Liu, Miqing (1990).《現代翻譯理論》(*Studies on Translation Today*). Nanchang: Jiangxi Education Publishing House.

Liu, Zhongde, ed. (1998).《英漢語比較與翻譯》(*Comparative Studies of English and Chinese*). Qingdao: Qingdao Press.

Luo, Xinzhang (1984).《翻譯論集》(*An Anthology of Translation Theory*). Beijing: The Commercial Press.

Luo, Xuanmin and She Xiebin, eds. (1997).《外語・翻譯・文化》(*Foreign Languages, Translation and Culture*). Changsha: Hunan Science and Technology Press.

Ma, Zuyi (1984).《中國翻譯簡史》(*A Concise History of Chinese Translation*). Beijing: Foreign Translation Press.

Mou, Zongsan (1983).《中國哲學十九講》(*19 Lectures on Chinese Philosophy*). Taipei: Student Bookshop.

Mou, Zongsan (1963).《中國哲學的特質》(*The Characteristics of Chinese Philosophy*). Taipei: Student Bookshop.

Mou, Zongsan (1980).《中西哲學之會通十四講》(*14 Lectures on the Interface between Chinese and Western Philosophy*). Taipei: Student Bookshop.

Tan, Zaixi (1998a).〈翻譯學必須重視中西譯論對比研究〉(The Significance of Chinese-Western Comparative Studies in Translation Studies).《中國翻譯》(*Chinese Translators Journal*), Vol. 2, No. 12, pp. 12–16.

Tan, Zaixi (1993).《跨語交際》(*Interlingual Communication*). Guilin: Lijiang Publishing.

Tan, Zaixi (1984).《奈達論翻譯》(*Nida on Translation*). Beijing: Foreign Translation Press.

Tan, Zaixi (1998b). "On the *Routledge Encyclopedia of Translation Studies.*" *Journal of Translation Studies*, No. 2, pp. 86–91.

Wang, Kefei (1997).《翻譯文化史論》(*Cultural History in Translation*). Shanghai: Shanghai Foreign Languages Education Press.

Wong, Wang-chi (1997).〈重釋「信、達、雅」── 論嚴復的翻譯理論〉("Xin, Da, Ya": On Yan Fu's Translation Theories), *Journal of Translation Studies*, No. 1, pp. 36–62.

Xu, Jun, ed. (1998).《翻譯思考錄》(*Reflections on Translation*). Wuhan: Hubei Education Press.

Xu, Siyuan (1997).《中西文化回眸》(*Reflections on Chinese and Western Culture*). Shanghai: Huadong Normal University Press.

Yang, Zijian and Li Ruihua, eds. (1990).《英漢對比研究論文集》(*Anthology of English-Chinese Contrastive Studies*). Shanghai: Shanghai Foreign Languages Education Press.

Yang, Zijian and Liu Xueyun, eds. (1994).《翻譯新論‧1983–1992》(*New Anthology of Translation, 1983–1992*). Wuhan: Hubei Education Press.

Zhang, Borang (1997).〈翻譯本體論的斷想〉(Contemplation on the Ontology of Translation). In Zhang Borang and Xu Jun, eds.《譯學論集》(*Selected Essays on Translation Studies*). Nanjing: Yilin Press, pp. 55–63.

Zhang, Borang and Xu Jun, eds. (1997).《譯學論集》(*Selected Essays on Translation Studies*). Nanjing: Yilin Press.

Works in English

Alvarez, R. and M. C. Vidal, eds. (1996). *Translation, Power and Subversion.* Clevedon: Multilingual Matters.

Baker, Mona, ed. (1998). *Routledge Encyclopedia of Translation Studies.* London and New York: Routledge.

Barthes, Roland (1974). *S/Z.* Trans. Richard Miller. Oxford: Blackwell.

Bassnett, Susan and André Lefevere (1998). *Constructing Cultures: Essays on Literary Translation*. Clevedon: Multilingual Matters Ltd.

Bhabha, Homi K. (1994). *The Location of Culture*. London and New York: Routledge.

Chan, Sin-wai (1995). *A Topical Bibliography of Translation and Interpretation: Chinese-English, English-Chinese*. Hong Kong: The Chinese University Press.

Chan, Sin-wai and David E. Pollard, eds. (1995). *An Encyclopaedia of Translation: Chinese-English, English-Chinese*. Hong Kong: The Chinese University Press.

Chang, Nam-fung (1996). "Toward a Better Theory of Equivalent Effect." *Babel*, Vol. 42, No. 1, pp. 1–17.

Cheyfirz, Eric (1991). *The Poetics of Imperialism: Translation and Colonization from the Tempest to Tarzan*. New York and London: Oxford University Press.

Delisle, J. and J. Woodsworth, eds. (1995). *Translators through History*. Amsterdam: John Benjamins.

Feng, Yu-lan (c.1948). *A Short History of Chinese Philosophy*. London: Collier Macmillan.

Holmes, James (1988). *Translated! Papers in Literary Translation and Translation Studies*. Amsterdam: Rodopi.

Jin, Di and Eugene Nida (1984). *On Translation: With Special Reference to Chinese and English*. Beijing: Foreign Translation Press.

Lau, D. C., tr. (1963). *Tao Te Ch'ing*. Hong Kong: The Chinese University Press.

Lefevere, André, ed. (1992). *Translation, History, Culture: A Sourcebook*. London and New York: Routledge.

Lefevere, André, ed. (1978). "Translation Studies: The Goal of the Discipline." In J. Holmes, J. Lambert and R. van den Broek, eds. *Literature and Translation*. Leuven: ACCO, pp. 234–35.

Liu, Ching-chih (1998b)."Translation Syllabuses at the Tertiary Level in Hong Kong." *Translation Quarterly*, Nos. 9–10, pp. 29–84.

Lynn, R. J., tr. (1984). *The Classic of Changes*. New York: Columbia University Press.

Lynne, Bowker, *et. al.*, eds. (1998). *Bibliography of Translation Studies*. Manchester: St. Jerome.

Niranjana, Tejaswini (1992). *Siting Translation*. California: University of California Press.

Robinson, Douglas (1997). *Translation and Empire: Postcolonial Theories Explained*. Manchester: St. Jerome.

Shuttleworth, Mark and Moira Cowie (1997). *Dictionary of Translation Studies*. Manchester: St Jerome.

Snell-Hornby, Mary (1995). *Translation Studies: An Integrated Approach*. Revised Edition. Amsterdam: John Benjamins.

Venuti, Lawrence (1998). *The Scandals of Translation*. London: Routledge.

Yip, Wai-lim (1969). *Ezra Pound's Cathay*. Princeton: Princeton University Press.

Effective Bilingualism and Hong Kong Government Translators — The Way Forward

Michael Chuen Kam-hung
Official Languages Agency
The Government of the Hong Kong Special Administrative Region

Translation services flourish in Hong Kong with good historical reason. As a place where East meets West, Hong Kong has had a long history of bilingualism. The Official Languages Ordinance, enacted in 1974, stipulates that English and Chinese are the official languages of Hong Kong, and that both languages enjoy equal status in official communication between the Government or any public officers and members of the public. While the Ordinance establishes the legal status of Chinese as a medium of communication between the Government and the public, English was still predominantly used within the civil service in the years that followed. At that time, government documents ranging from internal papers to letters to the public were mostly drafted in English. Hence, translation services were often required when the Government wished to communicate with the public in Chinese.

There are a number of grades in the civil service which provide translation and interpretation services, namely the Law Translation Officer, Police Translator and Court Interpreter grades and the Chinese Language Officer (CLO) and Simultaneous Interpreter grades under the Official Languages Agency (OLA). In so far as the number of employees is concerned, the HKSAR Government is the largest employer of translators in Hong Kong. Among the grades mentioned above, the CLO grade has the largest establishment and handles the most government documents both in terms of quantity and variety, so I will, therefore, make close reference to the work of the CLO grade in addressing my topic today.

The initial set-up of the CLO grade comprised about 200 officers in three ranks. It has now expanded to over 550 officers in five ranks, namely CLOII, CLOI, SCLO, CCLO and PCLO. Of them, some 160 are working at the OLA headquarters, while the rest are posted to bureaux and departments. The types of documents handled by CLOs vary from department to department, with the majority being official documents related to departmental administration and policies. The development toward a more open and accountable government has generated an increasing number of official documents, including policy briefs, consultation papers, consultancy documents and investigation reports. To name a few, we have policy addresses by the Chief Executive, budget speeches by the Financial Secretary, annual reports on Hong Kong, the recently-published inquiry report on the new airport, as well as a range of booklets, leaflets and forms distributed at the District Offices. All these documents are published in both Chinese and English. Last year, the official documents translated by the OLA headquarters alone amounted to a wordcount of 4.5 million. While the number of words serves to reflect the workload, an analysis of the figure will shed light on the changes in the nature, trend and direction of translation work in the Government in recent years.

As I mentioned earlier, English has been, until quite recently, the major working language in the civil service. As a result, communication between the Government and the public often had to rely on translation, mainly from English to Chinese. Hong Kong's reunification with China has brought about many changes, one of which is the growing importance attached to the Chinese language. Article 9 of the Basic Law states: In addition to the Chinese language, English may also be used as an official language by the executive authorities, legislature and judiciary of the Hong Kong Special Administrative Region. There have been diversified views as to whether Article 9 implies a primary role for Chinese and a secondary one for English, or whether both languages share equal importance. But we know one thing for sure. While the Government may use English in accordance with Article 9 of the Basic Law, Chinese will certainly be the language widely used for internal and external communication. The "new status" of the Chinese language has also brought about changes to our translation duties.

First, there have been changes in the types of documents to be translated from English to Chinese. Given the Government's determination to transform its language culture, and with the rising importance of the Chinese language, a growing percentage of less complex documents for day-to-day communication with the public are drafted in Chinese. The demand for English-to-Chinese translation service for this type of documents will fall. On the other hand, owing to new language habits and emerging operational needs, more and more documents which used to have English versions only now need to be translated into Chinese. What I am referring to are documents of a specialized and technical nature.

In the past, English was the primary working language in the Government and professional sectors. It was only logical that many specialized and technical documents were prepared in English only. This was also the case with our legal documents, as Hong Kong adopts the English common law system. But things are quite different now. To enhance transparency and communication with the public on the one hand, and to promote bilingualism and wider use of Chinese on the other, the Government has been providing Chinese versions to different types of documents. These range from legislation to contracts, tenders, as well as internal rules and regulations such as the Civil Service Regulations. These Chinese texts are no longer prepared just for the sake of reference, but rather to serve practical purposes. Given the variety and quantity of these documents, translation work in this area is expected to constitute the bulk of the workload for Government translators in the foreseeable future.

The "restructuring" of our translation services is also marked by an increasing demand for Chinese-to-English translation. Likewise, this has to do with the wider use of Chinese in the civil service. In 1995, the Government published the *Report of the Working Group on the Use of Chinese in the Civil Service*, setting out its policy to develop a civil service biliterate in Chinese and English and trilingual in Cantonese, English and Putonghua. The Report also called for greater use of Chinese in Government. Since then, we have seen civil servants switching to Chinese in drafting official documents. Many speeches and some of the committee papers are now prepared in Chinese and translated into English afterwards. By and large, while English-to-Chinese translation still accounts for the greater part of the translation work in the Government, the demand for Chinese-to-English translation is on the increase.

Judging from the above trend of development and the practical uses of the translation of official documents, the Government will put equal emphasis on both Chinese-to-English and English-to-Chinese translation in future.

The wider use of Chinese in the Government, both internally and externally, has another impact on the work of the CLOs. With more and more civil servants using Chinese in official business, CLOs are expected to play an active role in drafting Chinese documents and vetting Chinese drafts prepared by subject officers.

On the "restructuring" of our translation services and the way ahead, I must now come to how Government translators should equip themselves in the new environment. I mentioned earlier that translation of documents of a specialized and technical nature would form a major part of our CLOs' job in future. The technicality of the context of these documents, coupled with the terminology and complex sentence structures involved, has very often made comprehension and translation of the texts a formidable task for the translators. They must therefore be proficient in both the source and target languages to be able to handle the job competently. It will be an added advantage, of course, if they possess some knowledge in the relevant fields. The increasing demand for Chinese-to-English translation also calls for further enhancement in English on the part of the translators. They have to master the English language in order to produce skilful renditions faithful to the original texts. All in all, a good command of both the Chinese and English languages remains to be the requisite basic skills for Government translators, and this is particularly true now as both languages are enjoying equal status.

As to the way forward for translation services in the Government, we will be putting equal emphasis on both the English and Chinese languages while attaching equal importance to quality as well as productivity. As announced in last year's Policy Address the Government is implementing an Enhanced Productivity Programme with the objective of raising the overall productivity of the civil service by 5%. How to cope with an ever-increasing workload without compromising the quality of the service is bound to be a new challenge faced by the Government translators.

As the saying goes, "There is no limit to knowledge." I believe this means more to language workers, including translators, than to anyone else. Language lives, and is constantly evolving. To be a highly proficient translator, one cannot but keep updating one's knowledge. Learning is a life-long process, and it is the only way to equip ourselves for any challenges and difficulties we may encounter as translators. We have developed from a language culture that uses English predominantly to one that gives equal status to both English and Chinese. As to our translation services, we are attaching importance to quality as much as productivity. Whatever the changes ahead, translators who are well equipped with the professional skills can always keep abreast of the times.

Hong Kong's Bilingual Laws Programme*

Tony Yen Yuen Ho
Department of Justice
The Government of the Hong Kong Special Administrative Region

I would like to talk about the historical setting first, and then identify certain difficulties and problems that arise in legal translation. I shall then discuss how these difficulties and problems can be resolved and how judges and the legal profession use Chinese in their everyday legal work.

As we all know, the working language of lawyers and judges used to be English. For a long time after Hong Kong was occupied by Britain over 150 years ago, all local laws and regulations that affected the livelihood and rights and obligations of the people of Hong Kong had been drawn up solely in English, and ratified and put into effect by the law-making body in that language. However, the majority of the population is Chinese-speaking. If the laws, a tool regulating the norms of behaviour of both the administration and the general public, continue to be in a language unfamiliar to them, how can we say that the legal system is a perfectly just system?

Supposing we were involved in litigation or had some legal problems concerning our rights that had to be resolved in a court of law, but the judge on the bench presiding over the court would only use a language that we do not understand, or are not too familiar with, and even your lawyer would not put forward your arguments in a way that you can understand, then would you say that your rights have been guaranteed, or that the law has helped you? In our society, the importance of democracy and governance

---

* This is the English translation of the speech given by Mr. Tony Yen at the "Symposium on Translation in Hong Kong: Past, Present and Future" held by The Chinese University of Hong Kong on 19 March 1999.

by the rule of law are often emphasized, but if the law is not expressed in a language that people do understand, how can you expect the public to understand the law, know their rights and obligations, and be law-abiding citizens? This language barrier was an impediment to the popularization of the rule of law and good civic education. It only helped to create an unfair situation.

In the 1960s and 1970s, as people became more aware of the unfairness of the situation, a movement calling for an increased use of the Chinese language gradually gained force. The government finally recognized that the legal system should not operate solely in English, and at least the written language that was familiar to most of its citizens should also be used as a legal language so that they could understand more easily the system and all the laws that related to them.

The government eventually began its Bilingual Laws Programme in 1986. One of the most important items on the agenda was to render into Chinese more than 20,000 pages of statutes that had been drawn up and enacted in English only in Hong Kong over a period extending for more than a hundred years. Also, since 1989, draft legislation has to be prepared in both English and Chinese for submission to the Legislative Council for discussion and ratification.

Full legislative bilingualism is a historic and unprecedented move. We experienced tremendous difficulties in the preparatory stage as we did not have enough qualified personnel at the start of the project. Also, legal language, like many other technical languages, has its own peculiar and unique terminology and it is often difficult to find equivalent expressions in the other language when translating the common law. To express English and American legal concepts in Chinese is not easy at all.

Notwithstanding these difficulties, the Law Drafting Division finally completed the translation of all the laws in Hong Kong before the Reunification.

The following is a rather brief account of some of the difficulties we faced. First, we realized that many of the statutes of current laws had been indiscriminately copied from existing English statutes of over 200 years of age, and that they were laden with outdated concepts or antiquated English expressions. Many sentences ran into two to three hundred words without a full stop, presenting us with great difficulty in translating them into Chinese. We had to parse these long sentences into several shorter ones before we could do anything to them.

Our greatest difficulty in translating the laws was the relatively rigid nature within which we had to operate. We did not have the flexibility to change the original text by rearranging the word order, nor could we employ a free-style of translation. We had to grasp all the legal elements of the English source text, and account for every one of them in the Chinese translation. Faced with these restraints, we used what is called the "hard translation" approach. More or less had to "match" the English text by a word-by-word equivalent. The result may not be pleasing, but we can't jettison accuracy for the sake of apparent smoothness. Law translation is different from other kinds of translation, for example the translation of literary and artistic works. Every word in a statute carries its own meaning that may define important rights and responsibilities, and a slight difference in wording can mean litigation, so the strictest attention has to be paid to accuracy. In order to achieve complete accuracy of the laws, sometimes we are bound to compromise the smooth flow of the text. Some of the legal provisions are thus not easy to read.

Certain legal terminology is not in general use in Chinese. Just take the transfer of property or real estate as an example. English has *transfer, give, convey, demise, devise, assign, bequeath* and so on. They all mean some sort of alienation of property rights, but there are not so many words to express the concept "to transfer property" in Chinese. The English words share a core meaning, that is, property changed hands, but the actual legal meaning of every word above is different. Some of these words indicate the outright transfer of property, others refer to a formal transfer and even a gift by will. Behind every word lies a different legal concept, we cannot just use a single Chinese word, for example, 轉讓 ("transfer"), to stand for these seven to eight English words. Risking criticism, sometimes we have to coin new words and expressions in order to bring out the different legal meanings in some specialized terms.

Didn't the gurus long ago coin many new words when they translated the Buddhist Scriptures and other foreign works? Today for example, we have words like *langman* 浪漫 (romantic), *youmo* 幽默 (humour), *datong* 大同 (great harmony), *shijie* 世界 (world) and *pudu* 普渡 (universal salvation), in the Chinese lexicon that bear specific meanings. Coinage of words has been around a long time and some coined words have been so frequently used that they have been well accepted, thus enriching the modern Chinese lexicon. Recent examples like *bashi* 巴士 (bus), *dishi* 的士 (taxi), *aizi* 愛滋 (AIDs), *wangzhi* 網址 (URL), *heike* 黑客 (hacker), and even *kala'ouke* 卡拉OK (Karaoke), all have gradually appeared in the

Chinese language and became a part of it. We feel that the translation of the laws may give rise to a similar phenomenon. When some of these words were first used, they were criticized by legal circles due to their unfamiliarity. We did that because we had no choice — we could not find an equivalent word in modern Chinese for some of the old legal concepts. As more newly coined words are used, the new generation of legal practitioners and paralegals will gradually become more used to them and will be more likely to accept them. This process will enrich Chinese legal usage.

To sum up, we can get around all these problems by a variety of means, but we feel that they are nevertheless no ideal path to a perfect Chinese text, mainly because of the limitations of the original text. Yet, the Department of Justice has to perform the urgent and heavy legislative tasks which will tie down our resources for two to three years before we can critically and carefully examine all statutes, and then redraft them again (as the provisions may require) in plain modern Chinese and English.

In the past, we could not touch the original English text. But in future we will be able to reorganize or divide into paragraphs some of those extremely antiquated and obscure English legislative provisions in the new legislative format and design, and to draft them again in plain language. This will also help iron out difficulties in the Chinese version.

We estimate that this task will commence at the end of 1999 and take at least seven to eight years before any obvious improvement can be seen. We hope that if you read the statutes when the work is completed, you will feel that the English and Chinese texts have been better written and easier to understand.

We will perform this task seriously because we think that the law is important. We hope that through these efforts, we will make legal language clearer and easier to understand, so that everyone will be interested in what the law means, have a better understanding of their own rights and obligations, hold a greater respect for the rule of law and thus have an even higher law-abiding spirit.

Presently all statutes are in both English and Chinese, the two texts enjoy equal legal status. In other words, the English version *and* the Chinese version can be equally cited in courts of law. Moreover, if there is any discrepancy in meaning between them, we cannot say that English or Chinese text will take precedence. Of course, translation is subject to linguistic restraints inherent in the source and target texts, so there is a chance that different people will come up with different meanings on the same text. I believe that this accounts for the apparent ambiguities in the

bilingual legislative texts. This may cause litigation, but we have an inter-
pretative guide, so the judges will have a ready reference on the interpretation of texts if any ambiguity between the two texts arises before them.
The text that best expresses the meaning of the principles enshrined in the
original legislation will be adopted, so there is no cause for alarm if the
Chinese and English texts appear to be somewhat different.

Now let's look ahead and talk about how we can promote the use of
Chinese in the legal field. As I have mentioned in the beginning, judges and
lawyers receive their legal training in English, so when they do legal work,
it is natural for their minds to switch immediately to the "English channel."
All university legal references, teaching materials and textbooks on the
common law have until very recently been mainly in English, so judges
and lawyers are used to using English as a working language. Yet, there is
a significant change in the attitude towards language use in recent years. In
the majority of cases in magistrate's courts Chinese is now used as the
medium of communication, and most of the magistrates are bilingual. But
when you get to the High Court the situation may be different. There are
many judges and lawyers in the Hong Kong legal circle who do not
understand Chinese, so that the case is better conducted in English if the
judge hearing that case and the lawyers representing the parties can't speak
Chinese. Hong Kong is an international city in which many foreign companies will run into legal problems from time to time, and big cases,
especially commercial ones, that are before the High Court, are generally
reported in English, so lawyers and judges tend to use English. This is
appropriate and causes no injustice. On the other hand, many criminal
cases like traffic offences, regulatory breaches of the Public Health and
Municipal Services Ordinance and cases of small claims are heard at a
lower level of the courts. Most legal proceedings involving local people are
conducted in these lower courts, and since the main issue is usually on the
finding of facts only, it will be easier to get to the truth if Chinese is used.
Everybody is able to understand the proceedings clearly, so peoples' rights
and justice are better preserved. In the High Court, however, English is
usually the more convenient medium since most documents are in English,
and parties do not generally feel that this creates any major problem.

All along we have been talking of a bilingual legal system. By bilingual we mean Chinese *and* English, not discarding English in favour of
Chinese or giving Chinese the superior status that English once had. A
bilingual system that emphasizes one language at the expense of another is
unfair. It is much fairer now to use both Chinese *and* English.

Judges and lawyers are diligently studying and raising their academic standards in Chinese. I hope that eventually in the future when matters reach the High Court, we will be able to present all our cases before bilingual judges.

In the past when we purchased a property we would see piles of property deeds which were all written in English only. Many people simply did not know what was in these documents; even people who understood English did not understand those documents, which made the situation even worse. The Law Society of Hong Kong has set up a task force to carry out research and translations of standard legal documents that people often need to sign. So when local people are involved in legal actions, they will all able to understand the relevant legal documents. The Law Society also shares with the Department of Justice the wish of improving on the form of outmoded and outdated English legal documents by using plain English, and refining the convoluted and incomprehensible legal clauses. These efforts will greatly help popularizing and upholding the law.

The Government, judges and lawyers are working hard for a bilingual legal system. I hope all of us will lend them our support.

Translation and the Internationality of Hong Kong

Zhang Longxi
Department of Chinese, Translation and Linguistics
City University of Hong Kong

As someone arriving in Hong Kong only recently, just a little more than eight months ago, I feel ill-equipped to discuss translation in Hong Kong in any depth. As a sort of outsider, however, I fancy myself capable of turning my blindness into some kind of a fresh insight into things that may be too obvious to be noticed by people inside, and which are nonetheless important for understanding Hong Kong. What I have to say will therefore be both obvious and, in my eyes at least, important for discussing translation in Hong Kong, particularly the future of translation.

Hong Kong is probably unique among the world's great cities in its bilingual programmes and services and its essential international character. Looking at comparable metropolises in the world — New York, London, Paris, Berlin, Beijing, Shanghai, just mention a few — the extent to which bilingualism reaches the various strata of society is probably much higher in Hong Kong than in any other place. I do not just mean the signs in both Chinese and English that you find in all kinds of shops, train and metro stations, government offices and academic institutions, the kind of thing that helps tourists to locate themselves in the labyrinth of a big city. In Hong Kong English still has a much more significant role to play than just to provide tourists with a survival kit, because in official communication, English is often the only language or, when there are bilingual texts, the authoritative one or the one that is legally binding. In courthouses and university classrooms, even in large department stores, English is still the major language. At the same time, Hong Kong is a Chinese community and the use of Chinese coexists with that of English in all aspects of life. A glance at any newsstand or a push of the TV remote control button will be sufficient to convince us of the coexistence of these two languages in media and in society at large, and it is this coexistence of languages that marks Hong Kong as a truly international city. Consequently, translation, and specifically translation between English and Chinese, becomes a thriving business in Hong Kong. This of course has much to do with the past of Hong Kong as a British colony, and there might be an argument, in this post-colonial phase, for a decrease in the use of English as part of the process of decolonization. Indeed, some might ask, if the Americans and the British only speak English, and the French only French, why should English be an important language in Hong Kong, which has always been predominantly Chinese in its population? Perhaps the rather popular idea of *muyu jiaoyu* or "mother-tongue education" arose in Hong Kong in such a context, and it has already generated a good deal of discussion. All these, of course, bear directly on the future of translation in Hong Kong. That is to say, whether translation will have a future here very much depends on the continual presence of bilingualism in the Hong Kong society.

Despite the political appeal of the argument for decolonization or localization, I believe that to turn Hong Kong into a monolingual society is not at all in the interest of Hong Kong and its people. It is commonly believed, though perhaps not really true, that most Americans don't learn any foreign language. But even if it were true, it is precisely what many American educators see as a serious problem. Derek Bok, a former President of Harvard University, laments over American "parochialism and lack of language skills," and the fact that "American students also lag behind their counterparts in other industrialized nations in their knowledge of foreign cultures and their ability to speak foreign languages." (Bok, 1990: 27, 36) As for the French, the stereotype of a Frenchman is a monolingual snob who never condescends to speak anything but his own language. As Count Antoine de Rivarol argued in 1784 in his pamphlet, *De l'universalité de la langue française,* that French should be the universal language. "What was the need for a universal language, asked the count, when a perfect language existed already?" The language was, of course, French (Eco, 1997: 300). French used to be the language of Europe's educated elite and the language of international affairs, but the situation changed dramatically after the Second World War, and English has long since replaced French as the *lingua franca.* Today, even the French would feel the limitations of their linguistic and cultural narcissism, and the establishment of a European Union would further promote the interactions, and with it translations, among the different nations in Europe. That is to say, translation as the necessary means for communication is clearly recognized in the West as crucial in this world of ours, in which it has become increasingly difficult, if not totally impossible, to indulge in self-imposed

isolation and parochialism. Internationality, in other words, is the characteristic of our times.

The future of Hong Kong depends very much on the continuation of its
being a truly international metropolis, a great centre of world finance, a
major seaport, and one of Asia's large manufacturers of consumer goods.
After the return to Chinese sovereignty and the establishment of the Hong
Kong SAR in 1997, Hong Kong now occupies the unique position of being
part of China and yet at the same time an autonomous region with its
capitalist system intact and distinct from the mainland. The recent debate
on the rule of law in Hong Kong and how does this relate to its status as an
autonomous SAR is very instructive. Under such circumstances, the legal
and political significance of Hong Kong becomes more prominent and its
connections with the outside world very important not only for Hong Kong
but for China as well. Genuine bilingualism and the use of English for
various purposes thus have more than just a practical value, and I would
argue that the attractiveness of Hong Kong as a great city owes much to its
bilingualism, its international appeal. Without the coexistence of two languages (or three, if we count Putonghua as a third), Hong Kong would not
be what it is. As we step into a new century and a new millennium, we shall
see more interactions among different nations and cultures, and because of
its special location and history, Hong Kong has always been a place where
the East meets the West. It is an ideal location for East-West comparative
study of the various aspects of social and cultural life. Looking into the
future, there is no doubt that both the government and the people of Hong
Kong have realized the challenge this great city faces in preserving its
international character and its unique position of being the place where the
Chinese and the Western coexist. Here again, translation is crucial. It plays
an important part in education, social service, and communication. It
satisfies a practical need and also plays the role of a cultural characteristic
that shows the internationality of Hong Kong. In this sense, then, before
translation solves any practical problem of rendering a term or text from
one language into another, it is first and foremost an effort at cross-cultural
understanding, the evidence of the possibility of intercultural negotiations.

Therefore, the importance of translation in Hong Kong does not seem
to me a real problem, but the decline of bilingualism or the tendency
toward monolingualism is. It is perhaps appropriate at this point to venture
some comments on "mother tongue education," a slogan that seems to me
to cover up some of its possibly undesirable consequences under an emotionally attractive name. Who doesn't love his mother? And one's mother-

tongue? But to be closed off in one language, that of one's own, is not at all desirable or even useful at this late stage of the twentieth century. It is, to use another popular expression, to be trapped in "the prison house of language." I am not at all arguing against "mother-tongue education," and a lot of careful discussion is needed before we know what is the best way to teach our children language and culture. But I am not comfortable with the implied monolingualism, the self-enclosure of the mind in one's own language and culture, especially considering the fact that Hong Kong students have so far been exposed to more English and bilingual practice than their mainland counterparts. It would be a mistake to give up this small but significant advantage they have by cutting down English and lowering the standard in the teaching of English, and by reducing everything to Cantonese. I say so not because I come from Sichuan and do not speak Cantonese myself, for I don't advocate speaking the Sichuan dialect, either. The mother-tongue, like the blood that the mother gives to her child, will never be lost, and it is to the advantage of the child to grow up and be able to speak more languages than the mother-tongue. In matters related to language, like everything else, knowledge *is* power.

Mother-tongue and bilingualism are not mutually exclusive terms, but they do represent different mentalities and different visions. And of the two, it is bilingualism that will make translation a necessity and lead it to a better future. Of all Chinese communities, either on the mainland or overseas, Hong Kong is probably the most developed in its social structure and economic strength, and therefore it should also be the most promising in the development of other aspects of life, culture and education in particular. If translation by nature depends on a more open-minded attitude toward the rest of the world, a greater vision for the interactions of different nations and cultures, then it is important to go beyond the mentality of thinking only of one's own. Let me conclude with an old Chinese parable preserved in *Lü shi chunqiu* 《呂氏春秋》 about the lost bow. A man from the place of Jing lost his bow, but he does not try to find it, saying, "If a man from Jing lost his bow, it is going to be found by people of Jing. So why bother to search for it?" So the man seems to be generous and unselfish. But when Confucius heard what he said, Confucius remarks, "It would do if we take off the word *Jing*." But when Laozi heard this, he says, "It would do if we take off the word *man*." What the parable tells us is that true magnanimity will always go beyond the limitation of one's own locale and be open to people in other places, and indeed to the whole universe. And that, I believe, is the right attitude we should have when we look into the future of translation in Hong Kong.

References

Bok, Derek (1990). *Universities and the Future of America.* Durham: Duke University Press.

Eco, Umberto (1997). *The Search for the Perfect Language.* Trans. James Fentress. Oxford: Blackwell.

Notes on Contributors

Evangeline S. P. Almberg

Evangeline Almberg 吳兆朋 received her B.A. from the University of Hong Kong and her Ph.D. from the University of Stockholm. She has taught at the University of Hong Kong, the University of Stockholm, Lingnan College and The Chinese University of Hong Kong. During her sojourn in Sweden she also freelanced as a translator and interpreter for international bodies and public institutions. At present she is Professor at the Department of Translation, The Chinese University of Hong Kong.

Kenneth Au Kim-lung

Au Kim-lung 區劍龍 is Assistant Professor of the Department of Chinese, Translation and Linguistics, City University of Hong Kong where he teaches General Translation, and Commercial and Financial Translation. He has published papers in local and international journals about television subtitle translation, the legal language issue in Hong Kong and advertisement translation.

Gillian Bickley

Gillian Bickley came to Hong Kong in 1970 to join the Department of English at the University of Hong Kong as a lecturer. After taking up an appointment as Lecturer at the University of Auckland, New Zealand, which she held from 1974 to 1977, she returned to Hong Kong where she worked for the Hong Kong Examinations Authority as Subject Officer from 1979 to 1982. She then joined Hong Kong Baptist College (now Hong Kong Baptist University) where she is Associate Professor in the Department of English.

Elsie Chan Kit-ying

Elsie Chan 陳潔瑩 studied translation and interpretation at the City Polytechnic and The Chinese University of Hong Kong. She is an executive committee member of the Hong Kong Translation Society, member of the Institute of Linguists (MIL) and Accredited Translator of the Australian National Accreditation Authority for Translators and Interpreters (NAATI). She was a government translator before teaching translation at the City University of Hong Kong and is currently enrolled in a Ph.D. programme at the University of Warwick.

Chan Man Sing

Chan Man Sing 陳萬成 teaches translation and Chinese poetry at the University of Hong Kong.

Chan Sin-wai

Chan Sin-wai 陳善偉 teaches translation at The Chinese University of Hong Kong, where he is the Chairman of the Department of Translation. His teaching and research interests lie in the areas of machine translation, translation theory and Chinese-English Translation. His forthcoming publication is *A Translator's Chinese-English Dictionary.*

Leo Chan Tak-hung

Leo Chan 陳德鴻 is currently Associate Professor in the Department of Translation, Lingnan University. He taught previously at the City Polytechnic of Hong Kong, Georgetown University in Washington D.C. and the University of Maryland. His recent publications include *Masterpieces in Western Translation Theory* (2000; co-edited) and *The Discourse on Foxes and Ghosts* (1998). He is also Founding Editor of *Journal of Modern Literature in Chinese,* Editor of *Translation Quarterly* since 1997, and Advisory Board Member of *TTR: Traducation, Terminologie, Redaction.*

Carrie Chau Kam Hung

Carrie Chau 周錦紅 is a lecturer in Translation and Interpretation, Division of Language Studies, City University of Hong Kong. She obtained a Higher Diploma in Translation and Interpretation from Hong Kong Polytechnic and an M.A. in Translation from The Chinese University of Hong Kong. She has extensive experience in practical translation, publication and education. Her research interests include translation skills and development of multimedia packages for educational purposes.

Simon S. C. Chau

Simon Chau 周兆祥 is the author, translator and compiler of over 80 books and is a regular contributor to local and overseas magazines and journals. The University of Edinburgh awarded him a doctorate for his thesis on translation pedagogy. He is currently Head of the Translation Programme, Hong Kong Baptist University and Chief Examiner (Chinese) of the Institute of Linguists, UK.

Cheng Ting-au

Cheng Ting-au 鄭定歐 has degrees in French language and literature from Zhongshan University in China, a B.A. (Linguistics) from the University of Grenoble III and a M.A. and Ph.D. (Linguistics) from the University of Paris VII, France. His research interests include pedagogical lexicography, syntax (lexicon-grammar) as well as Cantonese linguistics and Romance linguistics. He has published widely in the above fields. He has worked in the Department of Chinese, Translation and Linguistics, City University of Hong Kong since 1986 and is now an Associate Professor.

Michael Chuen Kam-hung

Michael Chuen 川錦鴻 has been doing translation and interpretation work since joining the Hong Kong Government in 1966. He currently holds the position of Principal Chinese Language Officer, the Official Languages Agency of the Hong Kong SAR Government.

He Yuanjian

He Yuanjian 何元建 is an Associate Professor at the Department of Translation, The Chinese University of Hong Kong. He teaches translation, translation studies, grammar theory and comparative and Chinese syntax.

Eva Hung Wai Yee

Eva Hung 孔慧怡 received her B.A. (1st Honours) and M.Phil. degrees from the University of Hong Kong and her Ph.D. from London University. She has been the Director of the Research Centre for Translation, The Chinese University of Hong Kong and Editor of *Renditions* since January 1987. Her recent publications in translation studies include《翻譯・文化・文學》(*Translation, Literature, Culture*. Peking University Press, 1999),《亞洲翻譯傳統與現代動向》(合編楊承淑) (*Translation in Asia — Past and Present*, Peking University Press, 2000), and "The Role of the Foreign Translator in the Chinese Translation Tradition." (*Target*, 1999) She is also the editor/translator of ten titles of Chinese literature in English translation, including works by Eileen Chang, Xi Xi, Shu Ting and Wang Anyi. Eva Hung also writes creatively. She publishes fiction and essays in Chinese, and poetry in English.

Irene Ip Kwok Chun

Irene Ip 葉幗珍 is a lecturer in English, Division of Language Studies, City University of Hong Kong. She received her university education in Australia and Hong Kong, specialising in English language and literature. She has extensive teaching experience with tertiary students from different disciplines. Her research interests are curricula design, reading skills as well as the development of multimedia packages for educational purposes.

Lai Swee Fo

Lai Swee Fo 賴瑞和 received his B.A. in English literature from the National Taiwan University and obtained both his M.A. and Ph.D. in Chinese Studies from Princeton University. He gained his professional experience by working as a full-time translator for two major Chinese-language daily newspapers for four years, translating and editing international news stories. In addition, he has translated short stories by Ernest Hemingway, William Faulkner and Isaac Singer, as well as two plays by Edward Albee, *The Zoo Story* and *The Sandbox*. His current research interests include translation theory, news translation, translation teaching, and computer applications in translation.

David Lam Kui Kwong

David Lam 林鉅洸 obtained his Ph.D. from the University of Alberta and has served the China Patent Agent (H.K.) Ltd. as Legal Translator and the Bell-Northern Research and several government offices as senior staff. He is now a part-time lecturer at the Department of Translation, The Chinese University of Hong Kong, the School of Professional and Continuing Education, Hong Kong University, and the School of Continuing Education, Hong Kong Baptist University. He has translated the *History of China as Recorded in Stamps* (The commercial Press, 1995) and is author of 《21世紀高科技中譯英教材》(*An Overview of Hi-Tech & Science*) (Cosmos, 1999).

Paul Levine

Paul Levine has taught at the City University of Hong Kong in the areas of language and translation for the past fifteen years, and has been in charge of the Language and Translation Programme at the Open University of Hong Kong since 1998. At present his interests include the history of translation studies, comparative translation theory and translation pedagogy. His most recent publication is "A Re-examination of Nietzsche's Views on Language and Translation with Reference to Buddhist and Daoist Statements" in *Sino-German Relations Since 1800: Multidisciplinary Explorations* (Frankfurt: Peter Lang, 2000).

Li Defeng

Li Defeng 李德鳳 is Assistant Professor in the Department of Translation, The Chinese University of Hong Kong. He has taught translation and English in Hong Kong, Canada and Mainland China. His academic interests include translation studies, translation teaching research and second language learning and teaching. His present study in translation focuses on translation pedagogy and curriculum design and material development in translation. He has written for leading international journals such as *Target, Babel, Perspectives, TESOL Quarterly* and *Teaching and Teacher Education*.

Liu Ching-chih

Liu Ching-chih 劉靖之, a graduate of the University of London and the University of Hong Kong, is at present Professor and concurrently Director of the Centre for Literature and Translaton at Lingnan University; Honorary

Professor and Honorary Research Fellow at the Centre of Asian Studies at the University of Hong Kong. The research interests and publications of Professor Liu are wide-ranging and cover music, literature and translation. He also publishes music and book reviews on a regular basis.

Mak Wai Ho

Mak Wai Ho 麥偉豪 is a graduate of The Chinese University of Hong Kong. He worked as a language teacher on graduation, and later developed a keen interest in linguistics and translation when he undertook further studies in translation and interpretation. He has been teaching at the Division of Language Studies of the City University of Hong Kong since 1991. His special research interests include translation theories, discourse analysis, lexis, vocabulary acquisition, grammar and sociolinguistics.

Alan Tse Chung

Alan Tse Chung 謝聰 joined the City Polytechnic of Hong Kong in 1987 and has since been teaching principally translation and interpretation, and peripherally linguistics, in particular English phonetics and phonology as well as sociolinguistics. He obtained his doctorate in language and law from the University of Hong Kong in 1997. He is now a senior lecturer with the Division of Language Studies at the City University of Hong Kong. His specialized areas include translation, interpretation and language and the law.

Yau Wai Ping

Yau Wai Ping 邱偉平 received a B.A. in English Studies and Comparative Literature from the University of Hong Kong in 1988. He was also awarded the M.Phil. in Comparative Literature from the University of Hong Kong in 1996 with his thesis on the "root-searching" school in contemporary Chinese fiction. He is working on a Ph.D. thesis on the translation of modernist fiction in Hong Kong in the 1950's. He is at present a lecturer in the Department of Translation at Lingnan University.

Tony Yen Yuen Ho

Tony Yen 嚴元浩 started his civil servant career in the Government's

Legal Aid Department, where he was engaged in translation, administration, and civil and criminal litigation work from 1967 to 1986. He was transferred to the Department of Justice (formerly the Legal Department) in 1986 as a Crown Counsel. He became the Law Draftsman in 1995. As Law Draftsman, he oversees the drafting of all Hong Kong Ordinances and subsidiary legislation proposed by the government.

Tony Yen's many public service roles cover both legal and community issues. He is a member of the Law Reform Commission and the Committee on the Bilingual Legal System. He is a course adviser, external examiner, mentor and Court member respectively of four local universities. He is Vice-Chairman of the Neighbourhood Advice-Action Council, a voluntary agency that provides community services to young people, the disabled and the elderly. He is an executive committee member of the Scout Association of Hong Kong's Continuing Education Centre. He is also a director of the Kiangsu-Chekiang College.

Yiu Po Kwong

Yiu Po Kwong 姚普光 is a practising subtitler in Hong Kong and writes a language column in the *Ming Pao* newspaper. He has put out nine books on learning English through subtitles.

Zhang Longxi

Zhang Longxi 張隆溪 is Chair Professor of Comparative Literature and Translation at the City University of Hong Kong. Before joining the City University in 1998, he was Professor of Comparative Literature at the University of California, Riverside. He has published many articles in scholarly journals in both Chinese and English and is the author of 《二十世紀西方文論述評》 (*A Critical Introduction to Twentieth-century Western Theories of Literature*, Beijing: Sanlian, 1986), *The Tao and the Logos: Literary Hermeneutics, East and West* (Durham: Duke University Press, 1992), *Mighty Opposites: From Dichotomies to Differences in the Comparative Study of China* (Stanford: Stanford University Press, 1998), and most recently 《走出文化的封閉圈》(*Out of the Cultural Ghetto*, Hong Kong: The Commercial Press, 2000).

Index

Abridged translation, 89–90, 92

Abstract translation, 89, 92

Abusive translation, 170

Addison Wesley Longman China Limited, 50

Address translation, 215

Æsop's Fables, 13

Affinity-in-spirit and Affinity-in-form, 161

Ah Q, 32–33

Alexander, Lloyd, 22

Almberg, S.P. Evangeline 吳兆朋, xii, 42, 60, 261

American Literary Translators Association, 126

American Translators Association (ATA), 51, 126

An, Shigao 安世高, 235

Apple Daily, 141–142

Aristophanes, 170

Arrojo, Rosemary, 158

Art and Profession of Translation, The, 41

Artistry in Encountering Difficulty, 161

Asad, Talal, 158

ATA, abbreviation for American Translators Association, 51

Au, Kim-lung Kenneth 區劍龍, xiii, 10, 58–60, 261

Au, Oscar, 213

Au, Weng-hei, 49–50

Au-Yeung, Makey 歐陽漢玉, 60

Aubert, Francis Henrik, 188

Authentic translation, 92

Automatic multi-code identification, 215

B.A. Programme in Languages and Translation, 120

Bachelor of Arts in Translation and Interpretation, 206

Back-translation, 24–34

Baker, Mona, 160, 198–199

BALIS, abbreviation for Bachelor of Arts in Language Information Science, 206

Ball, J. Dyer, ix, 1–2, 4, 14–15; biography of, 1–2

BALT, abbreviation for B.A. Programme in Languages and Translation, 120, 122

Ban, Gu 班固, 1

Barkhudarov, Leonid, 163

Barme, Geremie R., 42

Bassnett, Susan, 82, 160, 238

BATI, abbreviation for Bachelor of Arts in Translation and Interpretation, 206

Beauvoir, Simone de, 21

Beijing Evening News, 146

Benjamin, Walter, 159–160, 163, 165–166, 171

Best Translation Project Awards, 49

Bible, The, 13

Bibliography of Sino-Japanese and Japanese-Chinese Translation, 75

Bibliography of Translation Studies, 237

Bickley, Gillian, ix, 261

Bilingual Laws Information System, 199

Bilingual Laws Programme, 250; difficulties faced in translation, 250–252; in Hong Kong, 250–254

Bilingualism, 245, 255–257; and Hong Kong government translators, 245–248; in Hong Kong society, 255–256

Bloom, Harold, 159

Board of Examiners, 11, 14–15

Bowen, George, 15

Bowring, John, 12

Bulletin, The 《譯訊》, 39–40

Cai, Siguo 蔡思果, same as Frederick Tsai, 200

CAL, abbreviation for Computer-assisted Learning, 129

Caldwell, Daniel Richard, 14

CALL, abbreviation for Computer-assisted Language Learning, xi, 129, 132–133

Cameron, K., 129

Camus, Albert, 21

Cantonese Made Easy, 1

Cantonese-Putonghua sight-translation, 144

Cantonese-Putonghua sight-translation training, 141; at City University of Hong Kong, 141–147; teaching format of, 144–146

CAT, abbreviation for computer-aided translation, 200–201

Catford, J.C., 157, 160, 164

CCP, abbreviation of Chinese Communist Party, 22, 33–35

Centre for Comparative Literature and Translation, 74, 76

Centre for Promotion of Chinese Culture, The, 40

Centre for Translation Projects, 74–75

Centre for Translation Studies, 40

Centre of Asian Studies, 40

Cha, Louis 查良鏞, 37–39

Chalmers, J., 14–15

Chan, Kit-ying Elsie 陳潔瑩, xiv, 59–60, 261–262

Chan, Man Sing 陳萬成, ix, 14, 262

Chan, P., 210

Chan, Sin-wai 陳善偉, xiii, 262

Chan, Tak-hung Leo 陳德鴻, xii, 42, 163, 262

Chan, W.K. Samuel, 209–210

Chan, Y.W. Terence, 210

Chang, Nam-fung, 163

Chang, Nancy 張蘭熙, 43

Chang, Ruogu 張若谷, 43

Chang, Tung 張同, 58

Changes and Development in Translation Theory, 161

Chau, Kam Hung Carrie 周錦紅, xi, 262

Chau, Kenneth 蔡天助, 60

Chau, S.C., Simon 周兆祥, xiv, 58, 263

Chen, John 陳佐舜, 43

Chen, K.J., 211

Chen, Longgen 陳龍根, 60

Cheng, C.C., 209–210

Cheng, Ting-au 鄭定歐, xii, 211, 263

Cheng, Yang-ping 鄭仰平, 43

Cheng Yu《成語》(*A Manual of Chinese Quotations*), 2

Cheung, Agnes 張燕萍, 59

Cheung, Ki-sun 張祺新, 56

Chew, C.H., 212

Chi, Pang-yuan 齊邦媛, 43

Chin, Roland, 213

China Review, 2, 11

Chinese Classics, 13

Chinese Communist Party (CCP), 22

Chinese Language and the Modern Chinese Cultural Enlightenment, 164

Chinese Language Officer (CLO), 86, 88, 100–101, 245

Chinese Reading Club, 2

Chinese teacher's allowance, 17

Chinese teacher's scheme, 17

Chinese translation studies, 228–237; importance of Hong Kong in, 237–239

Chinese Translators Journal, 162

Chinese University Language Translator, The 中文大學語言翻譯器 (CULT), 213

Chinese University of Hong Kong, The, 40, 44, 73, 77, 136; 160, 205

Chinese-English and English-Chinese Translation, 161–162

Chinese-English Bilingual Legis-lative Records(Hansard), 199

Chinese-English Dictionary in the Cantonese Dialect, 1

Chiu, Ka-man, Aman 趙嘉文, 59–60

Chow, Oi-wah 周愛華, 58

Chu, Chi-tai 朱志泰, 56–57

Chuen, Kam-hung Michael 川錦鴻, xiv, 263

Chung-Wai Literary Monthly, 165

City Polytechnic of Hong Kong (CPHK), 40, 98–99

City University of Hong Kong, xi–xii, 44, 97–98, 100–102, 106, 119–120, 123–124, 126, 130, 141, 160

CityU Linguists, 208

Civil Service Regulations, 247

Clarke, Jack, 221

CLO, abbreviation for Chinese Language Officer, 245–247

Coeval translation, 176

Cohen, Ralph, 159

Cohesion, 149, 151

Collected Essays on Translation 1983《翻譯叢論一九八三》, 41

Collected Essays on Translation 1986《翻譯叢論一九八六》, 41

Collected Essays on Translation 1988《翻譯叢論一九八八》, 41

Collected Essays on Translation 1991《翻譯新論集》, 41

College of Higher Vocational Studies, 98

College of Languages, Linguistics and Literature, 40

Commercial Press (HK) Limited, 50

Commercial translation, 87, 94

Companion for Chinese Translators, A《中國翻譯詞典》, 238

Complete translation, 91

Complete Works of Lu Xun, The, 34

Computer screen translation
    software, 214
Computer-aided translation
    (CAT), 200–201
Computer-assisted Learning
    (CAL), 129
Computer-assisted language
    learning(CALL), xi, 129–130
Conceptual-intentional System,
    183
Conference interpreter, 224
Confucian Analects, 13
*Contemporary Feminist Literary
    Criticism*, 159
*Contemporary Translation
    Theories*, 161–162, 176
Contextualized translation, 91
Contingent translation, 176
Court Interpreter, 100, 245
CPHK, abbreviation for City
    Polytechnic of Hong Kong, 40,
    98–99
CUHK, abbreviation for The
    Chinese University of Hong
    Kong, 40, 44, 73, 77, 136, 160,
    205
Culler, Jonathan, 159
CULT, abbreviation for The
    Chinese University Language
    Translator, 213
Cultural Revolution, 34, 80
Cultural translation, 158
Cultural turn, 157
Dao'an 道安, 232
de Beaugrande, Robert, 171
de Man, Paul, 160, 163, 171
Deane, Meredith, 16
Deep Blue, 201
Delisle, Jean, 164

Deng, Xiaoping, 135, 166
Dent-Young, John, 42
Department of Applied
    Linguistics, 98
Department of Chinese, Transla-
    tion and Linguistics, 98, 141,
    206
Department of Chinese, Univer-
    sity of Hong Kong, 208
Department of Chinese and
    Bilingual Studies, 207
Department of Computer Science,
    213
Department of Extra-mural
    Studies, 44
Department of Justice, 199, 252,
    254
Department of Languages, 98
Department of Translation,
    Lingnan University, 208
Department of Translation,
    The Chinese University of
    Hong Kong, ix, xiv, 207,
    213–214
Derrida, Jacques, 160, 163, 171
Descriptive translation studies,
    198
*Descriptive Translation Studies
    and Beyond*, 198
Dialogue & c, 13
Diary of a Madman, 32–33
Dictionary modification, 215
Dictionary of Chinese Translators
    《中國翻譯家辭典》, 238
Didactic translation, 190
Dilthey, Wilhelm, 165
Ding, Samuel 丁紹源, 57–59
*Dissertation Abstract
    International*, 197

Division of Humanities and Social Sciences, 98

Division of Language Studies, 97–98, 106

Division of Social Studies, 98

Dolet, Etienne, 176

Dong, Qiusi 董秋斯, 238

Download update, 215

Dream of the Red Chamber, see also *Red-chamber Dream*, 4

Dressler, Wolfgang, 171

Dublin City University, 160

Eagleton, Jennifer, xv, 146, 202

Eagleton, Terry, 159

Eitel, E.J., ix, 1–4, 7–8, 11–12, 14–15, 18; biography of, 1; method of translation, 2–4; translation of *Thousand-character Text*, 3

Electronic text, 197–199

Encyclopaedia of Translation, An, 237

Encyclopedia Britannica, 197

English-Chinese Cookery Book, The, 2

Enigmatic Parallelism of the Canton Dialect, 2

Eoyang, Eugene C. 歐陽楨, 42, 82, 176

Erostrate, 22

Erostratus, x, 21–22, 31–33, 35; the plot of the story, 22–23

Essays on Translation 《翻譯論集》, 41

Fagles, Robert, 198

Fan, Wen-mei 范文美, 42

Fang, Neng-hsun, xv

Federation Internationale des Traducteurs, 237

Fedorov, Andrei, 163

Feng Shui, 1

Feng, Xuefeng 馮雪峰, 33

Feng, Zikai 豐子愷, 198

Fenollosa, Ernest, 5

Financial Services Bureau, 185–186

Financial translation, 185–191; definition of, 186; in Hong Kong, 185–192

Financial translator, 185–191; challenges of, 187–190

FIT, abbreviation for International Federation of Translators, 50

Flotow, von Louise, 158

Foreign Language Teaching and Research, 162

Foreign Languages, 163

Foreign Languages and Translation, 163

Fou, Lei 傅雷, 50

Fou, Ts'ong 傅聰, 50

Fou Lei Foundation, 50

Fou Lei and His World, 51

Fu, Lei 傅雷, same as Fou Lei, 232, 235

Functional translation, 181–182

Fung, Pascale, 213

Gadamar, Hans-Georg, 159

Gallin, Bernard, 75

Gan, Kok Wee, 213

Gemet, Jacques, 166

Genji Monogatari 《源氏物語》 (*The Tale of Genji*), 198

Gentzler, Edwin, 176

Gillespie, Gerald, 159

Glossary of New English, A 《英語新辭辭彙》, 41

Gong, Jianming, 159

Government Education System, 9
Grey, George, 12
Guo, Baoquan 戈寶權, 43
Guo, Yinxing, 168
Gutzlaff, Charles, 10
Hansard, 199
Hatim, Basil, 171
Hatta, 5
HDTI, abbreviation for Higher
    Diploma of Translation and
    Interpretation, xi, 97–103, 105–
    106
He, Weijie, 161
He, Yuanjian 何元建, xiii, 198,
    263
Hermans, Theo, 82
Hickie, 170
Higher Diploma of Translation
    and Interpretation(HDTI), xi,
    97, 130; at City University of
    Hong Kong, 97–117; career
    development, 104–106; course
    design, 99–100, 103–104;
    history of, 97–98
Highlight and translate, 215
Hilbert, Paul, 22–33
Hirsch, E.D., 159, 165
*History of the Former Han
    Dynasty* 《漢書》, 1
HKBC, abbreviation for Hong
    Kong Baptist College, 40
HKP, abbreviation for the Hong
    Kong Polytechnic, 40
HKTS, abbreviation for the Hong
    Kong Translation Society, 37,
    41, 50, 52
HLTC, abbreviation for Human
    Language Technology Centre,
    212–213

Ho, Alloy, 16
Ho, Fuk, 16
Ho, H.C., 210
Ho, Ping-yu 何丙郁, 42
Ho, Shun-kan Ben 何信勤, 58–59
Ho, Tsung Chi, 16
Ho, Tung Robert, 16
Holmes, James S., 160, 179–180,
    228
Holub, 159
Holz-Mänttäri, Justa, 171
Homer, 197
Hong Kong Baptist College, 40,
    160
Hong Kong Baptist University, 44
Hong Kong Beliliosi Middle
    School, 1
Hong Kong Council for Academic
    Accreditation, 47
Hong Kong Examinations
    Authority, 47
Hong Kong Government Central
    School for (Chinese) Boys, 9,
    11, 15–16
Hong Kong Institute of
    Architects, 52
Hong Kong Legislative Council,
    10
Hong Kong Polytechnic, The, 40,
    76
Hong Kong Polytechnic
    University, The, 44, 160, 207
Hong Kong Productivity Centre,
    45
Hong Kong Trade Development
    Council, 45
Hong Kong Translation Society,
    The, x, 37–38, 45, 47, 50;
    establishment of, 37–39;

executive committees of, 56–61; Fou Lei Foundation, 50; Honorary Fellowship of, 42–43; major conferences, 53–54; organization of conferences and publication of proceedings, 40–41; publication of *Translation Quarterly*, 42; scholarships, 49–50; syllabus of Diploma and Advanced Diploma Examinations, 62–68

Hong Kong University of Science and Technology, The, 212

Honig, H.G., 180

Honorary Fellowship, 42–43

Hop Ying International Holdings Limited, 49

House, Julian, 180

Housman, L., 170

Hsia, S., 212

Hsin Hsing: Taiwan, A Chinese Village in Change, 75

Hsu, Sin-chu 許性初, 57–58

Hu, Gongze, 161

Hu, P.H. Jerome, 209, 212

Huai, Su 懷素, 3

Huang, Bangjie, 161–162

Huang, C.R., 211

Huang, Changning, 210

Huang, Guobin, same as Laurence K.P. Wong, 161

Huang, H.Y., 209

Human Language Technology Centre(HLTC), 212–213

Hung, Hing-sum, 213

Hung, Wai Yee Eva 孔慧怡, x, 264

Hung On-To Research Laboratory for Machine Translation, 213

In Search of Wealth and Power: Yen Fu and the West, 167

Infante, Guillermo Cabrera, 170

Infante's Inferno, 170

Instant screen translation, 215

Instant transliteration, 215

Institute of Linguists(IOL), 44, 50

Institute of Translating and Interpreting(ITI), 50

International Bibliography of Translations, 237

International Federation of Translators(FIT), 50

International Review of Chinese Linguistics, 209

Internet, 197, 223; and translation studies, 197–202

Interpreter training, 143–144

Investigation into Equivalence-in-effect, An, 161–162

IOL, abbreviation of Institute of Linguists, 44

Ip, Kwok Chun Irene 葉幗珍, xi, 264

Iser, Wolfgang, 159

ITI, abbreviation for Institute of Translating and Interpreting, 50

Jameson, Fredric, 159

Jao, Y.C. 饒餘慶, 40

Jauss, 159

Jean, Herbert, 163

Jin, Di 金隄, 42, 161–162, 228

Jin, Serena 金聖華, xv, 41–43, 50, 57–60, 200

Jin, Shenghua, 161, same as Serena Jin, 161

John Dos Passos and 1919, 21

Joly, H.B., 4

Journal of the Hong Kong Branch

of the Royal Asiatic Society, 11
Joyce, James, 198
Kao, George 高克毅, 42, 56, 74–75
Kasparov, Gary, 201
Ke, Ping, 161–162
Kong, Luan, 213
Kumarajiva 鳩摩羅什, 232, 235
Kusmaul, P., 180
Kwan, S.F. Anna, 211
Lai, B.Y. Tom, 209–210
Lai, C.C. Jane 黎翠珍, 60
Lai, Swee Fo 賴瑞和, xiii, 264
Lai, T.C., same as Lai Tim-cheong, 38–39, 41, 43, 50, 51
Lai, Tim-cheong 賴恬昌, 38, 56–61
Lam, Jacqueline 林錦薇, 59–60
Lam, Kui Kwong David 林鉅洸, xii, 264–265
Lam, Raymond, 211
Lam, Shan-mu 林山木, 39
Language and Translation, 162
Language Information Sciences Research Centre, 208
Lattimore, Richard, 198
Lau, Chi-ping 劉治平, 56–57
Lau, D.C. 劉殿爵, 40, 42
Lau, S.M. Joseph 劉紹銘, 42–43
Law Drafting Division, 250
Law Society of Hong Kong, The, 254
Law translation, 251
Law Translation Officer, 245
LC, abbreviation of Lingnan College, 40
Lee, Mein-ven 李勉民, 56–59
Lefevere, André, 82, 170, 178, 238

Legge, James, 12–14
Legislative Council, 199
Leong, C.K., 211–212
Lethbridge, H.L., 11–12
Leung, Bo-sang 梁寶生, 57–59
Leung, Joanne 梁寶珍, 59
Leung, M., 210
Leung, S.H., 211
Levine, Paul, xi, 265
Levine, Suzanne Jill, 170
Lewis, Philip, 170
Li, Defeng 李德鳳, xi, 265
Li, K.C. 李國章, 6–7
Li, Kam-kee 李錦祺, 59–60
Li, Zixiu, 159
Liang, Qichao 梁啟超, 236
Lie, Shing-chai Raymond 李成仔, 58
Lin, H.L., 210, 212
Lin, Tai-yi 林太乙, 43
Lin, Wen-yueh 林文月, 42–43
Lin, Wenyue 林文月, same as Lin Wen-yueh, 198
Lingnan College, 40
Lingnan University, 44, 160, 163
LISRC, abbreviation for the Language Information Sciences Research Centre, 210
LISRC Newsletter, 209, 212
Lister, Alfred, 15–16
Literary Current Monthly Magazine 《文藝新潮》, x, 21–22, 35
Literary Gazette 《文藝報》, 34
Liu, C.C., same as Liu Ching-chih, 41
Liu, Ching-chih 劉靖之, x, 10, 42–43, 50, 56–60, 126, 265–266
Liu, Jingzhi, same as Liu Ching-chih, 161

Liu, K.F. Godfrey, 211–212
Liu, Miqing 劉宓慶, 161–162, 228
Liu, Wei, 164–165
Lo, Chi-hong 羅志雄, 58–60
Lockhart, J. Stewart, ix, 1, 4–5, 15; biography of, 2
Loh, Shiu-chang, 213
Longman Asia Limited, 49
Lu, Xun, 22, 32–33, 235
Lui, Shu Ching, 142
Lun, Caeser S., 210–212
Luo, Miu, 21
Luo, Xinzhang, 232
Lutts, Andrew, 222
Lysrstrata, 170
Ma, Boliang 馬博良, 21
Ma, Lang 馬朗, x, 21–35
Ma, Meng 馬蒙, 38, 43, 56
Macdonnell, Richard, 14
Machine translation, 205–208, 212–216; at City University of Hong Kong, 206–212; at Hong Kong Baptist University, 208; at Hong Kong Polytechnic University, 207; at Hong Kong University of Science and Technology, 212–213; at Lingnan University, 208; at The Chinese University of Hong Kong, 207, 213–216; in Hong Kong, 205–217; research of, 208–216; teaching of, 205–208
Machine Translation Laboratory (MTL), xiv, 213–214
Mak, Wai Ho 麥偉豪, xi, 266
Malmqvist, Göran, 42
Mandarins, The, 21

Mapping Theory, 180
Marvell, Andrew, 166
Mason, Ian, 171
Masterpieces in Western Translation Theory, 163–164
Matricial norm, 177
McNaughton, William, 7
Mei, K. Kenneth, 209
Membership of Institute of Linguists, 44
Metzger, Thomas, 166
MIL, abbreviation for Membership of Institute of Linguists, 44, 105
Minford, John, xv, 42
Ming Pao, 133
Mitkov, R., 210
MLA International Bibliography, 197
Moi, Toril, 159
Mok, Wing Yin Rebecca, xv
Morozov, Mikhail, 163
Morrison, John Robert, 10
Morrison, Robert, 10
Mother-tongue education, 257–258
Mou, Zongsan 牟宗三, 237
Mounin, Georges, 160
Mouse-trailing word-translation, 215
MTL, abbreviation for Machine Translation Laboratory, 214–215
MultiTerm, 201
NAATI, abbreviation for Australian National Accreditation Authority for Translators and Interpreters, 105
Nankai University, 79
New Age, 217–224

New Anthology on Translation, 233

New Explorations in Translation, 161

New translation theories, 158–172

Newmark, Peter, 42, 157, 160, 175–176, 237

News translation, 87

Newsletter, 209

Nida, Eugene A., 42, 82, 160–163, 176, 205, 237

Niranjana, Tejaswini, 82, 158, 167, 171

Nord, Christiane, 171

"Occam's razor," 3

Odyssey, 197

Official Languages Agency (OLA), 245

Official Languages Ordinance, The, 245

OLA, abbreviation for Official Languages Agency, 245–246

On the Art of Translation, 161

On-line dictionary, 214

One Hundred Translations That Had an Impact on Modern Chinese Society, 164

Open University of Hong Kong, The, xi, 44, 119–121, 123–125; programme goals of, 120; translation programme at, 119–127

Operational norm, 176

Oriental Daily, 144

Original purport 案本, 232

Ouyang, Ruying, 142

Oxford University Press (HK) Limited, 49–50

Pan, Chiu-yin 潘朝彦, 57–58

Pan, F.K., 130

Pearce, T.W., 2, 8

Peirce, Charles, 177

Peking University Press, 82

Peng, Jingxi, 162

Police Interpreter, 100

Police Translator, 245

Polysystem, 176

Pong, S.L. Elizabeth 龐林淑蓮, 59

Poon, Hon-kwong Joseph 潘漢光, xv, 59–60

Pope-Hennessy, John, 1, 15–17

Pound, Ezra, 5, 237

Prescriptive theory, 176

Professional dictionaries, 215

Professional translator, 190

Qian, Zhongshu 錢鍾書, 232

Queen's College, 9

RCT, abbreviation for the Research Centre for Translation, 73–83

Reader's Digest Association Far East Limited, 50

Real-life translation, 190

Red-chamber Dream, 4

Reiss, Katharina, 160, 171

Renditions, xi, 75–76, 81

Report of the Working Group on the Use of Chinese in the Civil Service, 247

Research Centre for Translation, The (RCT), x, 73–74; book projects of, 75; cultural mission of, 80–81; founding of, 73; historical and cultural research at, 79; literary translation at, 76–78; organization of conferences and workshops, 78

Rethinking Translation, 158, 160
Richards, I.A., 159
Robinson, Douglas, 158
Robinson, Hercules, 12, 14
Routledge Encyclopedia of Translation Studies, 126
Russell, James, 15–16
Sacred Edict, The, 13
Sartre, Jean-Paul, x, 21–22
Sasanuma, 5
Schleiermacher, Friedrich, 165
Scholes, Robert, 159
School of Professional and Continuing Education(SPACE), 44
Schreiber, Morry, 51
Schwartz, Benjamin, 166–167
SCOPE, abbreviation for School of Continuing and Professional Education, 105
Securities and Futures Commission of Hong Kong, 189
Selection of the Most Recent Critical Essays in the West, A, 159
Selective translation, 88–89, 91
Seleskovitch, Danica, 163
Semi-through translation, 181–182
Sentence translation, 215
Seymour, Richard K., 41
Shang, Qin, 166
Sheng, Ning, 159
Shi, Bertrand, 213
Shi, Feng, 211
Short History of Western Translation Theories, A, 162
Shue Yan College, 44
Sight-interpretation, 142
Silone, Ignazio, 21

Simon, Sherry, 158, 170
Simultaneous Interpreter, 245
Sin, Carol, 211
Sin, King-kui, xv, 210–211
Sino-British Joint Declaration, x
Sino-United Publishing (Holdings) Limited, 50
Siting Translation, 158
Smith, C.C., 13, 15–16
Snell-Hornby, Mary, 160, 171
Socialist Realism, 34–35
Soong, Stephen C. 宋淇, 38–39, 41–42, 56–57, 74, 81
South China Morning Post, 133
Spiritual resemblance 神似, 232
StarTerm, 201
Steiner, George, 164
Stephen C. Soong Translation Studies Awards, 82
Stewart, Frederick, 14–17
Stock Exchange of Hong Kong, 185, 187
Stranger, The, 21
Student-interpreter, 9, 11, 13–17; examinations for 12–15
Studies on Translation Today 《現代翻譯理論》, 228
Sublime consummation 化境, 233
Subtitle, 193
Subtitling translation, 193–195
Sum, Priscilla, 211
Summary translation, 89–90, 92
Sun, Hsu-hsien Alex 孫述憲, 38–39, 56, 59
Sun, Maosong, 210
Sun, S.Y. Phillip 孫述宇, 38–39, 56–57
Surrogate translation, 176
TAC, abbreviation for Translators'

Association of China, 40, 50
Tan, Daming, 159
Tan, Zaixi 譚載喜, 162, 228
Tang, Dominic 鄧榮煜, 59–60
TAT, abbreviation for Translator'
    Association of Taiwan, 50
Team translation, 91
Technical translation, 135; and
    Arts students, 135–140
Terminology management, 201
Text reading, 215
Text translation, 215
Text translation software, 214–
    215
Textual-linguistic norm, 177
Theoretical theory, 176
Things Chinese, 1
Thinking-aloud, 180
Thousand-character Text 《千字
    文》, 1–2
Three Lectures in Buddhism, 1
Three-character Classic, 13
Through translation, 181
Tonnochy, M.S., 16
Toper, Pavel, 163
*Topical Bibliography of Transla-
    tion and Interpretation, A*, 238
Touching the Elephant, 162
Toury, Gideon, 82, 175–177, 198
Translating Revisited, 161
Translation aids, 228
*Translation and Interpreting:
    Bridging East and West*, 41
Translation courses, 44; at tertiary
    institutions in Hong Kong, 44
Translation criticism, 180, 228
Translation education, 225
Translation educator, 225
Translation examination, 44–49

Translation memory, 200–201
Translation Programme, the Open
    University of Hong Kong, 208
Translation Quarterly 《翻譯季
    刊》, 41–42
Translation research, 227
*Translation, Rewriting and the
    Manipulation of Literary
    Fame*, 178
Translation Scholarships, 49
Translation studies, 179–180, 182,
    227–228; in Hong Kong, 227–
    244
Translation theory, 157–174, 175–
    178, 228
Translation Unit, Department of
    English, 208
Translation-memory database,
    200–202
Translatology, 157, 223, 233–234
Translator, The, 160
Translator training, 85-86, 89, 91,
    228, in Hong Kong, 85–95
Translator's Handbook, A 《翻譯
    工作者手冊》, 41
Translators through History, 237
Translators' Association of China
    (TAC), 40, 50, 237
Translators' Association of
    Taiwan (TAT), 50
Trimetrical Classic 《三字經》, 1–2
True Story of Ah Q, The, 32–33
Tsai, Frederick 蔡濯堂, 42–43,
    51, 57
Tse, Chung Alan 謝聰, xii, 266
Tse, J., 212
Tseng, Ovid, 5
Tsou, B.K., 209–212
Tsou, Sarah 盧毓文, 60

Tung, Peter, 211

Tung, Yuan-fang, xv

Twenty-four Dynastic Histories, 199

Tytler, Alexander, 176

UGC, abbreviation for University Grants Committee, 42

Ulysses, 198

University and Polytechnic Grants Committee(UPGC), 46

University Grants Committee (UGC), 42

University of Hawaii, 40

University of Hong Kong, 40, 44, 160, 197

University of Manchester, 198

UPGC, abbreviation for University and Polytechnic Grants Committee, 46

Urban Council Public Libraries, 40; organization of translation conferences, 40

Venuti, Lawrence, 158, 160, 163, 165, 171

Vermeer, Hans J., 160, 171

Wade, W.J., 14

Wall, The, 21

Wang, Fengzhen, 159

Wang, S.Y. William, 209, 211

Wang, Tao, 14

Web page translation, 215

Weber, Max, 166

Wei, Zhiqiang, 198

Wen, Jieruo 文潔若, 198

Wheelwright, C.A., 170

Wilss, Wolfram, 164

Wodehouse, H.E., 17

Wong, Bosco 黃承義, 60

Wong, Candy 黃紹顏, 60

Wong, Chak-cheung Peter 王澤長, 38–39, 56

Wong, Hoi, 16

Wong, Ian 黃邦傑, 58–59

Wong, K.P. Laurence 黃國彬, 42

Wong, Kam-hung 黃金鴻, 40

Wong, Kun-lan, 16

Wong, P.K., 210

Wong, Shing, 15

Wong, Siu-kit 黃兆傑, 38–39

Wong, Wang Chi, xv

Woo, Henry 胡家為, 60

Woo, T., 212

Wordsworth, William, 166

World Today Press, 74

Wu, Dekai, 213

Xiao, Liming, 161

Xiao, Peifei, 166–167

Xiao, Qian 蕭乾, 43, 198

Xin, Xiaozheng, 168

Xu, Wenbo, 159

Xuanzang 玄奘, 149, 155, 232, 235

Yan, Fu 嚴復, 4, 165, 169, 176, 232, 239

Yang, Gladys 戴乃迭, 43

Yang, Jiang 楊絳, 43

Yang, Xianyi 楊憲益, 43

Yau, Lau-ting, 16

Yau, Pak-chun 姚柏春, 42, 56, 58

Yau, Wai Ping 邱偉平, x, 266

Ye, Junqian 葉君健, 43

Yen, Yuen Ho Tony 嚴元浩, xiv, 266–267

Yeung, Linda, 7

Yip, Wai-lim, 165–166

Yiu, Eddie 姚棟華, 61

Yiu, Po Kwong 姚普光, xiii, 266

Yu, Kwang-chung 余光中, 43

Yu, Qing, 21
Yu, Ye-lu 余也魯, 38–39, 56–57
Yue, Diana 余丹, xv, 58, 60
Zhang, Borang 張柏然, 238
Zhang, Jingyuan, 159
Zhang, Longxi 張隆溪, xiv, 267
Zhang, Xudong, 159
Zhao, Yi 趙翼, 2
Zhao, Yiheng, 158
Zhi, Qian 支謙, 232
Zhi, Yong 智永, 3
Zhou, Guangqing, 164
Zhou, Ning, 159
Zhou, Shuren 周樹人, pen name
    of Lu Xun, 235
Zou, Zhenhuan, 164